The West Coast Crisis

Drugs, Homelessness, and Despair in Modern America

Kyle Combs

Dedication

To my family and all those who have been impacted by drug addiction,

This book is dedicated to you. Your strength and resilience in the face of the challenges that addiction brings is an inspiration to all who know you. I know that drug addiction is a struggle that affects not just the individual, but also their loved ones and communities.

Through sharing stories and experiences, my hope is that this book can shed light on the realities of addiction, and help those who are currently struggling feel seen and heard. I also hope that this book can help break down the stigma surrounding addiction and encourage a greater understanding of the complexities involved.

To my family, I want to express my gratitude for your unwavering support and love. Your strength and commitment to our family have been a source of inspiration and comfort to me throughout my life.

To all those who are currently battling addiction or have in the past, know that you are not alone. Recovery is a journey that requires courage and commitment, but it is possible. Let us continue to support one another in the journey towards healing and hope.

With love and gratitude,
Kyle Combs

Preface:

This book is a culmination of my personal journey towards understanding the drug and homelessness crisis that is prevalent on the West Coast of the United States. I must admit that before stumbling upon the YouTube channel Soft White Underbelly, I was not aware of the severity and complexity of this issue. The stories shared on this platform opened my eyes to the reality of those who are struggling with addiction and homelessness.

As I delved deeper into this subject, I began to realize that drug addiction and homelessness are not unique to the West Coast but are widespread issues that affect communities across the United States. However, the West Coast has been hit particularly hard, and its cities have become the epicenter of this crisis.

It is important to note that I am not an expert on this subject. I am simply an individual who was moved by the stories shared on Soft White Underbelly and felt compelled to learn more. I have conducted extensive research and reading to understand the root causes of this crisis, the current state of affairs, and potential solutions.

This book is not meant to be a definitive guide or a scholarly work. Instead, it is a collection of my observations and reflections on this issue, based on the research I have conducted. I hope that this book will provide readers with a greater understanding of the drug and homelessness crisis and inspire them to get involved in efforts to address this issue.

Lastly, I want to express my gratitude to the creators of Soft White Underbelly for shedding light on this important issue and providing a platform for those who are often ignored or overlooked. Without their work, this book would not have been possible.

Introduction

As someone who has followed the drug epidemic and homelessness crisis on the American West Coast through news stories, documentaries, and books, I have been deeply affected by the stories of those impacted by these issues. While I am by no means an expert on this topic, I do believe that I am well informed about the realities of the crisis, and I am passionate about sharing what I have learned with others.

This book is the result of that passion, and my hope is that it will provide readers with a comprehensive understanding of the drug epidemic and homelessness crisis on the American West Coast. Through 25 chapters, I aim to explore the root causes of these issues, highlight the stories of those impacted, and examine the social, political, and economic factors that contribute to the crisis.

One of the inspirations for writing this book has been the YouTube channel Soft White Underbelly, which features interviews with people impacted by the drug epidemic and homelessness crisis. These interviews are raw, honest, and deeply moving, and they provide a window into the lived experiences of those often invisible to society. It is my hope that this book will similarly amplify the voices of those impacted by the crisis, and provide readers with a deeper understanding of the issues at hand.

Throughout the book, readers can expect to learn about the complex interplay of factors that have led to the drug epidemic and homelessness crisis on the American West Coast. We will explore the impact of structural inequality, racial discrimination, and the failures of social welfare systems, among other issues. We will also examine the ways in which individuals and communities have been affected by the crisis, and highlight the innovative strategies and models being used to address it.

While this book is not intended to offer a definitive solution to the drug epidemic and homelessness crisis, my hope is that it will inspire readers to take action and advocate for change. By shedding light on the realities of the crisis and the systemic factors that contribute to it, I hope to create a greater sense of urgency around these issues, and encourage readers to become part of the solution.

Ultimately, my goal with this book is to provide a comprehensive and compassionate exploration of the drug epidemic and homelessness crisis on the American West Coast. Through careful research, personal stories, and an unwavering commitment to social justice, I hope to spark meaningful conversations, inspire activism, and create a greater sense of empathy and understanding for those impacted by these issues. I firmly believe that by working together, we can create a society that is more just and equitable for all, and that the insights and knowledge gained from this book can play an important role in that process. Whether you are a community member, an advocate, a policymaker, or simply someone who cares about these issues, this book has something to offer.

As we embark on this journey together, it is important to recognize that the drug epidemic and homelessness crisis are not isolated problems, but rather symptoms of larger social and economic issues. To truly address these issues, we must be willing to confront the systems and structures that contribute to them, and work together to create a more just and equitable society for all.

With this in mind, I invite you to join me on a journey through the American West Coast, to explore the complexities of the drug epidemic and homelessness crisis, and to learn from the experiences of those impacted by these issues. It is my hope that by doing so, we can create a greater sense of empathy, understanding, and urgency around these critical issues, and work together to create a brighter future for all.

The Roots of Drug Use in America

The history of drug use in America can be traced back to the 19th century, when opium was widely used for medicinal purposes. However, with the influx of Chinese immigrants in the mid-1800s, opium smoking became more common and eventually led to the first drug prohibition laws. This was followed by the Harrison Narcotics Tax Act of 1914, which restricted the sale and distribution of opiates and cocaine, and the Prohibition era, which outlawed alcohol.

The post-World War II era saw the rise of the counterculture movement, which challenged traditional values and norms. This led to increased experimentation with drugs such as marijuana, LSD, and amphetamines, and a growing interest in Eastern spiritual practices that incorporated drug use.

The 1980s brought a new wave of drug use with the emergence of crack cocaine, which disproportionately affected low-income and minority communities. This led to a "war on drugs" mentality, with harsher sentencing laws and increased policing of drug activity.

At the same time, the 1980s saw a rise in homelessness, with a significant increase in the number of people living on the streets. Factors contributing to this included the deinstitutionalization of mental health facilities, cuts to social welfare programs, and a lack of affordable housing.

The 1990s saw some improvements in addressing homelessness, with the implementation of the first federal plan to end homelessness and the creation of supportive housing programs. However, the drug epidemic continued to ravage communities, with the emergence of new drugs such as methamphetamine and a growing opioid epidemic.

The early 2000s brought renewed efforts to address homelessness, with a focus on providing supportive housing and addressing the root causes of homelessness, such as poverty and lack of access to healthcare. However, progress has been slow, and the number of people experiencing homelessness has remained stubbornly high.

Today, drug use and homelessness continue to be pressing issues in America. The opioid epidemic has reached crisis proportions, with overdoses now the leading cause of accidental death in the country. Homelessness remains a persistent problem, with an estimated 580,000 people experiencing homelessness on any given night.

The factors contributing to these issues are many and complex, including poverty, lack of affordable housing, social inequality, and failures of the healthcare system. The historical context of drug use and homelessness in America provides important insights into the root causes of these issues and the challenges of addressing them.

Through a deep understanding of the historical context, we can develop more effective strategies for addressing drug use and homelessness in America. It is my hope that this book will provide readers with the knowledge and context necessary to do just that.

In the early 19th century, opium was widely used for medicinal purposes in the United States. However, with the influx of Chinese immigrants in the mid-1800s, opium smoking became more common and eventually led to the first drug prohibition laws. The Opium Exclusion Act of 1909 banned the importation of opium for smoking, and the Harrison Narcotics Tax Act of 1914 restricted the sale and distribution of opiates and cocaine.

During this time, morphine was also widely used as a painkiller and sedative. However, its addictive properties soon became apparent, and efforts were made to control its use. The Pure Food and Drug Act of 1906 required the labeling of products containing drugs such as morphine, and the Harrison Narcotics Tax Act further restricted its distribution.

The early 1900s also saw the rise of cocaine, which was initially used for medicinal purposes and as a local anesthetic. However, it quickly became popular for recreational use, particularly among middle and upper-class Americans. Cocaine was also a key ingredient in early versions of Coca-Cola.

The use of these drugs was influenced by various social and cultural factors. For example, opium smoking was initially popular among Chinese immigrants, who brought the practice with them to the United States. In contrast, the use of morphine and cocaine was more prevalent among white Americans, particularly in urban areas.

Efforts to regulate and control these drugs were driven by concerns about their negative effects on individuals and society as a whole. The Harrison Narcotics Tax Act was passed in part due to concerns about the impact of drugs on society, and efforts to control the use of morphine and cocaine were driven by concerns about addiction and dependency.

As the use of opium and morphine continued to increase, concerns about their addictive properties grew, leading to the first federal drug regulation law in 1906, the Pure Food and Drug Act. This law required labeling on products containing opiates and cocaine, and it was followed by the Harrison Narcotics Tax Act of 1914, which required doctors and pharmacists to register with the government and pay a tax to prescribe and dispense these drugs.

The regulation of drugs continued to evolve throughout the 20th century, with the enactment of the Comprehensive Drug Abuse Prevention and Control Act in 1970, which created a system for classifying drugs based on their potential for abuse and medical use. This system is still in use today and serves as the basis for drug regulation and scheduling.

Overall, the early history of drug use in America was shaped by a complex interplay of factors, including cultural norms, medical practices, and social and political concerns. These early efforts to regulate and control drugs set the stage for the ongoing debate over drug policy and the current drug epidemic in America.

The History of Homelessness

Homelessness has a long and complex history in America, with various social and economic factors contributing to the issue. Homelessness refers to the state of individuals or families who lack a fixed, regular, and adequate nighttime residence, and who may be living in shelters, cars, or on the streets.

One significant factor contributing to homelessness is poverty. Poverty has been a persistent issue in America, with cycles of economic boom and bust resulting in periods of widespread unemployment and financial instability. According to the National Alliance to End Homelessness, poverty is the primary cause of homelessness, as individuals who lack sufficient income and resources are unable to afford housing and may become homeless as a result.

Another factor contributing to homelessness is the lack of affordable housing. As housing costs have risen in many cities and towns across America, low-income individuals and families have been priced out of the housing market. The shortage of affordable housing has been exacerbated by the decline in public housing and the lack of investment in social welfare programs that provide housing assistance to those in need.

Other factors that contribute to homelessness include mental illness, addiction, domestic violence, and job loss. Homeless individuals and families may also face discrimination and social exclusion, which can make it more difficult for them to access housing, healthcare, and other essential services.

The history of homelessness in America dates back to the colonial era, with the first recorded instances of homelessness being found among soldiers and veterans returning from the Revolutionary War. Homelessness became a more widespread issue in the late 1800s and early 1900s, with the rise of urbanization and industrialization. During this time, many rural residents moved to cities in search of work, leading to overcrowding and poor living conditions.

The Great Depression of the 1930s resulted in a significant increase in homelessness, as millions of Americans lost their jobs and were unable to afford housing. The federal government responded to the crisis by establishing the Home Owners' Loan Corporation, which provided loans to homeowners facing foreclosure, and the Federal Housing Administration, which subsidized the construction of low-cost housing.

The 1960s saw a renewed focus on the issue of homelessness, with the establishment of the National Institute of Mental Health and the

Community Mental Health Act, which aimed to provide mental health services and support to individuals with mental illness. However, the deinstitutionalization of mental health facilities in the 1970s and 1980s resulted in many individuals with mental illness being released into the community without adequate support or resources.

The 1980s and 1990s saw a significant increase in the number of homeless individuals, as a result of cuts to social welfare programs, rising housing costs, and the crack cocaine epidemic. The Reagan administration's policies, such as the closure of mental health facilities and cuts to social welfare programs, are often cited as contributing to the increase in homelessness during this period.

Efforts to address the issue of homelessness have included the establishment of federal programs, such as the McKinney-Vento Homeless Assistance Act, which provides funding for homeless shelters, transitional housing, and support services. However, the challenges faced by homeless individuals and families remain significant.

Homeless individuals and families often face a range of challenges, including lack of access to healthcare, food insecurity, and exposure to violence and trauma. Homeless children are at particular risk of experiencing negative outcomes, such as poor academic performance, mental health issues, and chronic health conditions.

Media coverage of homelessness has been widespread, with documentaries such as "The Homestretch" and "Dark Days" exploring the lives of homeless individuals and families. News outlets have also covered the issue extensively, with stories about efforts to address the issue through housing initiatives, outreach programs, and advocacy efforts.

Efforts to address homelessness have been complex and multifaceted, and often involve collaboration between government agencies, non-profit organizations, and community groups. While progress has been made in some areas, the issue of homelessness remains a significant challenge for many communities in America.

The War on Drugs

The War on Drugs is a term used to describe the aggressive policies and laws implemented in the United States in the 1980s and 1990s aimed at reducing drug use and drug-related crime. These policies included increased criminalization of drug use, harsher sentencing laws, and increased policing of drug activity.

One of the most significant impacts of the War on Drugs was the disproportionate impact on communities of color and low-income individuals. The policies and laws implemented during this time resulted in a significant increase in the number of people incarcerated for drug-related offenses, with African American and Hispanic individuals being disproportionately affected.

The War on Drugs was also characterized by a focus on punishment rather than treatment and prevention. This approach was criticized for being ineffective in reducing drug use and drug-related crime, and for contributing to the stigma surrounding drug use and addiction.

In addition to the impact on individuals, the War on Drugs had broader social and economic impacts. The focus on criminalizing drug use and drug-related activity led to the destabilization of communities, particularly in urban areas, as families were torn apart by incarceration and addiction.

Many advocates argue that the War on Drugs failed to address the root causes of drug use and addiction, such as poverty, trauma, and lack of access to healthcare and social services. In recent years, there has been a growing recognition of the need for a public health approach to drug use and addiction, with a focus on harm reduction, treatment, and prevention.

The impact of the War on Drugs on homelessness is also significant. The criminalization of drug use and drug-related activity contributed to the criminalization of homelessness, as individuals experiencing homelessness were often targeted by law enforcement and faced barriers to accessing housing and services. As a result, the number of people experiencing homelessness increased, particularly in urban areas where the policies were most aggressively implemented. Homelessness became increasingly associated with drug use and addiction, perpetuating the stigma and further marginalizing those experiencing homelessness.

Some scholars and activists have also pointed out the role of the War on Drugs in exacerbating poverty and economic inequality. The policies and laws implemented during this time resulted in a significant increase in spending on law enforcement and incarceration, diverting resources away from social welfare programs and economic development initiatives.

Moreover, the War on Drugs had a chilling effect on public discourse around drug use and addiction, contributing to a culture of fear and shame around these issues. This, in turn, made it more difficult for individuals to seek help and access the resources they needed to address their drug use or addiction.

In recent years, there has been growing recognition of the need to reform drug policies and move away from the punitive approach of the War on Drugs. Many states have legalized or decriminalized the use of marijuana, and there have been efforts to shift resources towards prevention, treatment, and harm reduction programs.

Additionally, there has been a push to address the racial disparities in drug enforcement policies and to provide more support to communities affected by the War on Drugs. In 2018, the First Step Act was signed into law, which aimed to reduce mandatory minimum sentences for nonviolent drug offenses and provide more opportunities for rehabilitation and early release for incarcerated individuals.

However, there is still a long way to go in terms of addressing the harm caused by the War on Drugs. Many individuals, particularly those from marginalized communities, continue to be disproportionately affected by drug enforcement policies, and access to effective treatment and support services remains limited in many areas.

As society continues to grapple with the legacy of the War on Drugs, there is a growing recognition of the need for a more compassionate and evidence-based approach to drug use and addiction. This includes efforts to address the root causes of drug use and addiction, such as poverty and trauma, and to provide individuals with the support they need to heal and recover.

The Rise of Prescription Drug Abuse

The rise of prescription drug abuse in America has been a significant public health concern in recent years. Prescription drug abuse is the use of prescription drugs for non-medical purposes, such as to get high or to cope with emotional or psychological issues. This trend has been fueled by a variety of factors, including changes in the healthcare industry, increased access to prescription drugs, and the stigma associated with addiction.

One major factor contributing to the rise of prescription drug abuse is the increased availability of prescription drugs. Pharmaceutical companies have aggressively marketed their drugs to doctors and patients, leading to a dramatic increase in the number of prescriptions being written. Additionally, the internet has made it easier to obtain prescription drugs without a prescription, through illegal online pharmacies or drug dealers.

Another factor contributing to the rise of prescription drug abuse is the stigma associated with addiction. Many individuals who struggle with addiction to prescription drugs are reluctant to seek help because of the shame and judgment associated with addiction. This stigma also affects healthcare providers, who may be hesitant to prescribe medications to individuals who have a history of addiction.

The impact of prescription drug abuse on individuals and communities has been significant. Prescription drug abuse can lead to addiction, overdose, and death. It can also contribute to the spread of infectious diseases, as individuals who use prescription drugs may engage in risky behaviors such as sharing needles. Additionally, the cost of prescription drug abuse is high, both in terms of healthcare costs and lost productivity.

The rise of prescription drug abuse has been the subject of significant media coverage in recent years. Documentaries such as "Prescription Thugs" and "The Pharmacist" have explored the impact of prescription drug abuse on individuals and communities. News outlets have also covered the topic extensively, with stories about individuals who have struggled with addiction to prescription drugs, as well as efforts to address the problem through prevention and treatment programs.

Efforts to address the problem of prescription drug abuse have included increased regulation of prescription drugs, expanded access to addiction treatment, and public education campaigns. Some states have implemented prescription drug monitoring programs, which track the prescribing and dispensing of controlled substances. There has also been a growing focus on harm reduction strategies, such as needle exchange programs, which aim to reduce the spread of infectious diseases among individuals who use drugs.

Additionally, there has been a push for healthcare providers to receive education and training on the risks associated with prescribing opioid medications, and to use alternative treatments for pain management.

One notable initiative to address prescription drug abuse is the Centers for Disease Control and Prevention's (CDC) Guideline for Prescribing Opioids for Chronic Pain. This guideline provides recommendations for healthcare providers on how to safely and effectively prescribe opioids for chronic pain, while minimizing the risk of addiction and overdose.

Despite these efforts, prescription drug abuse remains a significant public health concern in the United States. According to the National Institute on Drug Abuse, over 10 million people in the United States reported misusing prescription opioids in 2019. Additionally, the

COVID-19 pandemic has exacerbated the problem, with increased stress and isolation leading to a rise in drug use and overdose deaths.

In conclusion, the rise of prescription drug abuse in America has been fueled by a variety of factors, including increased access to prescription drugs, aggressive marketing by pharmaceutical companies, and the stigma associated with addiction. The impact on individuals and communities has been significant, with addiction, overdose, and the spread of infectious diseases being major concerns. While efforts have been made to address the problem, prescription drug abuse remains a significant public health concern in the United States.

The Crack Epidemic

The crack epidemic of the 1980s was a devastating period in American history, characterized by a rapid increase in the use and distribution of crack cocaine, a highly addictive and potent form of cocaine. The epidemic had a profound impact on drug use and homelessness in America, contributing to the rise of addiction and poverty in many urban areas.

The crack epidemic was fueled by a number of social and economic factors, including poverty, unemployment, and systemic racism. Many low-income individuals and communities, particularly those in inner cities, were struggling to make ends meet in the 1980s. The economic recession of the early 1980s resulted in widespread unemployment, particularly among young African American men, who faced significant discrimination in the job market.

As the crack epidemic continued to ravage communities across America, policymakers responded with a harsh and punitive approach to drug use and addiction. The Anti-Drug Abuse Act of 1986 and the Anti-Drug Abuse Act of 1988 established mandatory minimum sentences for drug offenses, including lengthy prison terms for crack cocaine offenses. These laws disproportionately impacted communities of color, where crack cocaine use was more prevalent, and contributed to the rise of mass incarceration in America.

In addition to the punitive approach to drug use, efforts were made to address the root causes of the epidemic. The federal government established the Drug-Free Communities Program in 1989, which provided funding to community-based organizations to develop and implement drug prevention and education programs. The program also aimed to address the social and economic factors that contribute to drug use and addiction, such as poverty, unemployment, and lack of access to healthcare.

At the same time, the War on Drugs was ramping up, with increased law enforcement efforts and harsh mandatory minimum sentences for drug offenses. This led to a proliferation of drug trafficking organizations and a black market for drugs, including crack cocaine.

The crack epidemic was also fueled by the easy availability of crack cocaine and its low cost. Crack cocaine was highly addictive and could be produced cheaply, making it an attractive option for low-income individuals who were looking for a quick high. The crack epidemic led to a significant increase in drug use and addiction, as well as related issues such as homelessness, crime, and the spread of infectious diseases like HIV and AIDS.

The impact of the crack epidemic on American society was significant, particularly for low-income communities and communities of color. Many inner-city neighborhoods became hotspots for drug trafficking and violence, leading to increased poverty and the displacement of families and individuals. Homelessness also increased during this period, as many individuals struggling with addiction and other issues were unable to find stable housing.

The media played a significant role in shaping public perceptions of the crack epidemic. The media coverage of the crack epidemic was often sensationalized and focused on the negative aspects of addiction and drug use, rather than on the root causes of the problem. This led to a lack of understanding and empathy for individuals struggling with addiction, as well as for the communities affected by the epidemic.

In recent years, there has been a growing recognition of the role that systemic racism played in fueling the crack epidemic. Many African American communities were disproportionately impacted by the epidemic, both in terms of drug use and the related issues of poverty and homelessness. This has led to a renewed focus on addressing the root causes of drug addiction and homelessness, including poverty, unemployment, and systemic racism.

Efforts to address the impact of the crack epidemic have included increased access to addiction treatment and harm reduction programs, as well as reforms to the criminal justice system and drug policies. However, the legacy of the crack epidemic continues to be felt in many communities today, and there is still much work to be done to address the root causes of addiction and homelessness in America.

The crack epidemic had a significant impact on drug use and homelessness in America, and its legacy continues to be felt today. The rise of mass incarceration and the disproportionate impact of drug policies on communities of color have led to ongoing debates about drug policy and criminal justice reform. Efforts to address homelessness and housing insecurity have also continued, with a renewed focus on providing affordable housing and support services to those in need.

The Opiod Crisis

The opioid crisis is a public health emergency that has had a devastating impact on individuals, families, and communities across America. The crisis is characterized by the widespread use and abuse of opioid drugs, including prescription painkillers, heroin, and fentanyl. The opioid epidemic has led to a dramatic increase in overdose deaths, as well as rising rates of homelessness and related social and economic problems.

One of the primary factors contributing to the opioid crisis is the over-prescription of opioid painkillers. In the 1990s and 2000s, pharmaceutical companies promoted opioids as a safe and effective way to manage chronic pain, leading to a significant increase in the number of prescriptions written for opioids. However, many of these prescriptions were written for conditions that did not require opioids, such as back pain and headaches. This led to a rapid increase in the number of people who became addicted to opioids, as well as a significant increase in the number of opioid-related deaths.

Another factor contributing to the opioid crisis is the rise of fentanyl. Fentanyl is a synthetic opioid that is up to 100 times more potent than morphine and is often used to cut other drugs such as heroin. The widespread availability of fentanyl has led to a dramatic increase in overdose deaths, as even small amounts of the drug can be lethal. According to the Centers for Disease Control and Prevention (CDC), fentanyl was involved in more than 60% of opioid overdose deaths in 2019.

Poverty and unemployment are also significant factors contributing to the opioid crisis. People living in poverty are more likely to experience chronic pain and are less likely to have access to alternative forms of pain management, such as physical therapy. They are also more likely to experience social and economic stressors that can contribute to substance abuse and addiction. The loss of manufacturing jobs in many parts of the country has also contributed to the opioid crisis, as people who have lost their jobs may turn to drugs as a way of coping with the stress and uncertainty of unemployment.

The impact of the opioid crisis on individuals and communities has been devastating. According to the CDC, more than 750,000 people have died from opioid-related overdoses since 1999. In addition to the human toll, the opioid epidemic has had significant social and economic costs, including rising rates of homelessness. Homelessness is a common consequence of opioid addiction, as people who become addicted to opioids may lose their jobs, their homes, and their support networks. They may also be more likely to experience mental health problems and other social and economic challenges.

The opioid crisis has also had a significant impact on healthcare providers and the healthcare system as a whole. Many healthcare providers have been implicated in over-prescribing opioid painkillers, and some have faced legal action as a result. The crisis has also strained the healthcare system, as hospitals and clinics have struggled to manage the high volume of patients seeking treatment for opioid addiction and related health problems.

Efforts to address the opioid crisis have focused on a range of strategies, including improving access to addiction treatment and recovery services, reducing the over-prescription of opioid painkillers, and cracking down on the illegal production and distribution of fentanyl and other opioids. These efforts have been led by federal and state governments, as well as by community-based organizations and healthcare providers. However, the opioid crisis remains a significant public health emergency, and there is much work to be done to address the underlying social and economic factors that contribute to the crisis.

There have been several high-profile cases of doctors being prosecuted for their role in the distribution of opioids. In 2019, a federal jury in Boston found Dr. Joel Smithers guilty of illegally prescribing opioids, resulting in the death of a patient. Smithers, who ran a pain clinic in Virginia, was found to have prescribed opioids to patients who did not need them, and to have ignored warning signs that his patients were addicted to the drugs. He was sentenced to 40 years in prison.

In 2018, Dr. Atiq Durrani, a spine surgeon in Cincinnati, was sentenced to 20 years in prison for performing unnecessary surgeries and prescribing large amounts of opioids to patients. Durrani was found to have operated on patients who did not need surgery, and to have prescribed opioids to patients who did not need them, resulting in addiction and overdose.

In 2019, Dr. Thomas Merrill, a family medicine physician in New Hampshire, was sentenced to six years in prison for illegally prescribing opioids. Merrill was found to have prescribed opioids to patients without a medical need, and to have accepted cash payments in exchange for prescriptions. Several of Merrill's patients suffered from addiction and overdose.

These cases highlight the role that doctors can play in the opioid crisis, and the need for better regulation and oversight of opioid prescriptions. While many doctors prescribe opioids responsibly and ethically, there are others who contribute to the problem by over-prescribing or prescribing opioids without a medical need. Prosecuting these doctors can help to deter others from engaging in similar behavior, and can also provide justice for the victims of the opioid crisis.

The opioid crisis has had a devastating impact on individuals and communities across America. In addition to the thousands of deaths that occur each year from opioid overdoses, the crisis has also led to a rise in homelessness. Many individuals who become addicted to opioids are unable to hold down a job or maintain stable housing, and may end up on the streets as a result.

According to a report by the National Coalition for the Homeless, the opioid crisis has contributed to a significant increase in the number of homeless individuals in America. The report notes that many homeless individuals suffer from chronic pain and are prescribed opioids to manage their pain, which can lead to addiction and overdose. Additionally, many homeless individuals turn to opioids as a way to cope with the stress and trauma of living on the streets.

To address the opioid crisis and its impact on homelessness, a multi-faceted approach is needed. This approach should include better regulation of opioid prescriptions, increased access to addiction treatment and mental health services, and increased funding for affordable housing and social welfare programs. By addressing the root causes of the opioid crisis and providing support and resources to those affected by it, we can work towards ending this devastating epidemic and reducing the number of individuals who experience homelessness as a result.

The Intersection of Drug Use and Homelessness

The intersection of drug use and homelessness is a complex and multifaceted issue in America. Homelessness and substance use disorders are interconnected, with drug use often contributing to or resulting from homelessness. Homeless individuals with substance use disorders face unique challenges, including difficulty accessing treatment and support services, increased risk of overdose and infectious diseases, and stigma and discrimination from society. The impact of drug use on the broader homeless population also has significant implications for public health and safety.

Substance use disorders are a common issue among homeless individuals, with studies estimating that up to 75% of homeless individuals have a history of substance use. Homeless individuals may turn to drugs or alcohol as a coping mechanism for the trauma and stress of homelessness, or as a way to numb the physical and emotional pain of living on the streets. Substance use can also exacerbate the challenges faced by homeless individuals, making it more difficult to find stable housing, maintain employment, and access healthcare and other services.

The challenges faced by homeless individuals with substance use disorders are numerous. One significant barrier to treatment is the lack of access to healthcare and support services. Homeless individuals may struggle to access healthcare due to a lack of insurance or identification, as well as a lack of transportation or proximity to healthcare facilities. The stigma and discrimination faced by homeless individuals with substance use disorders can also make it more difficult to access treatment, as they may be viewed as undeserving or unworthy of support.

The risk of overdose and infectious diseases is also increased for homeless individuals with substance use disorders. Homeless individuals may use drugs in unsafe and unsanitary conditions, increasing the risk of infections such as HIV and Hepatitis C. The risk of overdose is also heightened, as homeless individuals may use drugs alone or in unfamiliar settings, without access to naloxone or other life-saving interventions.

The impact of drug use on the broader homeless population also has significant implications for public health and safety. Drug use in homeless encampments and shelters can create unsafe and unsanitary conditions, with discarded needles and drug paraphernalia posing a risk to both homeless individuals and the surrounding community. The use of drugs such as methamphetamine can also contribute to aggressive and violent behavior, creating a public safety risk.

Addressing the intersection of drug use and homelessness requires a comprehensive approach that addresses the root causes of both issues. This includes addressing poverty and economic inequality, increasing access to affordable housing, and providing healthcare and support services to homeless individuals with substance use disorders. Harm reduction strategies such as syringe exchange programs and naloxone distribution can also help to mitigate the risks associated with drug use.

In recent years, there has been a growing recognition of the need to address the intersection of drug use and homelessness in America. The opioid crisis, in particular, has brought attention to the challenges faced by homeless individuals with substance use disorders, and the need for a more compassionate and evidence-based approach to addressing the issue. However, much work remains to be done to ensure that homeless individuals with substance use disorders receive the support and care they need to overcome these intersecting challenges.

While harm reduction strategies like providing clean needles and medication-assisted treatment (MAT) have been shown to be effective in reducing drug use and improving health outcomes among homeless individuals, they are not a substitute for comprehensive, evidence-based addiction treatment.

Providing clean needles and medication like Suboxone can help prevent the spread of diseases like HIV and hepatitis C, and can reduce overdose deaths. However, they do not address the root causes of substance use disorders or provide the necessary support and resources for individuals to achieve and maintain recovery.

Instead of relying solely on harm reduction strategies, it is crucial for the government to invest in and prioritize access to evidence-based addiction treatment for homeless individuals. This includes providing a range of services, such as detoxification, outpatient and inpatient treatment, and ongoing support through counseling, case management, and peer support.

The lack of access to addiction treatment is a significant barrier for homeless individuals who are seeking to overcome substance use disorders. Homelessness can make it difficult to access traditional treatment services, such as transportation to appointments and stable housing during the recovery process. Additionally, many homeless individuals face stigma and discrimination when seeking treatment, which can discourage them from seeking help.

Providing comprehensive addiction treatment services to homeless individuals can have a significant impact on reducing drug use and improving health outcomes. In addition to improving physical health, addiction treatment can also address underlying mental health issues, improve social functioning, and increase the likelihood of finding and maintaining stable housing.

Investing in addiction treatment for homeless individuals is not only the right thing to do, but it is also cost-effective. Studies have shown that for every dollar invested in addiction treatment, there is a return of up to seven dollars in reduced healthcare costs, reduced criminal justice costs, and increased productivity.

In conclusion, while harm reduction strategies like providing clean needles and medication-assisted treatment are important in reducing drug use and improving health outcomes among homeless individuals, they should not be seen as a substitute for evidence-based addiction treatment. Homeless individuals with substance use disorders face unique challenges, including limited access to healthcare and stable housing, and it is crucial for the government to prioritize investment in comprehensive addiction treatment services to address these challenges.

Rather than solely focusing on harm reduction strategies, the government should prioritize providing homeless individuals with access to a range of addiction treatment services, including detoxification, outpatient and inpatient treatment, and ongoing support through counseling, case management, and peer support. By investing in addiction treatment for homeless individuals, not only will it improve their health outcomes and reduce drug use, but it will also have significant cost-effective benefits in reducing healthcare and criminal justice costs and increasing productivity. It is time for the government to take action and prioritize investment in evidence-based addiction treatment services for homeless individuals with substance use disorders.

Drug Use and Homelessness

Drug use and homelessness have been complex social issues throughout American history, with various responses attempted at the individual, community, and governmental levels. These responses have ranged from criminalization and punitive approaches to harm reduction strategies and comprehensive addiction treatment.

One of the earliest responses to homelessness and drug use in the United States was the establishment of almshouses and workhouses in the 19th century. These institutions provided housing and employment opportunities for individuals who were experiencing poverty, including those who struggled with addiction. However, these institutions often had harsh living conditions and did not address the underlying issues contributing to homelessness and addiction.

The 20th century saw a shift towards criminalizing drug use and homelessness, particularly during the War on Drugs in the 1980s and 1990s. The Anti-Drug Abuse Act of 1986 introduced mandatory minimum sentences for drug offenses and disproportionately affected communities of color. Additionally, laws criminalizing homelessness, such as anti-vagrancy laws, were enforced in many cities. These approaches led to mass incarceration and a lack of access to comprehensive addiction treatment for individuals who were struggling with addiction and experiencing homelessness.

In response to the failures of punitive approaches, harm reduction strategies began to emerge in the 1990s. Needle exchange programs were established to prevent the spread of HIV and hepatitis C among injection drug users. Additionally, medication-assisted treatment, such as methadone and buprenorphine, were introduced to reduce cravings and withdrawal symptoms and support long-term recovery.

Community-based programs also began to emerge, such as Housing First, which prioritizes providing permanent housing to individuals experiencing homelessness without requiring sobriety or compliance with treatment as a prerequisite. These programs have been shown to be effective in reducing homelessness and improving health outcomes among individuals with substance use disorders.

Advocacy efforts have also played a significant role in shaping responses to drug use and homelessness. The National Alliance to End Homelessness and the National Coalition for the Homeless have been instrumental in raising awareness and advocating for policies that prioritize access to housing and addiction treatment for individuals experiencing homelessness.

Despite these efforts, there is still a significant lack of comprehensive and compassionate approaches to addressing drug use and homelessness. While harm reduction strategies have been effective in reducing harm, they do not address the root causes of addiction and homelessness. Additionally, criminalization and punitive approaches have led to mass incarceration and a lack of access to addiction treatment for those who need it most.

A more comprehensive and compassionate approach is needed, which prioritizes access to evidence-based addiction treatment, affordable housing, and support services such as counseling, case management, and peer support. This approach should also address the underlying social determinants of health, such as poverty, unemployment, and systemic racism, which contribute to drug use and homelessness.

During the 1980s, the federal government's response to homelessness and drug use was largely focused on law enforcement and criminalization. The War on Drugs was launched by President Ronald Reagan, which resulted in increased funding for drug interdiction efforts and harsher penalties for drug-related offenses. The response to homelessness was similarly focused on criminalizing homelessness, with laws being passed in several cities and states that criminalized behaviors associated with homelessness, such as sleeping in public spaces.

However, as the homeless population continued to grow, community-based organizations and advocacy groups began to call for a more compassionate and comprehensive approach to addressing homelessness and drug use. In the 1990s, a shift towards harm reduction strategies began to take place, with the development of programs that provided clean needles, medication-assisted treatment, and other services to reduce the harms associated with drug use.

Advocacy groups, such as the National Coalition for the Homeless and the National Alliance to End Homelessness, also began to gain traction and influence policy at the federal level. In 1987, the McKinney-Vento Homeless Assistance Act was passed, which provided federal funding for homeless services and housing. The act was reauthorized in 2009 as the HEARTH Act, which focused on ending homelessness through prevention and rapid re-housing.

Despite these efforts, homelessness and drug use continue to be major issues in America today. The opioid crisis has led to a resurgence of harm reduction strategies, such as the provision of naloxone, a medication that can reverse opioid overdoses. However, the lack of access to comprehensive addiction treatment remains a significant barrier for homeless individuals.

In recent years, there has been a growing movement towards a Housing First approach, which prioritizes providing stable housing to homeless individuals as a first step towards addressing other issues, such as substance use disorders and mental health issues. The Housing First approach has been shown to be effective in reducing homelessness and improving health outcomes, and has been adopted by several cities and states across the country.

In conclusion, the responses to drug use and homelessness in America have evolved over time, with a shift towards more compassionate and comprehensive approaches in recent years. While harm reduction strategies and community-based programs have had some success in reducing the harms associated with drug use and homelessness, there is still a significant need for access to evidence-based addiction treatment and stable housing for homeless individuals.

The criminalization of drug use and homelessness has proven to be ineffective in addressing these issues, and has often led to further marginalization and harm for those experiencing homelessness and substance use disorders. A more compassionate and evidence-based approach, focused on providing comprehensive addiction treatment and stable housing, is necessary to truly address these issues and improve the lives of homeless individuals and communities across America.

Conclusion

In conclusion, drug use and homelessness have been intertwined issues in America for decades. Throughout history, the government's response to drug use and homelessness has been largely focused on criminalization and law enforcement, which has resulted in harmful and ineffective policies that have failed to address the root causes of these issues. These policies have disproportionately affected marginalized communities, including people of color, LGBTQ+ individuals, and those experiencing poverty.

However, there have also been important moments of progress, such as the development of harm reduction strategies and the passage of legislation to provide funding for homeless services and housing. These efforts have been led by community-based organizations and advocacy groups, who have pushed for a more compassionate and comprehensive approach to addressing drug use and homelessness.

Understanding this history is critical for addressing the current crisis of drug use and homelessness in America. It is important to recognize the failures of past policies and the harm they have caused, while also acknowledging the progress that has been made. We must recognize that drug use and homelessness are complex issues that cannot be solved through criminalization or punitive measures alone.

A more equitable and just society is needed to address these issues, one that recognizes the dignity and humanity of all individuals, regardless of their circumstances. This includes providing access to comprehensive addiction treatment, affordable housing, and supportive services, as well as addressing the root causes of poverty and systemic inequality.

As individuals, we can take action to advocate for change. This includes supporting community-based organizations and advocacy groups, speaking out against harmful policies and practices, and educating ourselves and others on the complex issues of drug use and homelessness. It also means recognizing and addressing our own biases and privileges, and working towards a society that values the inherent worth and dignity of all individuals.

In conclusion, drug use and homelessness are complex issues that require a comprehensive and compassionate response. By understanding the history of these issues and taking action towards a more equitable and just society, we can work towards a future where all individuals have access to the support and resources they need to thrive.

The Rise of Drug use and Homelessness on the West Coast

The West Coast of the United States is currently experiencing a significant crisis related to drug use and homelessness. Cities like San Francisco, Los Angeles, and Seattle have seen a sharp rise in the number of people experiencing homelessness, many of whom are struggling with substance use disorders. The issue has become so pronounced that it has attracted national attention, with media outlets reporting on the dire conditions in homeless encampments and the impact of the opioid epidemic on these vulnerable populations.

Understanding the unique factors that have contributed to the drug use and homelessness crisis on the West Coast is critical to addressing the issue and developing effective solutions. While homelessness and drug use are problems that exist across the country, the West Coast has been particularly hard hit by the crisis, with cities in California, Oregon, and Washington reporting some of the highest rates of homelessness in the country.

One factor that has contributed to the crisis is the high cost of housing on the West Coast. Cities like San Francisco and Los Angeles have some of the highest median home prices in the country, making it difficult for many people to afford housing. This has led to a shortage of affordable housing and a growing number of people living on the streets or in cars. The lack of affordable housing has also contributed to the displacement of low-income communities, many of whom are people of color, as gentrification has pushed them out of historically affordable neighborhoods.

Another factor contributing to the crisis is the availability of drugs. The West Coast has long been a hub for drug trafficking, with its proximity to Mexico and the Pacific Rim making it an attractive location for drug cartels. The opioid epidemic has also hit the West Coast particularly hard, with many people becoming addicted to prescription painkillers before turning to heroin or other illicit drugs.

The high availability of drugs has made it difficult for people struggling with addiction to get clean and has contributed to the high rates of overdose deaths in the region.

The crisis has been further compounded by the lack of access to mental health and addiction treatment services. Many homeless individuals struggle with mental health issues or addiction, but the high cost of treatment and the shortage of available services make it difficult for them to get the help they need. The criminalization of drug use and homelessness has also made it difficult for people to seek treatment, as they may fear being arrested or facing other legal consequences.

The drug use and homelessness crisis on the West Coast is a complex issue with many interrelated factors. It is important to understand these factors in order to develop effective solutions that address the root causes of the problem. In the following sections, we will explore the unique factors that have contributed to the crisis, including the high cost of housing, drug availability, and lack of access to treatment services. We will also examine some of the innovative approaches that have been taken to address the issue and highlight the need for a more comprehensive and compassionate approach to addressing homelessness and drug use in the region.

Housing Affordability

The West Coast has been hit particularly hard by the ongoing crisis of homelessness and drug use. One of the key factors that have contributed to this crisis is the high cost of living and lack of affordable housing in the region. This problem has been compounded by the rapidly increasing population and limited space available for new housing development. In this essay, we will discuss the impact of housing affordability on the rise of homelessness and drug use on the West Coast.

The West Coast, particularly cities like San Francisco, Los Angeles, and Seattle, have become some of the most expensive places to live in the country. The cost of living, including housing, food, and other essentials, has increased significantly in recent years, while wages have not kept up with this trend. This has resulted in a large number of people being unable to afford basic necessities, including housing. As a result, many have been forced to choose between paying for housing and other essentials, such as food and healthcare.

The lack of affordable housing has led to a rise in homelessness in the region. In fact, California alone has an estimated 151,000 homeless people, accounting for over one-quarter of the nation's total homeless population. The majority of these individuals are unsheltered, meaning they are living on the streets or in other public places. The lack of affordable housing has made it difficult for homeless individuals to find stable, long-term housing solutions.

In addition to contributing to homelessness, the high cost of living has also led to an increase in drug use on the West Coast. Individuals who are struggling to afford housing and other essentials may turn to drugs as a way to cope with the stress and anxiety of their situation. This is particularly true for those who are homeless, as they may be dealing with the additional stress of living on the streets and the trauma associated with homelessness.

Studies have found a strong correlation between homelessness and drug use. According to the National Coalition for the Homeless, individuals who are homeless are more likely to use drugs than those who are housed. The stress of homelessness, combined with the stigma and lack of access to resources, can make it difficult for homeless individuals to get the help they need to overcome their addiction.

The lack of affordable housing and high cost of living have also contributed to a rise in overdose deaths on the West Coast. Individuals who are unable to afford housing may be forced to live in unsafe or unsanitary conditions, which can increase their risk of overdose. In addition, the lack of affordable healthcare and access to addiction treatment services can make it difficult for individuals to get the help they need to overcome their addiction and avoid overdose.

In recent years, there have been efforts to address the housing affordability crisis on the West Coast. Cities like San Francisco and Seattle have implemented new policies aimed at increasing the supply of affordable housing, including rent control and the construction of new affordable housing units. However, there is still a long way to go in addressing this issue and providing stable, long-term housing solutions for those in need.

Furthermore, the lack of affordable housing has also contributed to a rise in gentrification in many West Coast cities. Gentrification is the process by which wealthier residents move into traditionally low-income neighborhoods, leading to rising property values and the displacement of longtime residents. This has made it even more difficult for low-income individuals to find affordable housing and has contributed to the rise in homelessness in the region.

The impact of the housing affordability crisis on the West Coast has also been felt in other areas. For example, the high cost of living has made it difficult for many individuals to save for retirement or other long-term goals. This can lead to a cycle of poverty and financial instability, making it even more difficult for individuals to escape homelessness and addiction.

To address the housing affordability crisis, it is crucial to understand the root causes of the issue. While efforts to increase the supply of affordable housing are important, they must be accompanied by broader structural changes that address income inequality and the lack of affordable healthcare and addiction treatment services. This requires a commitment to creating a more equitable and just society, one that prioritizes the needs of all individuals, regardless of their income or social status.

In recent years, there have been calls for a national housing affordability policy that would address the root causes of the crisis and provide long-term solutions for those in need. This would include investments in affordable housing, job training and education programs, and healthcare and addiction treatment services. However, progress on these issues has been slow, and it will require a concerted effort from policymakers, community leaders, and individuals across the country to make meaningful change.

In conclusion, the high cost of living and lack of affordable housing on the West Coast have contributed to the ongoing crisis of homelessness and drug use in the region. The lack of stable, long-term housing solutions has made it difficult for individuals to escape homelessness and addiction, while the high cost of living has made it difficult for many to afford basic necessities. Addressing these issues requires a commitment to creating a more equitable and just society, one that prioritizes the needs of all individuals, regardless of their income or social status. By working together to address the root causes of the housing affordability crisis, we can create a future where all individuals have access to safe, affordable housing and the resources they need to thrive.

Income Inequality

Another key factor that has contributed to the rise of drug use and homelessness on the West Coast is income inequality. The region has experienced significant economic growth in recent years, driven by the technology industry and other sectors. However, this growth has not been shared equally, and many individuals and families have been left behind.

Income inequality is a major issue in the United States, and it is particularly acute on the West Coast. According to a recent report by the Economic Policy Institute, the top 1% of earners in San Francisco earn 44 times more than the bottom 99%. This extreme income inequality has made it difficult for many people to afford basic necessities like housing and healthcare, which has contributed to the rise of homelessness and drug use.

In a city like San Francisco, where the median home price is over $1.5 million, many people simply cannot afford to live there. This has led to a situation where people are living in overcrowded and unsafe conditions or are forced to commute long distances to find affordable housing. The lack of affordable housing has also contributed to gentrification and displacement, as landlords and developers seek to profit from rising property values.

The high cost of healthcare is another factor that has contributed to the drug use and homelessness crisis on the West Coast. Many people, particularly those with lower incomes, cannot afford the high cost of medical care, prescription drugs, and mental health services. This lack of access to healthcare can make it difficult for people to manage chronic illnesses, addiction, and mental health issues, which can lead to homelessness and drug use.

Studies have shown that income inequality is closely linked to both homelessness and drug use. According to a report by the National Low Income Housing Coalition, people who earn less

than $15 per hour cannot afford a two-bedroom rental home in any state in the United States. This means that many low-income individuals and families are at risk of becoming homeless, as they simply cannot afford the high cost of housing. In addition, the stress and anxiety of financial insecurity can lead people to turn to drugs as a way to cope.

Homelessness and drug use also have a negative impact on economic inequality. Homelessness and drug addiction can make it difficult for individuals to maintain stable employment or advance their careers. The stigma associated with homelessness and addiction can also make it difficult for individuals to access resources and services that could help them improve their economic situation.

The impact of income inequality on the drug use and homelessness crisis is compounded by the racial and ethnic disparities that exist in the region. Communities of color, particularly Black and Indigenous communities, are disproportionately impacted by homelessness and drug addiction. This is due in part to systemic racism and discrimination in housing, healthcare, and employment.

In recent years, there have been efforts to address income inequality on the West Coast. Some cities have implemented minimum wage increases and other policies aimed at reducing economic disparities. However, more needs to be done to ensure that everyone has access to basic necessities like housing, healthcare, and education.

One approach to addressing income inequality and its impacts on drug use and homelessness is to implement progressive tax policies. By increasing taxes on the wealthy and corporations, governments can generate revenue to fund social programs aimed at reducing poverty, increasing access to healthcare, and providing affordable housing. For example, in 2018, Seattle passed a controversial "head tax" on businesses making more than $20 million a year to fund affordable housing and homeless services. However, the tax was later repealed after a backlash from businesses and the public.

Another approach is to increase access to education and job training programs. By providing individuals with the skills and knowledge they need to compete in the job market, governments can help reduce income inequality and increase economic mobility. In recent years, there has been a growing movement for tuition-free public college and university education, which would make it easier for low-income students to access higher education and increase their earning potential.

Finally, there is a need to address systemic issues such as discrimination and racism, which can contribute to income inequality and poverty. Communities of color, particularly Black and Indigenous communities, have been disproportionately impacted by the drug use and homelessness crisis on the West Coast. Addressing issues such as police brutality, redlining, and other forms of systemic racism can help create a more equitable society where everyone has access to basic necessities and the opportunity to thrive.

In conclusion, income inequality is a major contributor to the drug use and homelessness crisis on the West Coast. The high cost of living and lack of affordable housing and healthcare have made it difficult for many individuals and families to meet their basic needs. Governments, businesses, and communities need to work together to address this issue and create a more equitable society where everyone has the opportunity to succeed. By implementing policies such as progressive taxation, increasing access to education and job training, and addressing systemic issues of discrimination and racism, we can help reduce poverty and create a better future for all.

Mental Health and Addiction

The drug use and homelessness crisis on the West Coast is not only caused by economic factors but is also closely linked to mental health and addiction. Many people experiencing homelessness and substance abuse have underlying mental health conditions that are either untreated or undertreated due to a lack of access to healthcare and other resources.

Mental illness is a prevalent issue among the homeless population, with studies estimating that up to 30% of people experiencing homelessness have a serious mental illness. Common mental health conditions among this population include schizophrenia, bipolar disorder, and major depression. These conditions can make it difficult for individuals to maintain stable housing, employment, and relationships, leading to a higher risk of homelessness and substance abuse.

In addition, addiction is a significant issue among the homeless population, with studies showing that up to 70% of people experiencing homelessness have a history of substance abuse. Substance abuse can lead to a range of health problems, including chronic diseases like HIV/AIDS and hepatitis, and can exacerbate mental health issues.

The lack of access to mental health and addiction treatment exacerbates these issues. Many people experiencing homelessness and addiction do not have access to basic healthcare, let alone specialized mental health and addiction treatment. This can lead to a cycle of homelessness and addiction, as individuals are unable to access the resources they need to address their underlying mental health conditions and addiction issues.

The impact of the mental health and addiction crisis on the West Coast can be seen in the growing number of overdose deaths in the region. According to the National Institute on Drug Abuse, drug overdose deaths increased by 29% in California from 2019 to 2020, with fentanyl-related deaths increasing by 77%. The lack of access to addiction treatment and harm reduction services is a major contributor to this crisis.

There have been some efforts to address the mental health and addiction crisis on the West Coast. Cities like Seattle and San Francisco have implemented harm reduction programs, including needle exchange programs and safe injection sites, aimed at reducing the harm associated with drug use. These programs have been shown to be effective in reducing the spread of infectious diseases and preventing overdose deaths.

However, more needs to be done to address the underlying mental health and addiction issues that are driving the drug use and homelessness crisis. This includes increasing access to mental health and addiction treatment services, including medication-assisted treatment for opioid addiction. It also includes addressing the stigma associated with mental illness and addiction, which can prevent individuals from seeking the help they need.

In recent years, there has been increased awareness of the mental health and addiction crisis on the West Coast, with organizations and advocates pushing for more resources and support for those affected. However, there is still a long way to go in addressing these complex issues and providing the necessary resources and support to those in need.

In addition to limited access to mental health services, there is also a lack of addiction treatment options on the West Coast. Individuals struggling with addiction may not have access to affordable or effective treatment, which can lead to a cycle of homelessness and drug use. This lack of treatment options is particularly acute for those who are uninsured or underinsured, as addiction treatment can be expensive and may not be covered by insurance.

According to a report by the National Institute on Drug Abuse, only about 10% of people who need addiction treatment actually receive it. This treatment gap is even wider for homeless individuals, who face additional barriers to accessing care such as lack of transportation, stigma, and limited availability of treatment services.

The opioid epidemic has also played a significant role in the rise of drug use and homelessness on the West Coast. Opioid addiction can be particularly difficult to overcome, and the high cost of prescription opioids has led many individuals to turn to cheaper and more dangerous alternatives like heroin and fentanyl. The use of these drugs has led to a dramatic increase in overdose deaths on the West Coast, particularly in cities like San Francisco and Seattle.

In response to the opioid epidemic, there have been efforts to expand access to addiction treatment and harm reduction services on the West Coast. For example, some cities have implemented needle exchange programs, which provide clean needles and other supplies to reduce the risk of overdose and the spread of infectious diseases. In addition, some cities have implemented medication-assisted treatment (MAT) programs, which use medications like methadone and buprenorphine to help individuals overcome opioid addiction.

Despite these efforts, there is still a significant gap in access to addiction treatment and harm reduction services on the West Coast. Many individuals who need treatment are unable to access it, and the lack of effective treatment options can make it difficult for individuals to overcome addiction and avoid homelessness.

While harm reduction strategies such as providing clean needles and government-regulated drugs may be necessary to prevent immediate harm, the ultimate goal should be to help people overcome addiction and rebuild their lives. Providing access to comprehensive addiction treatment is critical in achieving this goal.

One of the biggest challenges in addressing addiction and mental health issues is the lack of access to treatment. Many people simply cannot afford the high cost of addiction treatment, and there is often a shortage of resources available for those who do seek help. This lack of access to treatment can exacerbate the drug use and homelessness crisis, as people who are struggling with addiction and mental health issues are unable to get the help they need to recover.

Studies have shown that evidence-based addiction treatment is effective in helping people overcome addiction and improve their mental health. This includes treatments such as cognitive-behavioral therapy, motivational interviewing, and medication-assisted treatment. However, not all addiction treatment centers are created equal, and there is a need for better treatment options and standards in the field.

Rehab centers need to implement better treatment options that are tailored to the individual needs of each patient. This includes providing a range of evidence-based therapies, as well as addressing underlying mental health issues that may be contributing to addiction. Treatment should also be long-term and provide ongoing support to help people maintain their recovery.

Another important factor in addressing addiction and mental health issues is reducing the stigma associated with these conditions. Many people who are struggling with addiction and mental health issues are afraid to seek help due to the stigma surrounding these conditions. By reducing stigma and promoting understanding, more people may be willing to seek help and access the treatment they need to recover.

In conclusion, the role of mental health and addiction in the drug use and homelessness crisis on the West Coast cannot be ignored. Limited access to treatment exacerbates these issues, and there is a need for better treatment options and standards in the field. By providing access to evidence-based addiction treatment, addressing underlying mental health issues, and reducing stigma, we can help people overcome addiction and rebuild their lives.

Climate and Geography

The West Coast of the United States has become a hotspot for the homelessness crisis. There are a variety of factors that contribute to this issue, including income inequality, mental health and addiction, and lack of affordable housing. However, one often overlooked factor is the mild climate and geography of the region, which has made it a desirable location for people experiencing homelessness.

The West Coast has a mild climate, with relatively stable temperatures throughout the year. The average temperature in San

Francisco, for example, ranges from 50 to 70 degrees Fahrenheit, with relatively little variation throughout the year. This mild climate makes it easier for people to survive outdoors, without the harsh winter conditions that can be deadly for people experiencing homelessness in other parts of the country.

In addition to the mild climate, the geography of the West Coast has also contributed to the concentration of homelessness in the region. The West Coast is home to a variety of natural features, including beaches, forests, and mountains, which can provide shelter and resources for people experiencing homelessness. For example, many people experiencing homelessness in Seattle camp in wooded areas, where they can find shelter and food.

The mild climate and geography of the West Coast have made it a desirable location for people experiencing homelessness, which has contributed to the concentration of the crisis in the region. According to a report by the Department of Housing and Urban Development, the West Coast accounts for nearly half of the homeless population in the United States, despite being home to only a quarter of the total population.

This concentration of homelessness has put a strain on local resources and has made it more difficult for cities and states to effectively address the crisis. For example, in Seattle, the city's Navigation Team, which is responsible for connecting people experiencing homelessness with services, has struggled to keep up with the demand for services. The team is often forced to prioritize people who are at risk of dying on the streets, leaving many others without access to the help they need.

The mild climate and geography of the West Coast have also contributed to the development of informal homeless encampments, where people live in tents and makeshift shelters. These encampments can be found in cities and towns throughout the region, including Seattle, Portland, and San Francisco. While these encampments provide a sense of community and security for people experiencing homelessness, they also present a variety of health and safety risks.

For example, many encampments lack basic sanitation facilities, which can lead to the spread of disease. In addition, the concentration of people in these encampments can make it easier for drugs and other illicit activities to thrive, which can exacerbate the drug use and addiction issues that contribute to the homelessness crisis.

In recent years, cities and states on the West Coast have implemented a variety of strategies to address the homelessness crisis, including increasing funding for affordable housing, providing more resources for mental health and addiction treatment, and investing in outreach and services for people experiencing homelessness. However, the mild climate and geography of the region will continue to present challenges, and addressing the crisis will require a multifaceted approach that takes these factors into account.

The mild climate and geography of the West Coast have made it an attractive location for people experiencing homelessness, which has contributed to the concentration of the crisis in this region. The mild climate makes it easier for people to survive outside without shelter, as they are less likely to experience extreme temperatures and weather conditions. This makes it more feasible for people to live outside and forgo traditional housing options. Additionally, the West Coast's geography provides ample opportunities for people to find hidden or secluded areas to set up makeshift homes, tents, or other forms of shelter.

For many years, the West Coast has been seen as a place of opportunity, where people can come and start a new life. The region's natural beauty, mild weather, and diverse cultural offerings have drawn people from all over the world. However, this influx of people has also put a strain on the region's housing market, leading to rising costs and decreased availability of affordable housing. This has forced many people onto the streets, where they are left to fend for themselves.

According to a report by the US Department of Housing and Urban Development (HUD), California has the highest rate of homelessness in the country, with an estimated 151,278 people experiencing homelessness on any given night. Oregon and Washington also have high rates of homelessness, with 14,607 and 21,577 people experiencing homelessness respectively. The mild climate and geography of the West Coast are major contributors to these high rates of homelessness, as they make it easier for people to survive outside without shelter.

Furthermore, the concentration of homelessness on the West Coast has created a feedback loop, where the presence of a large homeless population attracts more homeless people to the area. This is known as the "magnet effect," where people experiencing homelessness are drawn to areas where there are more services and resources available to them. As a result, the West Coast has become a hub for homeless services, with many organizations and government agencies working to provide support to people experiencing homelessness.

While the mild climate and geography of the West Coast have made it a desirable location for people experiencing homelessness, it is important to note that homelessness is not limited to this region. Homelessness is a national issue that affects communities across the country. However, the concentration of homelessness on the West Coast has made it more visible and has put a spotlight on the need for solutions to this crisis.

In recent years, there have been efforts to address homelessness on the West Coast. Cities and counties have implemented a range of policies and programs aimed at reducing homelessness, including increasing funding for affordable housing, providing more services to people experiencing homelessness, and implementing diversion programs that provide temporary shelter and support services to people in need. However, more needs to be done to address the root causes of homelessness, including poverty, mental illness, addiction, and the lack of affordable housing. By addressing these underlying issues, we can work towards ending homelessness on the West Coast and across the country.

Social and Legal Policies

Social and legal policies play a significant role in shaping the drug use and homelessness crisis on the West Coast. Many of these policies have contributed to the concentration of the crisis in this region, and have also hindered efforts to address these issues.

One key policy area is drug enforcement. For decades, the United States has pursued a "war on drugs" that has resulted in mass incarceration and criminalization of drug use. This approach has disproportionately affected low-income communities and communities of color, and has done little to address the underlying issues of addiction and drug use.

In recent years, there has been a growing recognition of the need for a more public health-oriented approach to drug use and addiction. Some cities on the West Coast, such as Seattle and San Francisco, have implemented harm reduction policies such as needle exchange programs and safe injection sites. These policies have been shown to reduce the spread of diseases like HIV and hepatitis C, and can also connect people who use drugs with healthcare and social services.

However, there are still many legal barriers to implementing these policies more widely. For example, safe injection sites are currently illegal under federal law, which has limited their implementation in the United States. Similarly, many states still have harsh drug laws that criminalize drug use and possession, which can make it difficult for people to access treatment and support.

Another policy area that has contributed to the homelessness crisis on the West Coast is housing policy. In recent decades, there has been a trend towards deregulation and privatization of the housing market, which has made it more difficult for people to access affordable housing. This has been particularly acute on the West Coast, where high demand for housing has driven up prices and made it difficult for low-income individuals and families to find stable housing.

Many cities on the West Coast have responded to the affordable housing crisis by implementing policies such as rent control and affordable housing mandates. However, these policies have faced opposition from landlords and developers, who argue that they will discourage investment in the housing market.

Finally, social policies related to homelessness have also contributed to the concentration of the crisis on the West Coast. Many cities have implemented punitive policies such as anti-camping laws and sweeps of homeless encampments, which can further traumatize already vulnerable individuals and make it more difficult for them to access services and support.

There have also been efforts to implement more compassionate and effective policies to address homelessness. For example, some cities have implemented "Housing First" policies, which prioritize providing stable housing for homeless individuals and families as a first step towards addressing other issues such as addiction and mental illness. These policies have been shown to be effective in reducing homelessness and improving outcomes for people who experience it.

However, despite these efforts, many challenges remain in implementing effective social and legal policies to address the drug use and homelessness crisis on the West Coast. One of the major challenges is political opposition from conservative groups and politicians who argue that policies such as safe injection sites and Housing First are "enabling" or "rewarding" bad behavior.

Another challenge is the lack of coordination and resources among different agencies and organizations working on these issues. Homelessness and drug use are complex problems that require a multi-faceted approach involving healthcare providers, social workers, law enforcement, and community organizations. However, these groups often work in silos and do not have the resources or capacity to effectively coordinate their efforts.

Additionally, there is a lack of investment in mental health and addiction treatment, which is critical to addressing the root causes of the crisis. Many people who experience homelessness and drug addiction also struggle with mental illness, and without access to treatment, it can be difficult for them to overcome these challenges and rebuild their lives.

To address these challenges, there is a need for a more coordinated and holistic approach to addressing the drug use and homelessness crisis on the West Coast. This approach should prioritize harm reduction policies such as safe injection sites and needle exchange programs, as well as investment in mental health and addiction treatment. It should also prioritize providing stable housing as a first step towards addressing other issues such as addiction and mental illness.

Finally, there is a need for greater public education and awareness about the root causes of the crisis and the importance of addressing it in a compassionate and effective manner. Many people still view homelessness and drug addiction as personal failings rather than systemic issues, and this stigma can make it more difficult to implement effective policies and programs.

In conclusion, social and legal policies have played a significant role in shaping the drug use and homelessness crisis on the West Coast. While there have been some efforts to address these issues, many challenges remain in implementing effective policies and programs. To address these challenges, there is a need for a more coordinated and holistic approach that prioritizes harm reduction, mental health and addiction treatment, and stable housing. Additionally, there is a need for greater public education and awareness to reduce stigma and increase support for these policies and programs.

Racial and Ethnic Disparities

Racial and ethnic disparities are a significant factor in the drug use and homelessness crisis on the West Coast. Communities of color are disproportionately affected by these issues, and historical and ongoing systemic racism has contributed to these disparities.

One key factor in racial and ethnic disparities in the drug use and homelessness crisis is economic inequality. Communities of color are more likely to experience poverty and economic hardship, which can contribute to both drug use and homelessness. According to a 2019 report by the National Alliance to End Homelessness, Black Americans are overrepresented in the homeless population, comprising 40% of homeless individuals despite making up only 13% of the general population. Similarly, a 2016 report by the Substance Abuse and Mental Health Services Administration found that poverty and unemployment were significant risk factors for substance abuse, and that Black and Hispanic individuals were more likely to experience poverty and unemployment than White individuals.

Another factor contributing to racial and ethnic disparities in the drug use and homelessness crisis is discrimination and criminalization. Communities of color are more likely to be targeted by law enforcement for drug offenses, even though drug use rates are similar across racial and ethnic groups. This can result in disproportionate criminalization and incarceration of communities of color, which can exacerbate economic and social disadvantages and contribute to homelessness.

Additionally, communities of color may face discrimination in accessing housing and employment, which can contribute to homelessness and economic hardship. For example, Black and Hispanic individuals may face discriminatory lending practices when attempting to purchase a home, making it more difficult to build wealth and access stable housing. Discrimination in the job market can also make it more difficult for individuals to maintain stable employment and access healthcare and other social services.

Historical and ongoing systemic racism has also contributed to racial and ethnic disparities in the drug use and homelessness crisis. For example, discriminatory housing policies such as redlining and segregation have limited access to affordable housing and contributed to economic inequality in communities of color. The War on Drugs, which has disproportionately affected communities of color, has also contributed to the criminalization and stigmatization of drug use and addiction in these communities.

Efforts to address racial and ethnic disparities in the drug use and homelessness crisis on the West Coast must take a holistic approach that addresses the root causes of economic inequality and discrimination. This includes policies that increase access to affordable housing and address discriminatory lending practices, as well as policies that promote economic opportunity and reduce criminalization of drug use and addiction.

There are also efforts to center the experiences and voices of communities of color in the development of policies and programs to address the drug use and homelessness crisis. For example, organizations such as the Black Homelessness Coalition in Seattle and the Black Community Development Project in San Francisco are working to address the specific needs of Black individuals experiencing homelessness and advocate for policies that center racial equity.

Overall, addressing racial and ethnic disparities in the drug use and homelessness crisis is a critical component of efforts to create more just and equitable communities on the West Coast and beyond.

Community-Based Responses

Community-based responses have been crucial in addressing the drug use and homelessness crisis on the West Coast. These responses have included harm reduction strategies, mutual aid groups, and grassroots advocacy efforts, among others.

Harm reduction strategies have been an important community-based response to the drug use crisis. Harm reduction is a public health approach that aims to reduce the harm associated with drug use, rather than focusing on abstinence or criminalization. Harm reduction strategies include needle exchange programs, safe injection sites, and overdose prevention education.

In the early 1990s, needle exchange programs were established in many cities on the West Coast, including San Francisco and Seattle, in response to the HIV/AIDS epidemic. These programs provide clean needles and other supplies to people who inject drugs, which can help reduce the spread of diseases like HIV and hepatitis C. Safe injection sites, which provide a safe and supervised environment for people to inject drugs, have been established in some cities, including Vancouver, Canada, and are currently being considered in some cities in the United States.

Mutual aid groups have also played an important role in addressing the drug use and homelessness crisis on the West Coast. Mutual aid is a form of community-based support that emphasizes collaboration, solidarity, and collective action. Mutual aid groups provide support and resources to people who use drugs, as well as to people experiencing homelessness and other forms of marginalization.

One example of a mutual aid group is the Homeless Youth Alliance, which was established in San Francisco in 1992. The group provides a range of services to young people experiencing homelessness, including access to showers, laundry facilities, and food, as well as harm reduction services like needle exchange and overdose prevention education. Other mutual aid groups include the San Francisco Community Health Engagement and Empowerment Project (CHEEP), which provides support and resources to people living with HIV/AIDS, and the People's Harm Reduction Alliance in Seattle, which provides harm reduction services to people who use drugs.

Grassroots advocacy efforts have also been an important community-based response to the drug use and homelessness crisis on the West Coast. Grassroots advocacy involves mobilizing individuals and communities to advocate for social and political change, often through direct action and community organizing.

One example of grassroots advocacy on the West Coast is the California Homeless Youth Project, which is a coalition of organizations and individuals working to address youth homelessness in California. The coalition engages in advocacy and policy work, as well as direct services and community organizing, to address the root causes of youth homelessness.

Other grassroots advocacy efforts include the Western Regional Advocacy Project, which works to address the criminalization of homelessness and advocate for housing as a human right, and the Seattle/King County Coalition on Homelessness, which advocates for policies and programs to address homelessness in the Seattle area.

In addition to harm reduction strategies, mutual aid groups, and grassroots advocacy efforts, other community-based responses have been important in addressing the drug use and homelessness crisis on the West Coast. One such response is the Housing First approach, which prioritizes providing housing to individuals experiencing homelessness without requiring them to meet certain conditions like sobriety or employment.

Housing First has been shown to be effective in reducing homelessness and improving health outcomes for individuals who have experienced long-term homelessness and have multiple health conditions. For example, a 2015 study found that Housing First programs in Seattle and Portland were associated with significant reductions in homelessness and emergency room visits, as well as improvements in mental health and substance use outcomes.

Community land trusts have also been an important community-based response to the housing crisis on the West Coast. Community land trusts are nonprofit organizations that acquire and hold land in trust for the benefit of the community, and can be used to provide permanently affordable housing. Community land trusts have been established in many cities on the West Coast, including San Francisco and Seattle, and have been effective in providing affordable housing to low-income and marginalized communities.

Finally, community-based responses have also included efforts to address the root causes of the drug use and homelessness crisis, including economic inequality and systemic racism. For example, some community organizations have focused on promoting economic justice and equitable access to affordable housing, while others have advocated for policy changes to address systemic racism and discrimination in housing, employment, and law enforcement.

Overall, community-based responses have been crucial in addressing the drug use and homelessness crisis on the West Coast, particularly in the face of limited government resources and political will. These responses have focused on providing support and resources to individuals experiencing homelessness and drug addiction, as well as advocating for systemic change to address the root causes of these issues.

Government Responses

Government responses to the drug use and homelessness crisis on the West Coast have been varied, but generally not sufficient to address the scale of the problem. The response of federal, state, and local governments has included funding for affordable housing, mental health and addiction treatment, and other services, but many argue that the response has been inadequate in both scale and effectiveness.

One major government response to the crisis has been funding for affordable housing. Housing affordability and availability are critical issues for people experiencing homelessness, and lack of access to affordable housing is a leading cause of homelessness. Federal funding for affordable housing programs has been reduced in recent years, which has made it more difficult for cities and states to address homelessness.

Many cities on the West Coast have responded to the crisis by allocating funding for affordable housing programs. In San Francisco, for example, voters passed a $600 million affordable housing bond in 2015 to fund the development of affordable housing units. Seattle has also increased funding for affordable housing programs in recent years.

However, critics argue that these efforts have been insufficient to address the scale of the problem. In San Francisco, for example, the number of homeless people increased by 17% between 2017 and 2019, despite increased funding for affordable housing programs. Many cities on the West Coast continue to face a shortage of affordable housing, particularly for people with extremely low incomes.

Another government response to the drug use and homelessness crisis has been increased funding for mental health and addiction treatment. Many people experiencing homelessness also struggle with mental health and addiction issues, and access to treatment can be critical for addressing these issues and reducing the risk of homelessness.

In recent years, many cities and states on the West Coast have increased funding for mental health and addiction treatment programs. In San Francisco, for example, the city has increased funding for behavioral health services, including substance abuse treatment, in recent years. Seattle has also increased funding for mental health and addiction treatment programs, including a new program to provide addiction treatment in jails.

However, critics argue that these efforts have been insufficient to address the scale of the problem. Many people experiencing homelessness still lack access to adequate mental health and addiction treatment, and the quality of treatment can vary widely depending on the provider and the location.

Other government responses to the crisis have included providing services like public toilets and hygiene stations to people experiencing homelessness, increasing funding for outreach and engagement programs, and implementing policies like "housing first" that prioritize providing housing to people experiencing homelessness.

However, many argue that these efforts have been insufficient to address the scale of the problem, and that more aggressive action is needed to address the root causes of homelessness and drug use, including systemic racism, economic inequality, and the criminalization of drug use and homelessness.

One factor that has hampered government responses to the drug use and homelessness crisis on the West Coast is a lack of coordination and collaboration between different levels of government, as well as between different agencies and service providers. Homelessness and drug use are complex issues that require a coordinated and comprehensive response, but many argue that the current system is fragmented and lacks clear leadership.

In recent years, there have been some efforts to address this issue. For example, in 2018, the state of California created the Homeless Coordinating and Financing Council to help coordinate state and local efforts to address homelessness. The council is responsible for developing a statewide plan to address homelessness and increasing coordination between different agencies and service providers.

Similarly, many cities on the West Coast have established new positions or agencies to coordinate responses to homelessness and drug use. In San Francisco, for example, the city established a new Department of Homelessness and Supportive Housing in 2018 to coordinate the city's response to homelessness.

However, critics argue that these efforts have been insufficient, and that there is still a lack of coordination and collaboration between different levels of government and between different agencies and service providers. Some argue that a more centralized and coordinated approach is needed to address the scale of the problem.

Another challenge facing government responses to the crisis is the criminalization of drug use and homelessness. Many people experiencing homelessness and drug addiction are subject to criminalization and punishment, rather than being provided with support and services to address their needs.

In recent years, some cities and states on the West Coast have implemented policies aimed at reducing the criminalization of homelessness and drug use. For example, in 2018, Seattle passed a law that prohibits landlords from discriminating against renters based on their criminal record, including past convictions for drug use or homelessness-related offenses.

Similarly, some cities on the West Coast have implemented "housing first" policies that prioritize providing housing to people experiencing homelessness, rather than requiring them to go through treatment or other programs before being provided with housing.

However, critics argue that more needs to be done to address the criminalization of homelessness and drug use, and to provide support and services to people experiencing homelessness and drug addiction, rather than punishing them. Many argue that the criminal justice system is ill-equipped to address these issues, and that more funding and resources need to be directed towards community-based responses like harm reduction and mutual aid.

Overall, while government responses to the drug use and homelessness crisis on the West Coast have included funding for affordable housing, mental health and addiction treatment, and other services, many argue that these responses have been insufficient to address the scale of the problem. A lack of coordination and collaboration between different levels of government and between different agencies and service providers, as well as the criminalization of drug use and homelessness, are among the factors that have hampered government responses to the crisis. To address these challenges, many argue that a more coordinated and comprehensive approach is needed, as well as a greater focus on community-based responses and addressing the root causes of homelessness and drug addiction.

Conclusion

In conclusion, the drug use and homelessness crisis on the West Coast has been caused by a complex set of factors, including economic inequality, systemic racism, lack of affordable housing, and inadequate access to mental health and addiction treatment. The crisis has been exacerbated by the opioid epidemic, which has led to a significant increase in drug use and overdose deaths.

The response of governments to the crisis has included funding for affordable housing, mental health and addiction treatment, and other services. While these efforts have helped some individuals, many argue that they have been insufficient to address the scale of the problem. More aggressive action is needed to address the root causes of homelessness and drug use.

To truly address the crisis, a comprehensive and compassionate approach is necessary. This includes increasing funding for affordable housing programs, expanding access to mental health and addiction treatment, and implementing policies that prioritize providing housing to people experiencing homelessness. It also involves addressing the root causes of the crisis, including systemic racism and economic inequality.

As individuals, we can take action to support community-based organizations working to address the crisis. We can also advocate for change at the local and national level, by contacting our elected officials and participating in community organizations. Only through collective action and compassionate policies can we hope to address the drug use and homelessness crisis on the West Coast and beyond.

Finally, it is important to recognize that the drug use and homelessness crisis on the West Coast is a complex issue that cannot be solved through one single approach. It requires a comprehensive and compassionate approach that takes into account the diverse needs and experiences of people experiencing homelessness and addiction.

This includes addressing the root causes of homelessness and drug use, such as systemic racism, economic inequality, and the criminalization of drug use and homelessness. It also requires increasing funding for affordable housing, mental health and addiction treatment, and other support services, as well as implementing policies like "housing first" that prioritize providing housing to people experiencing homelessness.

Ultimately, it is up to all of us to take action to address this crisis. We can advocate for change by contacting our elected representatives, volunteering with community-based organizations working to address homelessness and addiction, and supporting policies and initiatives that prioritize the needs and dignity of people experiencing homelessness.

In conclusion, the drug use and homelessness crisis on the West Coast is a devastating issue that affects thousands of people and has far-reaching consequences for our communities. While there is no easy solution, it is clear that we must take action to address this crisis with a comprehensive and compassionate approach that recognizes the complex needs and experiences of people experiencing homelessness and addiction. By working together and taking action, we can create a better future for all members of our community.

The Role of Poverty and Inequality in Drug Use and Homelessness

The drug use and homelessness crisis on the West Coast of the United States is a complex issue that has been ongoing for several decades. The crisis is characterized by a high prevalence of drug use and homelessness, which disproportionately affects low-income and marginalized communities. While the crisis is not unique to the West Coast, the region has been particularly hard hit due to a variety of economic and social factors.

The issue of homelessness on the West Coast has been the focus of extensive media coverage in recent years, with stories highlighting the visible presence of homeless encampments and the associated public health and safety concerns. The crisis has been exacerbated by the prevalence of drug use, particularly the use of opioids, which has led to an increase in overdose deaths and other health problems among people experiencing homelessness.

Poverty and inequality are key factors that have contributed to the drug use and homelessness crisis on the West Coast. Economic factors, including high housing costs, low wages, and limited access to affordable healthcare, have made it difficult for many people to maintain stable housing and access the resources needed to address drug addiction and other health problems.

Moreover, the crisis has disproportionately affected marginalized communities, including people of color, LGBTQ+ individuals, and people with disabilities, who face additional barriers to accessing healthcare and housing due to systemic inequalities and discrimination.

This essay will explore the role of poverty and inequality in exacerbating the drug use and homelessness crisis on the West Coast. Specifically, it will examine how economic factors have impacted people's lives and health outcomes, and how social inequalities have contributed to the disproportionate impact of the crisis on marginalized communities. Finally, it will discuss the importance of a comprehensive and compassionate approach to addressing the crisis, one that recognizes the interconnectedness of poverty, inequality, and health outcomes.

The link between poverty and drug use

Drug use and poverty are interrelated issues that are closely linked to the drug use and homelessness crisis on the West Coast. Poverty is one of the main drivers of drug use, and drug use can perpetuate poverty by creating a cycle of addiction, criminalization, and social exclusion. Understanding the link between poverty and drug use is essential to addressing the drug use and homelessness crisis on the West Coast.

Poverty is a major risk factor for drug use, and people living in poverty are more likely to use drugs than those who are economically stable. Poverty can lead to drug use in several ways. First, poverty can increase stress, anxiety, and social isolation, which can lead people to use drugs as a coping mechanism. Second, poverty can limit access to education, employment, and other opportunities, which can increase the likelihood of drug use as a way to escape the harsh realities of poverty. Third, poverty can increase exposure to social and environmental factors that contribute to drug use, such as crime, violence, and drug trafficking.

The link between poverty and drug use has been well documented in research studies. For example, a study published in the Journal of Adolescent Health found that poverty was a significant predictor of drug use among a sample of adolescents in the United States. The study found that adolescents living in poverty were more likely to use drugs than those who were not living in poverty. Another study published in the International Journal of Drug Policy found that poverty was a significant predictor of injection drug use among a sample of people who inject drugs in Vancouver, Canada.

Drug use can also perpetuate poverty by creating a cycle of addiction, criminalization, and social exclusion. Drug addiction can lead to job loss, financial instability, and social isolation, which can perpetuate poverty. People who use drugs are also more likely to be criminalized, which can make it harder to find employment, housing, and other opportunities. Criminalization can also lead to social exclusion and marginalization, further perpetuating the cycle of poverty.

The link between drug use and poverty has been highlighted in media coverage of the drug use and homelessness crisis on the West Coast. For example, a report by the Los Angeles Times found that poverty and drug addiction were major factors contributing to the homelessness crisis in Los Angeles. The report found that many people experiencing homelessness in Los Angeles were struggling with drug addiction and had limited access to treatment and support services.

Addressing the link between poverty and drug use requires a comprehensive approach that addresses the root causes of poverty, such as economic inequality, lack of access to education and employment, and social and environmental factors that contribute to poverty and drug use. This approach should also include expanding access to drug treatment and support services for people who use drugs, as well as addressing the criminalization and stigmatization of drug use.

Moreover, addressing poverty and drug use requires a recognition of the systemic and structural factors that contribute to these issues. Economic inequality, lack of affordable housing, and inadequate healthcare systems are just a few of the factors that perpetuate poverty and drug use. To address these issues, policymakers and community leaders must work together to implement policies and programs that create economic opportunities, provide affordable housing, and expand access to healthcare.

One effective approach to addressing poverty and drug use is harm reduction. Harm reduction strategies aim to minimize the negative consequences of drug use and provide support for people who use drugs. This approach recognizes that drug use is a complex issue that cannot be solved simply by criminalizing drug use or promoting abstinence. Harm reduction strategies include expanding access to clean needles, providing overdose prevention education and naloxone, and creating safe injection sites.

Furthermore, addressing poverty and drug use requires a compassionate and non-judgmental approach that prioritizes the health and well-being of individuals and communities. This approach recognizes that drug use is often a symptom of deeper social and economic issues and that people who use drugs are deserving of support, care, and respect. Stigmatization and criminalization of drug use only perpetuate the cycle of poverty and addiction, making it harder for people to access the support and resources they need to recover.

In conclusion, the link between poverty and drug use is a complex and multi-faceted issue that requires a comprehensive and compassionate approach. Poverty is a major risk factor for drug use, and drug use can perpetuate poverty by creating a cycle of addiction, criminalization, and social exclusion. Addressing poverty and drug use requires a recognition of the systemic and structural factors that contribute to these issues, as well as a commitment to harm reduction, compassionate care, and social and economic justice. By working together to address the root causes of poverty and drug use, we can create healthier and more equitable communities on the West Coast and beyond.

The link between poverty and homelessness

Poverty and homelessness are closely linked issues, with poverty being a significant risk factor for homelessness. Homelessness, in turn, can perpetuate poverty by limiting access to basic needs such as housing, healthcare, and employment. Understanding the link between poverty and homelessness is critical to addressing the homelessness crisis on the West Coast.

Poverty can lead to homelessness in several ways. First, poverty can make it difficult for people to afford housing, leading to housing instability and eventual homelessness. According to a report by the National Low Income Housing Coalition, there is a severe shortage of affordable housing in the United States, and many low-income households are forced to spend a disproportionate amount of their income on housing, leaving little left for other basic needs. This can lead to housing insecurity and eventual homelessness.

Second, poverty can limit access to healthcare and other social services, increasing the likelihood of becoming homeless. For example, people living in poverty may struggle to access mental health treatment or substance abuse treatment, leading to further deterioration of their physical and mental health and eventual homelessness.

Finally, poverty can lead to increased exposure to other risk factors for homelessness, such as domestic violence, job loss, and natural disasters. People living in poverty may lack the resources and social support necessary to cope with these events, leading to homelessness.

Homelessness, in turn, can perpetuate poverty by limiting access to basic needs and creating barriers to employment and other opportunities. Homelessness can lead to poor health outcomes, making it difficult for people to maintain employment or attend school. Homelessness can also lead to social isolation and stigma, making it difficult for people to build relationships and access support services. This can create a cycle of poverty and homelessness that is difficult to break.

The link between poverty and homelessness has been highlighted in media coverage of the homelessness crisis on the West Coast. For example, a report by The Guardian found that the high cost of housing and lack of affordable housing were major factors contributing to the homelessness crisis in San Francisco. The report also found that many people experiencing homelessness in San Francisco were struggling with poverty and had limited access to basic needs such as healthcare and social services.

Addressing the link between poverty and homelessness requires a comprehensive approach that addresses the root causes of poverty, such as economic inequality and lack of access to healthcare and social services. This approach should also include expanding access to affordable housing and support services for people experiencing homelessness, as well as addressing the stigma and criminalization of homelessness.

One approach to addressing homelessness is the Housing First model, which prioritizes providing stable housing for people experiencing homelessness as a first step toward addressing other needs such as healthcare and employment. The Housing First model has been successful in reducing homelessness and improving health outcomes for people experiencing homelessness in cities such as Seattle and Salt Lake City.

Another approach is to provide support services such as healthcare, mental health treatment, and substance abuse treatment for people experiencing homelessness. This can help address the underlying causes of homelessness and improve health outcomes, making it easier for people to maintain employment and housing stability.

Addressing the link between poverty and homelessness also requires addressing systemic issues such as economic inequality and lack of access to affordable housing. This can include policies such as increasing the minimum wage, providing tax incentives for affordable housing development, and expanding access to healthcare and social services.

In addition to policy solutions, addressing the link between poverty and homelessness also requires changing societal attitudes toward poverty and homelessness. This can include reducing stigma and criminalization of homelessness, as well as promoting empathy and understanding for people experiencing homelessness.

Overall, addressing the link between poverty and homelessness is essential to addressing the homelessness crisis on the West Coast. This requires a comprehensive approach that addresses the root causes of poverty and homelessness, provides support services for people experiencing homelessness, and changes societal attitudes toward poverty and homelessness.

Economic factors affecting health outcomes

Economic factors, such as income, education, and access to healthcare, have a significant impact on health outcomes, including drug use and homelessness. These factors can influence health outcomes in various ways, and understanding their impact is essential for developing effective policies to address health disparities.

Income is a significant predictor of health outcomes. People with lower incomes are more likely to experience poor health outcomes, such as chronic diseases, mental illness, and premature death. According to a report by the Centers for Disease Control and Prevention (CDC), people living in poverty are more likely to have health problems such as asthma, diabetes, heart disease, and stroke. Low-income individuals are also more likely to report experiencing poor mental health and substance abuse problems, including drug use and addiction.

One reason for this link is that people with low incomes often have limited access to healthy food, safe housing, and quality healthcare. Low-income neighborhoods often lack grocery stores that provide fresh produce and healthy food options, leading to higher rates of obesity and diet-related health problems. Additionally, people living in poverty are more likely to experience housing insecurity and homelessness, which can have negative health consequences.

Education is another significant predictor of health outcomes. People with higher levels of education tend to have better health outcomes and live longer than those with less education. According to the World Health Organization (WHO), higher levels of education are associated with a range of positive health outcomes, including lower rates of chronic diseases, fewer mental health problems, and a reduced risk of substance abuse and addiction.

Education can impact health outcomes in several ways. People with higher levels of education often have better-paying jobs, which can lead to greater access to healthcare and healthier living environments. Additionally, people with higher levels of education tend to have better health literacy, which can improve their ability to navigate the healthcare system and make informed decisions about their health.

Access to healthcare is also a critical factor in health outcomes. People without access to healthcare are less likely to receive preventive care, such as cancer screenings and vaccinations, and are more likely to experience health problems that require emergency care. The lack of access to healthcare can also contribute to health disparities based on race, ethnicity, and income.

The link between economic factors and health outcomes has been highlighted in media coverage of health disparities, including the drug use and homelessness crisis on the West Coast. For example, a report by The New York Times found that the high cost of healthcare was a significant barrier for people experiencing homelessness in San Francisco. The report found that many people experiencing homelessness in San Francisco lacked access to basic healthcare services and faced barriers to accessing mental health and substance abuse treatment.

Addressing the link between economic factors and health outcomes requires a comprehensive approach that addresses the root causes of health disparities, such as economic inequality and lack of access to healthcare and education. This approach should also include expanding access to healthcare and support services for people experiencing drug use and homelessness. Additionally, policies that address the social determinants of health, such as affordable housing, education, and food security, can help to mitigate the negative impact of economic factors on health outcomes.

The Affordable Care Act (ACA) is an example of a policy that aimed to increase access to healthcare and improve health outcomes. The ACA expanded Medicaid eligibility, provided subsidies for private insurance, and required insurers to cover essential health benefits. These provisions aimed to reduce healthcare costs and increase access to preventive care, which can improve health outcomes and reduce health disparities.

However, the ACA has faced significant opposition and challenges, with some arguing that it places an undue burden on businesses and individuals. Additionally, the ACA has not fully addressed the issue of affordability, with many people still struggling to afford healthcare despite the expansion of Medicaid and subsidies.

To address the link between economic factors and health outcomes, policymakers must continue to work towards increasing access to healthcare and addressing the root causes of economic inequality, including poverty, lack of education, and inadequate social services. This requires a collaborative effort between policymakers, healthcare providers, and community organizations to ensure that all people have access to the resources necessary to achieve and maintain good health.

In conclusion, economic factors such as income, education, and access to healthcare have a significant impact on health outcomes, including drug use and homelessness. People with lower incomes, less education, and limited access to healthcare are more likely to experience poor health outcomes and face health disparities. Addressing the root causes of economic inequality and expanding access to healthcare and support services can help to mitigate the negative impact of economic factors on health outcomes. Policies that address the social determinants of health, such as affordable housing, education, and food security, can also play a crucial role in improving health outcomes and reducing health disparities. It is essential to continue to work towards developing and implementing comprehensive policies that ensure that all people have access to the resources necessary to achieve and maintain good health. Only by addressing the root causes of health disparities can we hope to create a more equitable and just society where everyone has the opportunity to live a healthy and fulfilling life.

The impact of the opioid epidemic

The opioid epidemic is a public health crisis that has impacted communities across the United States. The epidemic has been particularly devastating for communities affected by poverty and inequality, exacerbating existing social and economic disparities. In this essay, I will analyze the impact of the opioid epidemic on these communities and explore how poverty and inequality have contributed to the epidemic.

The opioid epidemic is a result of the widespread use and abuse of prescription painkillers and illicit opioids such as heroin and fentanyl. According to the National Institute on Drug Abuse, opioids are responsible for the majority of overdose deaths in the United States, with over 70,000 deaths in 2019 alone. While the epidemic has affected people from all walks of life, it has disproportionately impacted communities affected by poverty and inequality.

One reason for this disparity is that people living in poverty are more likely to experience chronic pain and injury, which can lead to the use of prescription opioids. Poverty can also limit access to healthcare and result in inadequate pain management, leading individuals to turn to illicit opioids to manage their pain. According to a study by the National Bureau of Economic Research, individuals living in poverty are more likely to receive opioid prescriptions and are at a higher risk of opioid overdose.

The impact of the opioid epidemic on communities affected by poverty and inequality is significant. The epidemic has contributed to a rise in overdose deaths, infectious diseases such as HIV and Hepatitis C, and social and economic problems such as homelessness and job loss. In communities affected by poverty and inequality, the epidemic has exacerbated existing social and economic disparities, leading to a cycle of addiction, poverty, and poor health outcomes.

In addition to the impact on individual health, the opioid epidemic has also had a significant economic impact. According to a report by the Council of Economic Advisers, the opioid epidemic costs the U.S. economy over $500 billion annually in healthcare costs, lost productivity, and criminal justice costs. The economic impact of the epidemic is particularly devastating for communities affected by poverty and inequality, which often lack the resources and infrastructure necessary to address the epidemic's root causes.

The opioid epidemic has been the subject of extensive media coverage, with many stories highlighting the impact of the epidemic on communities affected by poverty and inequality. For example, a report by the New York Times documented the impact of the epidemic on communities in West Virginia, where poverty and opioid addiction are closely linked. The report described how the epidemic has devastated communities already struggling with poverty and unemployment, leading to a decline in social and economic well-being.

Addressing the impact of the opioid epidemic on communities affected by poverty and inequality requires a comprehensive approach that addresses the root causes of the epidemic. This approach should include expanding access to healthcare, increasing funding for addiction treatment, and addressing social and economic disparities that contribute to the epidemic.

One policy that has been proposed to address the impact of the opioid epidemic on communities affected by poverty and inequality is a "health in all policies" approach. This approach aims to integrate health considerations into all policy decisions, ensuring that policies address the social determinants of health, such as poverty and inequality, that contribute to the epidemic.

Another proposed policy to address the impact of the opioid epidemic is harm reduction. Harm reduction strategies aim to reduce the negative consequences of drug use, including overdose deaths and infectious diseases, without requiring individuals to stop using drugs. These strategies include providing access to clean syringes, naloxone (a medication used to reverse opioid overdoses), and addiction treatment.

Harm reduction has been effective in reducing overdose deaths and infectious diseases in communities affected by the opioid epidemic. For example, a study in Vancouver, Canada, found that a harm reduction program that provided access to clean syringes and naloxone reduced overdose deaths by 35%. Harm reduction has also been shown to be cost-effective, with a study by the National Bureau of Economic Research finding that harm reduction programs that provide access to clean syringes and naloxone are cost-effective compared to traditional addiction treatment.

However, harm reduction strategies have faced significant opposition, with some arguing that they enable drug use and do not address the root causes of the opioid epidemic. In communities affected by poverty and inequality, harm reduction strategies may be particularly controversial, as they are often seen as a band-aid solution that does not address the underlying social and economic factors that contribute to the epidemic.

Addressing the impact of the opioid epidemic on communities affected by poverty and inequality also requires addressing the stigmatization of drug use and addiction. Stigma can prevent individuals from seeking help for their addiction and can lead to discrimination and social exclusion. In communities affected by poverty and inequality, where drug use and addiction may be more prevalent, stigma can further exacerbate existing social and economic disparities.

Media coverage of the opioid epidemic has also contributed to the stigmatization of drug use and addiction. For example, media coverage has often portrayed people with addiction as moral failures or criminals, rather than individuals struggling with a chronic disease. This type of coverage can reinforce stereotypes and contribute to the stigmatization of addiction.

To address the impact of the opioid epidemic on communities affected by poverty and inequality, policymakers must work to address the root causes of the epidemic, including poverty, inadequate healthcare, and social and economic disparities. This requires a comprehensive approach that integrates healthcare, addiction treatment, harm reduction, and social and economic policies.

In conclusion, the opioid epidemic has had a devastating impact on communities affected by poverty and inequality, exacerbating existing social and economic disparities. Addressing the impact of the epidemic requires a comprehensive approach that addresses the root causes of the epidemic, including poverty and inequality. This approach should include expanding access to healthcare, increasing funding for addiction treatment, harm reduction, and addressing the stigmatization of drug use and addiction. By taking a comprehensive approach, policymakers can help to reduce the impact of the opioid epidemic on communities affected by poverty and inequality and improve health outcomes for all.

The role of systemic racism

Systemic racism is a pervasive and persistent issue in American society that has contributed to poverty and inequality for marginalized communities. It has also played a significant role in the drug use and homelessness crisis affecting these communities. In this essay, I will examine how systemic racism has contributed to poverty and inequality and the impact it has had on the drug use and homelessness crisis.

Systemic racism refers to the ways in which policies, practices, and societal norms perpetuate racial inequalities, resulting in unequal access to resources and opportunities for people of color. Historically, systemic racism has been used to justify policies and practices that have contributed to poverty and inequality for marginalized communities, including redlining, mass incarceration, and discrimination in employment and education.

One of the ways in which systemic racism has contributed to poverty and inequality is through the concentration of poverty in communities of color. According to a report by the National Low Income Housing Coalition, people of color are disproportionately represented in the lowest income brackets, with African Americans and Latinos experiencing poverty rates more than double those of white Americans. This concentration of poverty limits access to resources and opportunities, making it difficult for individuals and families to escape poverty and achieve economic mobility.

The impact of systemic racism on poverty and inequality has also contributed to the drug use and homelessness crisis affecting marginalized communities. For example, the War on Drugs, a series of policies and practices implemented in the 1980s to combat drug use, disproportionately targeted communities of color. This resulted in a significant increase in the number of people of color being incarcerated, leading to higher rates of unemployment and poverty, as well as a cycle of addiction and recidivism.

The impact of systemic racism on the drug use and homelessness crisis is also evident in the disproportionate number of people of color experiencing homelessness. According to the National Alliance to End Homelessness, people of color are overrepresented in the homeless population, with African Americans representing 40% of the homeless population, despite making up only 13% of the general population. This overrepresentation is due in part to systemic racism, which limits access to affordable housing, healthcare, and other resources necessary to maintain stable housing.

The impact of systemic racism on poverty and inequality and the drug use and homelessness crisis is a topic of extensive media coverage. For example, a report by the Washington Post documented the impact of systemic racism on the drug use and homelessness crisis in Baltimore, where redlining and discriminatory housing policies have contributed to concentrated poverty and limited access to resources. The report highlighted how these policies have resulted in higher rates of drug use and homelessness in communities of color.

Addressing the impact of systemic racism on poverty and inequality and the drug use and homelessness crisis requires a comprehensive approach that addresses the root causes of systemic racism. This approach should include policies and practices that promote racial equity, such as the dismantling of discriminatory housing policies, increased funding for affordable housing and healthcare, and the implementation of criminal justice reform that addresses the disproportionate impact of the War on Drugs on communities of color. It is also essential to promote anti-racism education and advocacy to challenge societal norms that perpetuate systemic racism and to increase awareness of its impact on marginalized communities.

Furthermore, it is essential to support community-led solutions that empower marginalized communities and address their specific needs. For example, initiatives such as community land trusts, which promote community control over land and housing, have been successful in addressing housing insecurity and displacement in communities of color. Additionally, harm reduction approaches that prioritize the health and well-being of individuals struggling with addiction, rather than punitive measures, have been successful in reducing overdose deaths and promoting recovery.

In conclusion, systemic racism has played a significant role in perpetuating poverty and inequality for marginalized communities and has contributed to the drug use and homelessness crisis affecting these communities. Addressing the impact of systemic racism requires a comprehensive approach that addresses the root causes of racial inequality and promotes racial equity. By implementing policies and practices that prioritize the needs of marginalized communities and promoting anti-racism education and advocacy, we can work towards a more just and equitable society for all.

The impact of gentrification

Gentrification is a complex and multifaceted issue that has become increasingly prevalent in many urban areas. It refers to the process by which more affluent residents move into a neighborhood, often leading to the displacement of low-income residents and changes in the character of the neighborhood. Gentrification has been linked to a variety of social issues, including the displacement of low-income communities and the exacerbation of the drug use and homelessness crisis.

One of the primary impacts of gentrification is the displacement of low-income communities. As more affluent residents move into a neighborhood, property values tend to increase, and landlords may choose to raise rents or sell their properties to wealthier buyers. This can make it difficult for low-income residents to afford housing in the area, leading to displacement and potentially homelessness.

The impact of gentrification on displacement is well-documented. According to a study by the National Community Reinvestment Coalition, between 2000 and 2012, gentrification was responsible for the displacement of approximately 135,000 African American and Hispanic residents in the United States. The impact of gentrification on displacement has also been observed in cities across the country, including San Francisco, where rising housing costs have led to the displacement of many long-term residents.

The displacement of low-income communities as a result of gentrification has also had an impact on the drug use and homelessness crisis. Displaced residents may be forced to move to areas with fewer resources and support systems, making it difficult to access healthcare, employment, and other resources necessary to maintain stable housing and avoid substance abuse.

The impact of gentrification on the drug use and homelessness crisis is particularly evident in areas with a high concentration of poverty and limited access to resources. In these areas, gentrification can exacerbate existing social issues by increasing housing costs and pushing low-income residents to areas with even fewer resources and support systems.

The impact of gentrification on the drug use and homelessness crisis is a topic of extensive media coverage. For example, a report by the New York Times documented the impact of gentrification on the drug use and homelessness crisis in San Francisco's Mission District, where rising housing costs have led to the displacement of many long-term residents and an increase in the number of people experiencing homelessness.

Addressing the impact of gentrification on displacement and the drug use and homelessness crisis requires a comprehensive approach that addresses the root causes of gentrification. This approach should include policies and practices that promote affordable housing and support for low-income communities, such as rent control measures, community land trusts, and increased funding for affordable housing initiatives. Additionally, efforts to prevent displacement and support those who are already displaced should be prioritized, including emergency housing assistance, job training programs, and access to healthcare and other resources necessary for stability and recovery.

Another impact of gentrification on the drug use and homelessness crisis is the disruption of social networks and community cohesion. Low-income communities are often close-knit, and displacement can lead to the breakdown of social networks and support systems. This can lead to increased isolation, mental health issues, and substance abuse.

Studies have also shown that the displacement of low-income communities can lead to an increase in drug-related activity in the surrounding areas. For example, a study published in the Journal of Urban Health found that the displacement of low-income communities in San Francisco's Tenderloin neighborhood led to an increase in drug-related activity in neighboring areas.

Gentrification can also lead to a concentration of poverty in specific areas, making it difficult for low-income residents to access resources and support systems necessary for recovery and stability. This concentration of poverty can perpetuate cycles of drug use and homelessness, as residents are unable to access the resources and support necessary to break these cycles.

The impact of gentrification on the drug use and homelessness crisis has also been documented in popular media. For example, the documentary film "The Overnighters" follows the impact of the oil boom in North Dakota on the local community, including the displacement of low-income residents and an increase in drug use and homelessness.

Addressing the impact of gentrification on the drug use and homelessness crisis requires a coordinated effort that includes the involvement of local communities, policymakers, and organizations dedicated to addressing these issues. One potential solution is to implement community land trusts, which allow residents to collectively own and manage housing and land in their communities. This can provide a stable and affordable housing option for low-income residents, while also preserving community cohesion and social networks.

Another potential solution is to implement policies that protect tenants from displacement, such as rent control measures, just cause eviction laws, and affordable housing requirements for new developments. These policies can help to ensure that low-income residents are not pushed out of their homes and communities due to rising housing costs.

Overall, the impact of gentrification on the drug use and homelessness crisis is a complex and multifaceted issue that requires a comprehensive approach to address. By prioritizing affordable housing, supporting low-income communities, and promoting community cohesion, policymakers and organizations can work to mitigate the negative impact of gentrification and support those who are most vulnerable to displacement and homelessness.

Solutions to address poverty and inequality

Poverty and inequality are persistent issues that affect millions of people around the world. Despite significant progress in reducing global poverty rates in recent years, inequality remains a major challenge, particularly in developed countries. There are a number of potential solutions to address poverty and inequality, including policies to increase access to affordable housing, healthcare, and education, as well as efforts to address systemic racism and gentrification.

One of the most effective solutions to address poverty and inequality is to increase access to affordable housing. The high cost of housing is one of the primary drivers of poverty, particularly in urban areas where housing costs are often prohibitively high. There are several policies that can help increase access to affordable housing, including rent control measures, community land trusts, and increased funding for affordable housing initiatives.

Rent control measures are policies that limit the amount that landlords can charge for rent. These policies are designed to prevent landlords from raising rents to unaffordable levels, which can help ensure that low-income residents can remain in their homes. While rent control has been a controversial policy in some areas, research has shown that it can be an effective tool for reducing poverty and inequality, particularly in areas with high housing costs.

Community land trusts are another potential solution to address poverty and inequality. These trusts are nonprofit organizations that purchase and manage land for the benefit of the community. They can help ensure that land remains affordable and accessible to low-income residents, even as property values rise. Community land trusts have been successful in many areas, including Burlington, Vermont, where they have helped increase access to affordable housing for low-income residents.

Increased funding for affordable housing initiatives is another potential solution to address poverty and inequality. This can include funding for the construction of new affordable housing units, as well as subsidies to help low-income residents afford housing in areas where rents are high. Efforts to increase funding for affordable housing have been successful in some areas, including San Francisco, where voters recently approved a bond measure to fund affordable housing initiatives.

In addition to policies to increase access to affordable housing, there are a number of other potential solutions to address poverty and inequality. These include policies to increase access to healthcare and education, as well as efforts to address systemic racism and gentrification.

Access to healthcare is a critical component of reducing poverty and inequality. Without access to affordable healthcare, many low-income residents are unable to access the care they need to maintain their health and wellbeing. Policies to increase access to healthcare can include expanding Medicaid coverage, providing subsidies to help low-income residents afford health insurance, and investing in community health clinics and other healthcare facilities in low-income areas.

Education is another important tool for reducing poverty and inequality. Access to quality education can help individuals develop the skills and knowledge they need to succeed in the workforce and improve their economic outcomes. Policies to increase access to education can include increasing funding for public schools, providing subsidies to help low-income students afford college, and investing in vocational training programs and apprenticeships.

Efforts to address systemic racism and gentrification are also critical components of reducing poverty and inequality. Systemic racism refers to the ways in which policies, practices, and institutions perpetuate racial inequality, often through the unequal distribution of resources and opportunities. Efforts to address systemic racism can include policies to promote equity and inclusion, such as affirmative action programs and anti-discrimination laws.

Gentrification, as discussed earlier, can exacerbate poverty and inequality by pushing low-income residents out of their homes and neighborhoods. Efforts to address gentrification can include policies to protect renters from eviction and displacement, as well as programs to increase access to affordable housing in gentrifying neighborhoods. In addition, efforts to promote equitable development, such as community land trusts and inclusionary zoning policies, can help ensure that the benefits of economic development are shared by all residents.

In conclusion, poverty and inequality are complex issues that require multifaceted solutions. Policies to increase access to affordable housing, healthcare, and education, as well as efforts to address systemic racism and gentrification, can all help reduce poverty and inequality. It is important to recognize that these issues are interconnected, and that addressing one can have a positive impact on the others. For example, increasing access to affordable housing can also improve access to healthcare and education, as residents are more likely to have stable housing and be able to afford basic necessities.

It is also important to acknowledge the historical and systemic factors that have contributed to poverty and inequality, particularly for marginalized communities. Addressing these underlying issues, such as structural racism and economic disenfranchisement, is critical to creating long-term solutions to these complex issues.

Finally, it is important to involve communities and stakeholders in the development and implementation of these solutions. Effective policies and programs require input and buy-in from those directly impacted by poverty and inequality. By working together, we can create more equitable and just societies that provide opportunities and resources for all.

The importance of community-based solutions

The drug use and homelessness crisis is a complex issue that affects communities across the United States. While there are a number of policy solutions that can help address these challenges, community-based solutions are also critical to supporting individuals who are experiencing homelessness and addiction. Grassroots organizations and community-led initiatives have an important role to play in addressing these issues, as they can provide more targeted and responsive support to individuals and families in need.

One of the most important reasons why community-based solutions are so critical is that they are often better equipped to understand the unique needs of their communities. Unlike top-down policy solutions, which can be inflexible and fail to address the specific needs of local communities, community-based solutions are able to adapt and respond to the needs of their neighbors. These solutions often involve individuals and families who have direct experience with the challenges of homelessness and addiction, which can help build trust and credibility within the community.

Grassroots organizations and community-led initiatives can also play an important role in providing support and services to individuals who are experiencing homelessness and addiction. These organizations can provide access to housing, healthcare, and other critical services, often in ways that are more accessible and responsive than traditional service providers. For example, many grassroots organizations offer harm reduction services, such as clean needle exchanges, which can help prevent the spread of infectious diseases and reduce the risk of overdose. Other organizations may provide access to job training programs, mental health services, or legal support.

Community-based solutions can also help build social capital and promote community resilience. When individuals come together to address common challenges, they can build relationships and networks that help strengthen the social fabric of their communities. These relationships can help individuals build the skills and connections they need to succeed, even in the face of adversity. For example, community-led initiatives that focus on housing and employment can help individuals build the skills and connections they need to secure stable housing and gainful employment, which can help break the cycle of poverty and homelessness.

There are a number of successful community-based solutions that have been developed to address the drug use and homelessness crisis. For example, in Seattle, Washington, the LEAD (Law Enforcement Assisted Diversion) program is a community-led initiative that provides individuals with access to housing, healthcare, and other support services, as an alternative to arrest and incarceration. The program is designed to help individuals who are engaged in low-level drug offenses and other non-violent crimes, and has been shown to reduce recidivism rates and improve outcomes for participants.

In San Francisco, California, the Homeless Youth Alliance is a grassroots organization that provides support and services to young people who are experiencing homelessness and addiction. The organization offers a range of services, including harm reduction, housing assistance, and job training, and has been successful in helping young people build the skills and connections they need to succeed. The organization is staffed by individuals who have direct experience with homelessness and addiction, which helps build trust and credibility within the community.

Another example of a successful community-based solution is the Housing First model, which has been implemented in a number of cities across the United States, including Salt Lake City, Utah and Houston, Texas. The Housing First model prioritizes providing stable and permanent housing for individuals experiencing homelessness, without requiring them to meet certain criteria, such as being clean and sober or having a job. By providing housing first, individuals are able to stabilize their lives and access critical services and support, such as healthcare and job training, which can help them address underlying issues, such as addiction and mental illness.

Community-based solutions can also be more cost-effective than traditional service providers. By leveraging the resources and expertise of local communities, grassroots organizations and community-led initiatives can often provide more efficient and effective support services than larger, more bureaucratic service providers. For example, the cost of providing housing and support services through the Housing First model has been shown to be lower than the cost of emergency shelter and hospitalization for individuals experiencing chronic homelessness.

However, community-based solutions do face some challenges. One of the biggest challenges is the lack of resources and funding available to grassroots organizations and community-led initiatives. These organizations often rely on grants and donations to fund their programs, which can make it difficult to sustain their operations over the long term. Additionally, community-based solutions may face resistance from local governments and law enforcement agencies, who may be skeptical of their ability to address complex social issues.

Despite these challenges, community-based solutions remain an important tool for addressing the drug use and homelessness crisis. By leveraging the resources and expertise of local communities, grassroots organizations and community-led initiatives can provide targeted and responsive support to individuals and families in need. By building social capital and promoting community resilience, community-based solutions can help individuals build the skills and connections they need to succeed, even in the face of adversity. And by providing more efficient and cost-effective support services, community-based solutions can help reduce the overall cost of addressing the drug use and homelessness crisis.

Conclusion

The drug use and homelessness crisis is a complex issue that affects communities across the United States. While there are a number of policy solutions that can help address these challenges, community-based solutions are also critical to supporting individuals who are experiencing homelessness and addiction. Grassroots organizations and community-led initiatives have an important role to play in addressing these issues, as they can provide more targeted and responsive support to individuals and families in need.

The key advantage of community-based solutions is that they are better equipped to understand the unique needs of their communities. These solutions often involve individuals and families who have direct experience with the challenges of homelessness and addiction, which can help build trust and credibility within the community. Grassroots organizations and community-led initiatives can also provide more accessible and responsive support to individuals who are experiencing homelessness and addiction. By building social capital and promoting community resilience, community-based solutions can help individuals build the skills and connections they need to succeed, even in the face of adversity.

There are a number of successful community-based solutions that have been developed to address the drug use and homelessness crisis, such as the LEAD program in Seattle, Washington and the Homeless Youth Alliance in San Francisco, California. These organizations provide access to housing, healthcare, harm reduction services, and other critical support services, as alternatives to arrest and incarceration.

However, in order to effectively address poverty and inequality and, in turn, the drug use and homelessness crisis, a comprehensive approach is needed. This includes addressing systemic issues such as affordable housing, access to healthcare, and poverty, as well as providing targeted support to individuals and families who are experiencing homelessness and addiction. While community-based solutions are an important part of this approach, they must be supported by government policy and resources to be truly effective.

To that end, it is important for readers to take action and support community-based organizations working to address these issues. This can include donating time or money, attending community events, or simply spreading awareness of the issue. By working together and supporting community-based solutions, we can help create more resilient and equitable communities that support all individuals and families, regardless of their circumstances.

The Impact of the Criminal Justice System on Drug Use and Homelessness

The drug use and homelessness crisis is a pervasive issue that has affected communities across the United States for decades. According to recent data from the Department of Housing and Urban Development, over half a million people were experiencing homelessness on any given night in 2020. Additionally, the opioid epidemic has led to a surge in drug overdose deaths, with over 90,000 deaths reported in the United States in 2020 alone. These issues have a devastating impact on individuals and families, and also pose significant social and economic costs to communities.

One factor that has contributed to the persistence of these issues is the criminal justice system. The criminalization of drug use and other low-level offenses has led to the mass incarceration of individuals, particularly those from low-income communities and communities of color. This has disrupted families, undermined economic stability, and perpetuated cycles of poverty and homelessness. Policing practices, such as the use of stop-and-frisk tactics and aggressive enforcement of drug laws, have also contributed to the over-criminalization of marginalized communities and eroded trust between law enforcement and the communities they serve.

In addition, the War on Drugs, which began in the 1970s, has resulted in the adoption of harsh drug laws that have done little to address the root causes of drug addiction and instead have led to the disproportionate punishment of individuals from marginalized communities. These policies have also led to a lack of access to harm reduction and treatment services for individuals struggling with addiction, further exacerbating the drug and homelessness crisis.

The impact of the criminal justice system on drug use and homelessness is a complex and multifaceted issue that requires a comprehensive understanding of the interplay between social, economic, and political factors. In this essay, we will explore the role that the criminal justice system has played in perpetuating the drug and homelessness crisis, looking at the impact of mass incarceration, policing practices, and drug laws. We will also examine the ways in which community-based solutions and policy reform can help address these issues and promote greater social and economic justice for individuals and communities impacted by these crises.

Mass incarceration

Mass incarceration has had a profound impact on drug use and homelessness in the United States, particularly for communities of color. The War on Drugs, initiated in the 1970s, led to an increase in policing, mandatory minimum sentencing laws, and harsher penalties for drug offenses. As a result, the U.S. has the highest rate of incarceration in the world, with over 2.3 million people behind bars.

The impact of mass incarceration on drug use and homelessness is twofold. Firstly, the criminalization of drug use has led to a significant increase in the number of people who are incarcerated for drug offenses. According to a report by The Sentencing Project, more than 456,000 people were incarcerated for drug offenses in 2017. Many of these individuals are serving lengthy sentences for nonviolent offenses, such as drug possession, that do not pose a threat to public safety.

Moreover, the impact of mass incarceration is disproportionately felt by communities of color. Black Americans are nearly four times more likely to be arrested for drug offenses than white Americans, despite similar rates of drug use. This is often attributed to racial bias in policing practices, such as racial profiling and targeting of communities of color. The consequences of this racial bias are dire: it perpetuates the cycle of poverty and homelessness, creates deep-seated trauma, and disintegrates communities.

The impact of mass incarceration goes beyond the individuals who are incarcerated. It also has negative effects on families and communities. Mass incarceration creates a cycle of poverty and joblessness, with many individuals being released from prison with few employment opportunities, making it difficult to access housing and support services. According to a report by the Brennan Center for Justice, families with incarcerated loved ones experience economic hardship, social stigma, and reduced access to public services.

Furthermore, the cost of mass incarceration is staggering, with the U.S. spending $80 billion annually on corrections. This money could be better spent on prevention, rehabilitation, and community-based programs that provide support for individuals who are experiencing homelessness and addiction.

In recent years, there has been a growing movement to reform the criminal justice system and reduce mass incarceration. This movement has gained support from both sides of the political spectrum and includes initiatives such as sentencing reform, drug policy reform, and investments in community-based solutions. Advocates of reform argue that reducing the number of people who are incarcerated for nonviolent offenses can help reduce the cycle of poverty and homelessness, and allow individuals to access the support services they need to rebuild their lives.

Overall, the impact of mass incarceration on drug use and homelessness is significant. The criminalization of drug use has led to an increase in the number of people who are incarcerated for nonviolent offenses, disproportionately affecting communities of color. The consequences of mass incarceration extend beyond those who are incarcerated, impacting families and communities and perpetuating the cycle of poverty and homelessness. Reform of the criminal justice system is needed to address these issues, and to support community-based solutions that provide support and services to individuals who are experiencing homelessness and addiction.

The impact of mass incarceration is felt most acutely by communities of color, who are disproportionately targeted by law enforcement and more likely to be sentenced to longer prison terms for drug offenses. According to data from the Bureau of Justice Statistics, Black Americans are more than three times as likely to be incarcerated as white Americans, and Hispanic Americans are 1.4 times as likely to be incarcerated as white Americans. This disparity is even more pronounced for drug offenses, with Black Americans being almost six times more likely to be incarcerated for drug offenses than white Americans, despite similar rates of drug use.

The negative impact of mass incarceration on families and communities cannot be overstated. When individuals are incarcerated, their families and communities are often left to pick up the pieces. Children of incarcerated parents are more likely to experience poverty, homelessness, and mental health issues, and are more likely to become involved in the criminal justice system themselves. Incarceration also creates economic hardship for families, as incarcerated individuals are often the primary breadwinners, and the costs of maintaining contact with incarcerated loved ones can be prohibitively expensive.

The impact of mass incarceration on communities of color is often compounded by other factors, such as lack of access to quality healthcare and education, housing discrimination, and environmental racism. These factors can create a cycle of poverty and disadvantage that makes it difficult for individuals and families to escape the effects of mass incarceration.

Despite the negative impact of mass incarceration on drug use and homelessness, there are signs of progress. In recent years, there has been a growing recognition of the need to reform the criminal justice system, and a number of initiatives have been launched to address issues such as mandatory minimum sentences and the use of private prisons. In addition, there has been a growing movement to decriminalize drug use and possession, and to treat drug addiction as a public health issue rather than a criminal justice issue.

In conclusion, mass incarceration has had a profound impact on drug use and homelessness in the United States, particularly for communities of color. The negative effects of mass incarceration are felt not only by individuals who are incarcerated, but also by their families and communities. While there are signs of progress in addressing these issues, much work remains to be done to create a more just and equitable criminal justice system. By working to address issues such as mandatory minimum sentences, private prisons, and drug laws, we can begin to create a system that promotes healing and recovery, rather than punishment and retribution.

Policing practices

Policing practices have played a significant role in perpetuating the drug use and homelessness crisis in the United States. The use of stop and frisk, racial profiling, and the militarization of police forces has disproportionately impacted communities of color and led to negative outcomes for individuals who are experiencing homelessness and addiction.

Stop and frisk policies, which allow police officers to stop and search individuals based on "reasonable suspicion," have been widely criticized for disproportionately targeting people of color. In New York City, for example, the majority of individuals subjected to stop and frisk were black or Latino, despite the fact that these groups represented a minority of the city's population. Stop and frisk has been linked to an increase in arrests for low-level drug offenses, which can lead to incarceration and exacerbate the cycle of poverty and homelessness.

Racial profiling is another policing practice that has had a negative impact on communities of color. Racial profiling refers to the practice of targeting individuals based on their race or ethnicity, rather than on their behavior or actions. This can lead to biased policing practices, where officers are more likely to stop, search, and arrest people of color, even when they have not committed a crime. Racial profiling can contribute to a sense of mistrust between law enforcement and communities of color, which can make it more difficult for police to effectively address drug use and homelessness.

The militarization of police forces has also had a negative impact on communities across the United States. Militarization refers to the use of military-grade weapons and tactics by police officers. This includes the use of SWAT teams, armored vehicles, and other equipment designed for use in combat situations. The use of militarized tactics can lead to an escalation of force, which can result in injury or death for both police officers and civilians. In addition, the use of militarized tactics can create a sense of fear and intimidation in communities, which can further undermine trust between law enforcement and community members.

The negative impact of policing practices on drug use and homelessness has been well-documented in the media. For example, in a 2016 article in The New York Times, reporter Nikita Stewart documented the impact of stop and frisk on communities of color in New York City. According to the article, stop and frisk had a disproportionate impact on black and Latino communities, and led to a significant increase in low-level drug arrests. The article also noted that many individuals who were subjected to stop and frisk were later found to be innocent.

In a 2018 report for The Marshall Project, journalist Simone Weichselbaum examined the impact of police practices on individuals who are experiencing homelessness. The report noted that police officers often use homelessness as a pretext for conducting searches and making arrests, even when there is no evidence of criminal activity. The report also highlighted the negative impact of criminalizing homelessness, noting that this approach can make it more difficult for individuals to access housing, employment, and other resources.

Moreover, the negative impact of policing practices on drug use and homelessness has also been documented through research studies. For example, a study published in the Journal of Drug Issues found that policing practices, including stop and frisk, were associated with increased drug use among young adults in New York City. The study also noted that individuals who were stopped and searched by police were more likely to report increased drug use in the following months.

Another study published in the Journal of Urban Health found that the use of militarized tactics by police, such as SWAT teams, was associated with an increase in civilian deaths and injuries during police raids. The study also noted that the use of militarized tactics was more likely in communities of color and low-income neighborhoods.

The negative impact of policing practices on drug use and homelessness has led to calls for reform and alternative approaches to addressing these issues. Community-based organizations, such as harm reduction programs and homeless outreach teams, have been effective in reducing harm and improving outcomes for individuals who are experiencing homelessness and addiction. These organizations prioritize the needs of individuals and work to build trust and rapport with the communities they serve.

In conclusion, policing practices have played a significant role in perpetuating the drug use and homelessness crisis in the United States. Stop and frisk policies, racial profiling, and the militarization of police forces have disproportionately impacted communities of color and led to negative outcomes for individuals who are experiencing homelessness and addiction. Reforming policing practices and investing in community-based organizations that prioritize harm reduction and outreach can help address these issues and improve outcomes for all individuals.

Drug laws

Drug laws in the United States have had a significant impact on the drug use and homelessness crisis. The criminalization of drug use and possession, combined with harsh mandatory minimum sentencing laws, has contributed to a cycle of poverty, incarceration, and homelessness for individuals who struggle with addiction.

One of the key ways that drug laws perpetuate the crisis is through the criminalization of drug use and possession. Despite growing recognition of addiction as a public health issue, drug use and possession remain criminal offenses in many parts of the country. This means that individuals who struggle with addiction are at risk of arrest and incarceration, even when they are not engaging in harmful or criminal behavior.

The criminalization of drug use and possession has also contributed to racial disparities in the criminal justice system. According to the Drug Policy Alliance, black Americans are almost four times more likely to be arrested for drug offenses than white Americans, despite similar rates of drug use. This has led to a disproportionate impact on communities of color, who are more likely to experience poverty, homelessness, and other negative outcomes as a result of incarceration.

Another way that drug laws contribute to the crisis is through mandatory minimum sentencing laws. These laws require judges to impose a minimum sentence for certain offenses, regardless of the individual circumstances of the case. Mandatory minimum sentencing laws have been criticized for limiting judicial discretion, perpetuating racial disparities, and contributing to mass incarceration. For individuals who struggle with addiction, mandatory minimum sentencing laws can make it more difficult to access treatment and other support services.

The negative impact of drug laws on drug use and homelessness has been widely documented in the media. In a 2020 report for NPR, journalist Beth Schwartzapfel examined the impact of mandatory minimum sentencing laws on individuals who struggle with addiction. According to the report, mandatory minimum sentencing laws have contributed to the "overcriminalization" of drug use and possession, and have made it more difficult for individuals to access treatment and other support services. The report also highlighted the racial disparities in the criminal justice system, noting that black Americans are more likely to be sentenced to mandatory minimum sentences than white Americans.

In a 2021 article for The Guardian, journalist Jamiles Lartey examined the impact of drug laws on individuals experiencing homelessness. The article noted that criminalizing drug use and possession can make it more difficult for individuals to access housing and other resources, as many landlords and employers are hesitant to work with individuals with criminal records. The article also highlighted the negative impact of mandatory minimum sentencing laws on individuals who struggle with addiction, noting that these laws can make it more difficult to access treatment and other support services.

Furthermore, drug laws have also contributed to the spread of homelessness among individuals who struggle with addiction. In many cases, individuals who are arrested for drug offenses may lose their jobs, housing, and social support networks, which can contribute to their becoming homeless. According to a 2019 report by the National Coalition for the Homeless, substance abuse is a leading cause of homelessness in the United States, with an estimated 25% to 35% of people experiencing homelessness struggling with addiction.

The criminalization of drug use and possession has also led to a lack of access to healthcare and harm reduction services for individuals who use drugs. In many cases, individuals who use drugs may avoid seeking medical treatment or harm reduction services out of fear of arrest or stigma. This can contribute to the spread of infectious diseases, such as HIV and hepatitis C, among people who use drugs.

Additionally, drug laws have had a significant impact on the availability and pricing of drugs in the United States. The War on Drugs, which began in the 1970s, has led to a focus on reducing drug supply through aggressive law enforcement tactics, rather than on addressing the root causes of drug use and addiction. This has led to a significant increase in the price of drugs, as well as a shift towards more dangerous and potent substances, such as fentanyl.

The high cost of drugs has made it more difficult for individuals who struggle with addiction to access treatment and other support services. According to a 2019 report by the National Institute on Drug Abuse, the high cost of drugs is a major barrier to accessing treatment, with many individuals citing financial reasons for not seeking help. This has contributed to a cycle of poverty, addiction, and homelessness for many individuals who struggle with drug use.

In recent years, there has been growing recognition of the negative impact of drug laws on drug use and homelessness. Many states have begun to adopt harm reduction strategies, such as syringe exchange programs and medication-assisted treatment, as a way of addressing the public health implications of drug use. In addition, there has been growing support for the decriminalization of drug use and possession, as a way of reducing the negative impact of drug laws on individuals who struggle with addiction.

In conclusion, drug laws have played a significant role in perpetuating the drug use and homelessness crisis in the United States. The criminalization of drug use and possession, combined with harsh mandatory minimum sentencing laws, has contributed to a cycle of poverty, incarceration, and homelessness for individuals who struggle with addiction. To effectively address the crisis, policymakers must adopt harm reduction strategies and work towards the decriminalization of drug use and possession. This approach will not only improve public health outcomes but also reduce the negative impact of drug laws on individuals and communities across the United States.

Overcrowding in prisons

Overcrowding in prisons is a major issue that has significant impacts on drug use and homelessness in the United States. The lack of access to treatment, negative effects on mental health and well-being, and high rates of recidivism all contribute to perpetuating the cycle of addiction and homelessness.

One of the primary impacts of overcrowding in prisons is the lack of access to treatment for individuals who struggle with addiction. Prisons are often ill-equipped to provide adequate treatment for addiction, and many individuals leave prison without receiving the support they need to overcome their addiction. This lack of access to treatment can contribute to high rates of recidivism, as individuals who struggle with addiction are more likely to return to drug use and criminal behavior after release from prison.

In addition to the lack of access to treatment, overcrowding in prisons can also have negative effects on mental health and well-being. Prisons are often overcrowded and understaffed, which can lead to unsafe conditions and a lack of access to basic necessities like food, water, and medical care. These conditions can be particularly harmful for individuals who struggle with mental health issues or addiction, as they may not receive the care and support they need to manage their conditions effectively.

The negative impact of overcrowding in prisons on drug use and homelessness has been well-documented in the media. In a 2021 report for The Marshall Project, journalist Abbie VanSickle examined the impact of overcrowding on individuals who struggle with addiction. According to the report, overcrowding can make it more difficult for individuals to access treatment and other support services, as prisons are often unable to provide adequate care. The report also noted that overcrowding can contribute to high rates of recidivism, as individuals who struggle with addiction are more likely to return to drug use and criminal behavior after release from prison.

In a 2018 article for The New York Times, journalist Jan Hoffman examined the impact of overcrowding on mental health and well-being. According to the article, overcrowding can contribute to high rates of violence and suicide in prisons, as individuals are forced to live in close quarters with limited resources and support. The article also noted that overcrowding can exacerbate mental health issues and make it more difficult for individuals to manage their conditions effectively.

Overcrowding in prisons also has a significant impact on homelessness. When individuals are released from overcrowded prisons without adequate support or resources, they are at increased risk of becoming homeless. This is particularly true for individuals who struggle with addiction, as they may not have the skills or resources necessary to maintain stable housing and avoid relapse.

The negative impact of overcrowding on homelessness has been highlighted in a number of media reports. In a 2021 report for The Guardian, journalist Jamiles Lartey examined the impact of overcrowding on individuals experiencing homelessness. According to the report, overcrowding can make it more difficult for individuals to access resources like housing and employment, as landlords and employers are often hesitant to work with individuals with criminal records. The report also noted that overcrowding can contribute to high rates of recidivism and homelessness, as individuals who struggle with addiction are more likely to return to drug use and criminal behavior after release from prison.

In order to address the negative impact of overcrowding in prisons on drug use and homelessness, it is essential to invest in alternatives to incarceration that prioritize treatment and support for individuals who struggle with addiction. This includes increasing access to evidence-based treatment programs, expanding access to mental health care, and investing in supportive housing programs that can help individuals maintain stable housing and avoid relapse. By prioritizing treatment and support over incarceration, we can help break the cycle of addiction and homelessness that is perpetuated by overcrowded prisons.

Reentry challenges

Reentry, the process of reintegrating into society after incarceration, is often a difficult and challenging experience for individuals who have been incarcerated. The challenges faced by formerly incarcerated individuals can include difficulties finding housing, employment, and access to healthcare, all of which can have significant implications for their overall health and well-being.

One of the most significant challenges faced by individuals returning to society after incarceration is finding affordable and stable housing. According to a 2020 report from the Prison Policy Initiative, formerly incarcerated individuals are almost 10 times more likely to experience homelessness than the general population. This is due in part to a lack of affordable housing options, as well as discrimination against individuals with criminal records by landlords and housing providers. The lack of stable housing can make it more difficult for individuals to access other resources, such as healthcare and employment, and can contribute to a cycle of poverty and homelessness.

Another significant challenge faced by individuals reentering society after incarceration is finding employment. According to a 2018 report from the Prison Policy Initiative, formerly incarcerated individuals are almost five times more likely to be unemployed than the general population. This is due in part to the stigma associated with having a criminal record, as well as legal barriers to employment such as occupational licensing restrictions. The lack of access to stable employment can make it more difficult for individuals to access other resources, such as housing and healthcare, and can contribute to a cycle of poverty and recidivism.

Access to healthcare is another significant challenge faced by individuals reentering society after incarceration. Many individuals who have been incarcerated have chronic health conditions or mental health issues that require ongoing treatment, but struggle to access care due to a lack of insurance or limited access to healthcare providers. According to a 2018 report from the National Academy for State Health Policy, states vary widely in their efforts to connect individuals leaving incarceration with healthcare services. The lack of access to healthcare can have significant implications for the health and well-being of individuals reentering society after incarceration, and can contribute to a cycle of poor health outcomes and recidivism.

The challenges faced by individuals reentering society after incarceration have been widely documented in the media. In a 2021 report for NPR, journalist Lisa Pickoff-White examined the challenges faced by individuals returning to the Bay Area in California after incarceration. The report highlighted the difficulty of finding affordable housing in the Bay Area, where rents are among the highest in the country, and noted the impact of the COVID-19 pandemic on housing insecurity. The report also noted the difficulty of finding employment for individuals with criminal records, and highlighted the work of organizations that provide job training and support to individuals reentering society after incarceration.

In a 2020 article for The Marshall Project, journalist Nicole Lewis examined the challenges faced by individuals with mental health issues who are reentering society after incarceration. The article noted that individuals with mental health issues are overrepresented in the criminal justice system, and often struggle to access the care they need while incarcerated. Upon release, they often face a lack of access to mental health services and may experience stigma and discrimination when seeking care. The article highlighted the importance of providing access to mental health services as part of the reentry process, and noted the work of organizations that provide mental health services to individuals reentering society after incarceration.

In conclusion, the challenges faced by individuals reentering society after incarceration are significant and wide-ranging. The lack of affordable housing, stable employment, and access to healthcare can have significant implications for the health and well-being of individuals reentering society after incarceration, and can contribute to a cycle of poverty and recidivism. It is important for policymakers, service providers, and communities to work together to address these challenges and support individuals as they reintegrate into society.

Criminalization of homelessness

The criminalization of homelessness refers to laws and policies that make it illegal to engage in certain activities associated with homelessness, such as sleeping in public or panhandling. While these laws are often framed as a way to address public safety concerns or improve the appearance of public spaces, they have significant negative consequences for individuals who are experiencing homelessness.

One of the most common forms of criminalization of homelessness is laws that prohibit sleeping in public spaces, such as sidewalks or parks. These laws, often referred to as "sit/lie" or "camping" ordinances, criminalize basic human needs such as sleeping, sitting, or resting. According to the National Law Center on Homelessness and Poverty, more than 200 cities in the United States have enacted sit/lie or camping ordinances in recent years. In some cases, violations of these laws can result in fines or even arrest, leading to further cycles of poverty and criminalization.

The criminalization of sleeping in public spaces has a significant impact on the physical and mental health of individuals experiencing homelessness. Without access to safe and stable housing, individuals experiencing homelessness are often forced to sleep in public spaces, such as sidewalks or parks. Criminalizing this behavior not only puts individuals at risk of arrest and incarceration but also disrupts their sleep and exacerbates existing health problems.

Another common form of criminalization of homelessness is laws that prohibit panhandling, or soliciting donations in public spaces. These laws, which are often justified as a way to address concerns about public safety or nuisance behavior, have a significant impact on the ability of individuals experiencing homelessness to earn a living and meet their basic needs. In some cases, violations of these laws can result in fines or even arrest, further compounding the challenges faced by individuals who are already struggling to make ends meet.

The criminalization of homelessness has significant negative consequences for the well-being of individuals experiencing homelessness, as well as for broader society. According to a report by the National Law Center on Homelessness and Poverty, criminalization policies do not address the root causes of homelessness, such as poverty, lack of affordable housing, and inadequate social services. Instead, these policies often serve to further marginalize and stigmatize individuals who are already vulnerable, leading to cycles of poverty, criminalization, and homelessness.

The negative impact of criminalization of homelessness on individuals and society has been widely documented in the media. In a 2021 article for The Guardian, journalist Jamiles Lartey examined the impact of criminalization policies on individuals experiencing homelessness in Los Angeles. According to the article, criminalization policies have made it more difficult for individuals to access basic services such as healthcare and employment, and have led to the arrest and incarceration of individuals who are already struggling to make ends meet. The article also noted that criminalization policies do not address the root causes of homelessness, such as poverty and lack of affordable housing.

In a 2020 report for NPR, journalist Claudia Escobar examined the impact of criminalization policies on individuals experiencing homelessness in Texas. According to the report, criminalization policies have led to the arrest and incarceration of individuals who are already struggling with mental illness or substance abuse issues. The report also noted that criminalization policies do not address the underlying causes of homelessness, and instead serve to further marginalize and stigmatize individuals who are already vulnerable.

In conclusion, the criminalization of homelessness has significant negative consequences for individuals experiencing homelessness, as well as for broader society. Criminalizing basic human needs such as sleeping in public spaces or panhandling only serves to further marginalize and stigmatize individuals who are already vulnerable, and does not address the root causes of homelessness. Instead, policymakers should focus on addressing the underlying causes of homelessness, such as poverty and lack of affordable housing, and providing individuals with access to the basic services and support they need to thrive

Alternatives to incarceration

Alternative approaches to incarceration have gained attention in recent years as a way to address the root causes of drug use and homelessness. Traditional incarceration has been criticized for its inability to address the underlying issues that often lead to criminal behavior, such as poverty, addiction, and mental health challenges. Here we will explore several alternative approaches to incarceration, including drug courts, diversion programs, and restorative justice, and their potential to address these underlying issues.

Drug courts are specialized court programs that aim to address addiction and substance abuse issues among non-violent offenders. These courts offer a combination of intensive treatment and supervision, along with regular court appearances and drug testing. According to the National Institute of Justice, drug courts have been found to reduce drug use and recidivism rates, as well as save money compared to traditional incarceration. By addressing the root cause of drug use and criminal behavior, drug courts offer a more effective and sustainable approach to reducing drug use and homelessness.

Diversion programs are another alternative to incarceration that aims to address the root causes of criminal behavior. These programs provide individuals with alternatives to incarceration, such as community service, counseling, or treatment programs, in lieu of traditional sentencing. Diversion programs can be particularly effective for individuals with mental health or addiction issues, who may be better served by receiving treatment and support services rather than being incarcerated. According to the National Institute of Justice, diversion programs have been found to reduce recidivism rates and offer cost-effective alternatives to incarceration.

Restorative justice is a philosophy of justice that emphasizes repairing harm caused by criminal behavior, rather than punishment. Restorative justice programs bring together the victim, offender, and community to address the harm caused by the offense and develop a plan for repair and reconciliation. This approach aims to address the underlying issues that often lead to criminal behavior, such as trauma, poverty, and social inequality. Restorative justice programs have been found to reduce recidivism rates and promote healing and reconciliation for both the victim and offender.

The potential benefits of these alternative approaches to incarceration extend beyond addressing the root causes of drug use and homelessness. They also offer a more cost-effective approach to addressing these issues. Traditional incarceration is a significant drain on resources, both in terms of the financial cost and the impact on families and communities. Alternative approaches such as drug courts and diversion programs have been found to save money compared to traditional incarceration, while also reducing recidivism rates and improving outcomes for individuals.

Furthermore, alternative approaches to incarceration prioritize rehabilitation and support, rather than punishment. This approach can help individuals who are struggling with addiction or mental health issues to access the support and treatment they need to overcome their challenges and build a successful life. By providing individuals with the resources and support they need to address the root causes of their criminal behavior, alternative approaches to incarceration can reduce the likelihood of future criminal behavior and promote healthier and more productive communities.

While alternative approaches to incarceration offer a promising solution to the challenges of drug use and homelessness, they are not without their challenges. One of the biggest challenges is access to resources and funding. Many alternative programs require significant resources to implement, such as drug treatment programs or counseling services. Without adequate funding, these programs may not be able to provide the level of support needed to be effective.

Another challenge is the stigma associated with criminal behavior, particularly among individuals who have been incarcerated. This stigma can make it difficult for individuals to access employment, housing, and other resources needed to successfully reintegrate into society. Addressing these challenges will require a shift in public perception and a commitment to providing support and resources to individuals who are working to rebuild their lives.

In conclusion, alternative approaches to incarceration offer a promising solution to the challenges of drug use and homelessness. By addressing the root causes of criminal behavior and prioritizing rehabilitation and support, these programs offer a more effective and sustainable approach to reducing recidivism rates and promoting healthier communities. However, addressing the challenges associated with funding and stigma will be critical to the success of these programs.

Community-based solutions

Community-based solutions play a crucial role in addressing the complex issues of drug use and homelessness. These issues are not only complex but also multifaceted, and they require a comprehensive approach that involves the participation of multiple stakeholders, including individuals, families, communities, and government agencies.

Grassroots organizations and community-led initiatives have emerged as a powerful force in the fight against drug use and homelessness. These organizations are often led by individuals who have personal experience with these issues and have a deep understanding of the challenges and barriers that individuals face when trying to access services and support. They are often better equipped to develop solutions that are tailored to the specific needs of their communities and are more likely to gain the trust and support of those who are most affected by these issues.

One example of a successful community-based solution is the Housing First approach, which prioritizes providing stable, permanent housing as a first step in addressing homelessness. This approach recognizes that without stable housing, it is almost impossible for individuals to address other issues that may be contributing to their homelessness, such as mental health and substance abuse. The Housing First approach has been shown to be effective in reducing homelessness and improving outcomes for individuals with complex needs.

Another example of a community-based solution is the Harm Reduction approach, which aims to reduce the negative consequences of drug use, rather than focusing on stopping drug use altogether. This approach recognizes that for many individuals, drug use is a chronic condition that requires ongoing support and care. Harm reduction strategies may include providing access to clean needles and syringes, opioid replacement therapy, and overdose prevention education. Harm reduction has been shown to be effective in reducing the spread of infectious diseases, such as HIV and hepatitis C, and reducing drug-related deaths.

Community-based solutions also play a crucial role in addressing the social determinants of drug use and homelessness, such as poverty, unemployment, and lack of access to healthcare. Community-led initiatives may include job training programs, community health clinics, and financial assistance programs to help individuals and families meet their basic needs. These initiatives not only provide critical support to individuals and families but also help to strengthen communities and promote social inclusion.

In addition to these initiatives, community-based solutions also involve promoting community engagement and participation in decision-making processes. This includes creating opportunities for individuals and families to have a voice in shaping policies and programs that affect their lives. It also involves promoting community-led research and evaluation to identify the most effective solutions and to ensure that programs and policies are responsive to the needs of the community.

In conclusion, community-based solutions play a critical role in addressing the complex issues of drug use and homelessness. These solutions involve the participation of multiple stakeholders, including grassroots organizations, community-led initiatives, government agencies, and individuals and families affected by these issues. By working together, these stakeholders can develop comprehensive solutions that address the root causes of drug use and homelessness, promote social inclusion, and improve outcomes for individuals and communities.

Conclusion

In conclusion, the drug use and homelessness crisis in the United States requires a comprehensive approach that addresses the underlying causes of these issues. The criminal justice system has traditionally relied on punitive measures such as incarceration, but this approach has proven ineffective in addressing the root causes of drug use and homelessness. Alternative approaches, such as drug courts, diversion programs, and restorative justice, offer promising solutions that prioritize treatment, support, and rehabilitation rather than punishment.

However, the success of these alternative approaches depends on systemic change within the criminal justice system, as well as a shift in societal attitudes towards drug use and homelessness. Community-based solutions, including grassroots organizations and community-led initiatives, play a crucial role in addressing these issues and advocating for harm reduction, social justice, and community-based solutions.

It is important for individuals to take action and support policies and initiatives that prioritize these values. This includes supporting community-based organizations, advocating for policy changes, and supporting harm reduction efforts such as safe injection sites and expanded access to healthcare and social services. By working together towards systemic change, we can create a more just and equitable society that prioritizes the health and well-being of all individuals, including those who are experiencing drug use and homelessness.

The Role of Mental Health Issues in Drug Use and Homelessness

Mental health issues have become a growing concern in modern society, affecting individuals from all walks of life. The impact of mental health issues on those who are experiencing drug use and homelessness is a significant issue that cannot be ignored. The lack of access to mental health services is one of the root causes of drug use and homelessness, and it has contributed to the crisis that we are currently facing.

Individuals experiencing mental health issues often struggle with substance use as a way to cope with their symptoms. It is estimated that up to one-third of people experiencing a mental health condition also struggle with substance abuse. In turn, substance abuse can lead to homelessness, as individuals may be unable to maintain employment or housing due to their addiction.

The link between mental health issues and drug use and homelessness is complex and multifaceted. The stigma surrounding mental health issues often prevents individuals from seeking help, and the lack of access to mental health services can exacerbate their condition. The impact of this link is not only felt by the individual but also by society as a whole.

As a society, it is our responsibility to understand the relationship between mental health issues, drug use, and homelessness. We must work together to address the root causes of this crisis and provide individuals with access to the support and services they need to improve their mental health and well-being. This requires a comprehensive and coordinated approach, which prioritizes harm reduction, social justice, and community-based solutions.

In the following sections, we will explore the link between mental health issues and drug use and homelessness in more detail. We will examine the impact of the lack of access to mental health services and discuss the need for systemic change to effectively address this crisis. Through a greater understanding of this link, we can begin to develop effective solutions that will support individuals experiencing mental health issues, substance abuse, and homelessness, and help them to achieve better outcomes.

The prevalence of mental health issues among individuals experiencing homelessness

According to the National Alliance to End Homelessness, mental health issues are prevalent among individuals experiencing homelessness. Approximately one-third of people experiencing homelessness have a serious mental illness, such as schizophrenia, bipolar disorder, or major depression. Additionally, over half of people experiencing homelessness have a history of some form of mental health condition.

The prevalence of mental health issues among individuals experiencing homelessness is significantly higher than in the general population. In fact, the Substance Abuse and Mental Health Services Administration (SAMHSA) estimates that 20-25% of the general population has a mental health condition, compared to the 30-35% of individuals experiencing homelessness who have a serious mental illness.

The impact of untreated mental health conditions on individuals experiencing homelessness can be devastating. Mental health conditions can make it difficult for individuals to maintain stable housing and sobriety. Without proper treatment, individuals may struggle to manage their symptoms, which can lead to erratic behavior, difficulty following through on obligations, and difficulty holding down a job or maintaining a steady income. This, in turn, can make it difficult to afford basic necessities such as food, clothing, and housing, which can lead to homelessness.

Moreover, individuals with mental health conditions who are experiencing homelessness are more likely to become involved with the criminal justice system. They may be arrested for non-violent offenses related to their homelessness, such as loitering or panhandling, or for drug-related offenses. Incarceration, in turn, can exacerbate mental health issues, leading to a cycle of instability and criminalization.

The impact of untreated mental health conditions on individuals experiencing homelessness extends beyond the individual level and affects the larger community as well. Homelessness and substance use can lead to increased emergency department visits, hospitalizations, and other costly services. According to the National Coalition for the Homeless, homeless individuals with mental health conditions are three times more likely to be admitted to a hospital and four times more likely to require emergency medical services.

Furthermore, untreated mental health conditions among individuals experiencing homelessness can have a negative impact on public safety. Individuals with untreated mental health conditions may be more likely to engage in behaviors that are perceived as threatening or dangerous, which can lead to increased calls to law enforcement and a greater burden on public safety resources.

Overall, the prevalence of mental health issues among individuals experiencing homelessness is alarmingly high. The impact of untreated mental health conditions can be devastating, leading to instability, homelessness, and criminalization. Understanding the link between mental health issues, drug use, and homelessness is crucial in developing effective strategies to address the crisis.

The connection between mental health issues and substance abuse

The connection between mental health issues and substance abuse is complex and multifaceted. Mental health issues can contribute to substance abuse and addiction, and substance abuse can also exacerbate mental health problems. According to the National Institute on Drug Abuse, individuals with mental health disorders are more likely to use drugs or alcohol than those without mental health issues. In fact, it has been estimated that approximately 30-50% of individuals with mental health disorders also have a substance abuse disorder.

One of the key factors that contribute to the link between mental health issues and substance abuse is self-medication. Individuals with untreated mental health conditions may turn to drugs or alcohol as a way to cope with their symptoms. For example, someone with depression may use drugs to numb their feelings of sadness, while someone with anxiety may use alcohol to calm their nerves. This pattern of self-medication can quickly spiral into addiction, as the individual becomes dependent on the substance to cope with their mental health issues.

Furthermore, some substances can directly contribute to the development of mental health issues. For example, research has shown that long-term use of certain drugs, such as methamphetamine or cocaine, can lead to changes in brain chemistry that increase the risk of developing mental health disorders such as depression or anxiety.

It is also important to note that substance abuse can worsen existing mental health conditions. For example, alcohol abuse can worsen symptoms of depression or anxiety, while drug use can trigger psychosis or other severe mental health disorders.

The combination of mental health issues and substance abuse can create a vicious cycle, where one problem exacerbates the other, making it difficult for individuals to seek help and overcome their challenges.

In order to address the link between mental health issues and substance abuse, it is important to take a holistic approach to treatment. This means addressing both the mental health condition and the substance abuse disorder simultaneously. Treatment options may include therapy, medication, and support groups.

It is also important to ensure that individuals with mental health issues have access to proper treatment and support services. Unfortunately, many individuals experiencing homelessness and addiction do not have access to mental health services, due to financial barriers or a lack of resources. This can create a significant barrier to recovery, as untreated mental health issues can make it difficult for individuals to maintain stable housing and sobriety.

Overall, the connection between mental health issues and substance abuse is complex and requires a comprehensive approach to address. By understanding this link and prioritizing access to mental health services and substance abuse treatment, we can work towards improving the lives of individuals experiencing homelessness and addiction.

The impact of trauma on mental health

Trauma is a significant factor in the development of mental health issues and substance abuse, particularly among individuals who are experiencing homelessness. Trauma can refer to a range of experiences, such as physical or sexual abuse, neglect, violence, or the sudden loss of a loved one. These experiences can be deeply distressing, and the impact of trauma can last for years, affecting an individual's physical and emotional well-being, relationships, and overall quality of life.

Trauma can be particularly detrimental for individuals who are already struggling with mental health issues, as it can exacerbate their symptoms and make it more challenging to manage their condition. For example, studies have shown that individuals with post-traumatic stress disorder (PTSD) are at a higher risk of developing substance use disorders, particularly if their trauma involved physical or sexual assault.

Trauma can also lead to a range of mental health issues, including anxiety, depression, and borderline personality disorder. These conditions can make it difficult for individuals to maintain stable housing and sobriety, as they may struggle to cope with the symptoms of their condition or turn to drugs or alcohol as a way to self-medicate.

One of the ways in which trauma can impact an individual's ability to cope is through the development of maladaptive coping strategies. These are coping mechanisms that may have been helpful in the short-term but become harmful in the long run. For example, an individual who has experienced trauma may turn to drugs or alcohol as a way to cope with their distressing feelings or memories. Although this may provide temporary relief, it can quickly become a pattern of self-medication that leads to addiction.

The impact of trauma on mental health and substance abuse is well-documented in the literature. A study published in the Journal of Substance Abuse Treatment found that individuals with a history of childhood abuse or neglect were more likely to have a history of substance abuse, and to report higher levels of depression and anxiety than those without such a history.

Furthermore, research has shown that trauma can have a lasting impact on an individual's brain chemistry and functioning. For example, studies have found that individuals who have experienced trauma may have decreased activity in the prefrontal cortex, the part of the brain responsible for decision-making, impulse control, and emotional regulation. This can make it more challenging for individuals to resist the urge to use drugs or alcohol, even when they know it is harmful.

Trauma can also impact an individual's ability to maintain stable housing. For example, someone who has experienced homelessness as a result of domestic violence may struggle to find safe and stable housing due to fear of further violence. This can lead to a cycle of homelessness, as the individual may turn to drugs or alcohol as a way to cope with the stress of their living situation.

It is important to note that trauma-informed care is critical for individuals who have experienced trauma and are struggling with mental health issues or substance abuse. This approach involves understanding the impact of trauma on an individual's life and tailoring treatment accordingly. For example, trauma-informed care may involve providing a safe and supportive environment, focusing on building trust and rapport with the individual, and providing access to evidence-based treatments such as cognitive-behavioral therapy or eye movement desensitization and reprocessing.

In conclusion, trauma is a significant factor in the development of mental health issues and substance abuse among individuals experiencing homelessness. The impact of trauma can be long-lasting, affecting an individual's ability to cope and maintain stable housing. It is essential that we prioritize trauma-informed care and evidence-based treatments to address the impact of trauma on mental health and substance abuse. By doing so, we can better support individuals in their recovery and work towards ending the cycle of homelessness and addiction.

The role of stigma in accessing mental health services
Stigma surrounding mental health issues is a significant barrier to accessing mental health services for many individuals. This stigma can manifest in a number of ways, including societal attitudes towards mental illness, fear of discrimination, and self-stigma. Unfortunately, this stigma can contribute to a cycle of untreated mental health conditions and substance abuse.

Societal attitudes towards mental illness play a significant role in stigma. Negative stereotypes and discrimination towards individuals with mental health issues are prevalent in many societies. These attitudes can be reinforced by media portrayals of mental illness as violent or unpredictable, which can contribute to fear and misunderstanding. This can lead to individuals with mental health issues being ostracized, discriminated against, and even feared. This fear can also extend to healthcare providers, who may be hesitant to provide treatment to individuals with mental health issues due to concerns about violence or liability.

Fear of discrimination is another factor that can prevent individuals from seeking mental health treatment. Discrimination can take many forms, such as employment discrimination, housing discrimination, or denial of insurance coverage. This fear can be particularly acute for marginalized populations, such as individuals experiencing homelessness or those with a history of incarceration. These populations are already vulnerable to discrimination and may fear that seeking mental health treatment will further stigmatize them.

Self-stigma is another significant barrier to accessing mental health services. Self-stigma refers to the internalization of negative attitudes and stereotypes about mental illness. This can lead to feelings of shame, guilt, and hopelessness. Individuals who experience self-stigma may be reluctant to seek mental health treatment due to concerns about being perceived as weak or flawed.

Stigma surrounding mental health issues can contribute to a cycle of untreated mental health conditions and substance abuse. Individuals who are hesitant to seek mental health treatment may turn to drugs or alcohol as a way to cope with their symptoms. This can lead to addiction, which can further exacerbate mental health issues. Additionally, the shame and guilt associated with self-stigma can make it difficult for individuals to seek help for their substance abuse.

The impact of stigma on access to mental health services has been well-documented. A 2017 study published in the Journal of Health and Social Behavior found that stigma was a significant barrier to seeking mental health treatment for both African American and white individuals. The study found that African American individuals were more likely to experience stigma related to mental health issues, which may contribute to the higher rates of untreated mental health conditions and substance abuse among this population.

Efforts to reduce stigma surrounding mental health issues have been ongoing for many years. The World Health Organization has launched a campaign called "Depression: Let's Talk" aimed at increasing awareness of depression and reducing stigma surrounding mental health issues. Additionally, there has been a push to integrate mental health services into primary care settings, which may reduce the stigma associated with seeking mental health treatment.

In conclusion, stigma surrounding mental health issues is a significant barrier to accessing mental health services for many individuals. Societal attitudes towards mental illness, fear of discrimination, and self-stigma all contribute to this issue. This stigma can contribute to a cycle of untreated mental health conditions and substance abuse, which can further exacerbate mental health issues. Efforts to reduce stigma surrounding mental health issues are ongoing and are critical to improving access to mental health services for all individuals.

The impact of the lack of access to mental health services
The lack of access to mental health services has become a major concern in many societies, as it contributes to a range of issues such as drug use and homelessness. Despite the growing awareness of mental health issues, there are still limited resources available to support individuals who require treatment. This often leads to long wait times and an inability to access the care needed.

The impact of the lack of access to mental health services can be seen in the growing rates of drug use and homelessness in many communities. People who struggle with mental health issues are often more vulnerable to addiction, as they may use drugs or alcohol as a means of coping with their symptoms. Additionally, the stress of living with a mental illness can also lead to substance abuse as individuals try to self-medicate to alleviate their distress.

Homelessness is also a common issue for individuals who lack access to mental health services. Without proper treatment and support, people with mental health conditions may find it challenging to maintain employment, housing, and relationships. This can lead to a cycle of poverty and homelessness that is difficult to break.

One of the major barriers to accessing mental health services is the limited availability of resources. Many communities have a shortage of mental health professionals, which can lead to long wait times for appointments. In some cases, people may need to wait weeks or even months to see a psychiatrist or therapist. This can be particularly challenging for individuals who require urgent care, as delays in treatment can lead to further deterioration of their mental health.

Another challenge is the cost of mental health services. Even if people have insurance, the cost of copays and deductibles can be prohibitive. For those without insurance, the cost of treatment can be even more significant. As a result, many people may avoid seeking care altogether, which can lead to a worsening of their mental health conditions.

The lack of access to mental health services can also have a significant impact on families and communities. When individuals with mental health issues do not receive appropriate treatment, their conditions can worsen, leading to higher rates of hospitalizations and emergency room visits. This can place a strain on healthcare systems and result in increased costs for both individuals and society as a whole.

In conclusion, the lack of access to mental health services has become a significant concern in many societies, contributing to issues such as drug use and homelessness. Limited resources and long wait times can prevent individuals from receiving the care they need, leading to a worsening of their conditions and a range of negative impacts on families and communities. It is essential to prioritize mental health services and increase access to care to address these challenges and support individuals in need.

The impact of deinstitutionalization on mental health
Deinstitutionalization refers to the closure of mental health institutions and the movement of patients with mental health conditions into community-based care. This approach was first introduced in the 1960s with the goal of providing more humane and effective treatment for individuals with mental illness. However, the unintended consequences of deinstitutionalization have had a significant impact on the mental health crisis, including the lack of access to mental health services and increased rates of homelessness.

One of the primary impacts of deinstitutionalization on mental health is the closure of mental health institutions. The closure of institutions led to the reduction of inpatient mental health services, leaving individuals with mental health conditions without access to the intensive care and support they require. This has contributed to the lack of access to mental health services, particularly for individuals with severe mental illness.

The lack of access to mental health services has contributed to the increased rates of homelessness among individuals with mental health conditions. Without proper treatment and support, individuals with mental illness may find it challenging to maintain employment, housing, and relationships. This can lead to a cycle of poverty and homelessness that is difficult to break. Additionally, the closure of mental health institutions meant that many people who were previously institutionalized were released into communities without adequate support, leading to an increase in the number of homeless individuals with mental health conditions.

Deinstitutionalization also had unintended consequences on the criminal justice system. The closure of mental health institutions resulted in an increase in the number of individuals with mental health conditions in prisons and jails. Many of these individuals require mental health services, which are not readily available within the criminal justice system. This has resulted in a significant burden on the criminal justice system and has contributed to the cycle of incarceration and recidivism.

Moreover, the shift to community-based care was not adequately supported, and many individuals with mental health conditions were not able to access the care they needed. This has resulted in a lack of continuity of care, inadequate support, and a failure to provide adequate housing for individuals with mental health conditions. The lack of support for individuals with mental health conditions has resulted in significant gaps in care, leading to a range of negative consequences for both individuals and society.

In conclusion, the impact of deinstitutionalization on mental health has been significant, leading to the lack of access to mental health services and increased rates of homelessness. The closure of mental health institutions has left many individuals with mental health conditions without access to intensive care and support, contributing to a cycle of poverty and homelessness. The unintended consequences of deinstitutionalization have had a significant impact on the criminal justice system, contributing to the cycle of incarceration and recidivism. It is essential to address these challenges by increasing access to mental health services, providing adequate support and housing, and addressing the root causes of homelessness and poverty.

The need for integrated care

Integrated care is the coordination of mental health and substance abuse treatment, with the goal of addressing the root causes of drug use and homelessness. It is an essential component of providing comprehensive care for individuals with co-occurring mental health and substance abuse disorders. Integrated care involves the collaboration of various healthcare professionals, including mental health providers, substance abuse counselors, primary care physicians, and social workers.

One of the primary benefits of integrated care is improved outcomes for individuals with co-occurring mental health and substance abuse disorders. Integrated care provides a more holistic approach to treatment, addressing both the mental health and substance abuse issues simultaneously. This approach can lead to better treatment adherence, increased engagement in care, and improved overall health outcomes.

Integrated care can also improve access to care for individuals with co-occurring disorders. Many individuals with co-occurring disorders face significant barriers to accessing care, such as limited resources and long wait times. Integrated care can help to reduce these barriers by providing more comprehensive and accessible services, which can increase the likelihood of individuals receiving the care they need.

Moreover, integrated care can reduce healthcare costs by decreasing the need for emergency department visits and hospitalizations. Individuals with co-occurring disorders often have complex healthcare needs and may require frequent hospitalizations or emergency care. By providing more comprehensive and coordinated care, integrated care can reduce the need for these costly interventions, ultimately reducing healthcare costs.

In addition to improving outcomes and reducing healthcare costs, integrated care can also improve quality of life for individuals with co-occurring disorders. By addressing the root causes of drug use and homelessness, integrated care can help individuals achieve greater stability in their lives, leading to improved overall well-being.

However, despite the benefits of integrated care, there are several challenges to its implementation. One of the primary challenges is the fragmentation of the healthcare system. Mental health and substance abuse treatment are often provided by separate systems, which can make it difficult to coordinate care effectively. Additionally, there may be stigma surrounding mental health and substance abuse disorders, which can make it challenging to provide integrated care in a non-judgmental and supportive environment.

In conclusion, integrated care is essential in addressing the root causes of drug use and homelessness among individuals with co-occurring mental health and substance abuse disorders. By providing more comprehensive and coordinated care, integrated care can improve outcomes, reduce healthcare costs, and improve quality of life for individuals with co-occurring disorders. While there are challenges to implementing integrated care, it is crucial to address these challenges to provide more accessible and effective care for individuals with co-occurring mental health and substance abuse disorders.

The role of harm reduction

Harm reduction approaches are an important aspect of addressing the drug use crisis, particularly for individuals who struggle with substance abuse disorders. Harm reduction is a public health strategy that aims to reduce the negative consequences associated with drug use, without necessarily requiring abstinence from drug use. Harm reduction approaches include providing access to clean needles, overdose prevention medication, and other supportive services, such as counseling and peer support.

One of the primary benefits of harm reduction approaches is that they can prevent overdose deaths. Overdose deaths are a significant concern in the drug use crisis, particularly with the rise of opioid use. Harm reduction approaches, such as providing access to overdose prevention medication like naloxone, can save lives by reversing the effects of an opioid overdose. Additionally, providing access to clean needles can prevent the transmission of infectious diseases, such as HIV and hepatitis C, which can be spread through shared needles.

Harm reduction approaches can also improve outcomes for individuals with substance abuse disorders by reducing the negative consequences associated with drug use. For example, providing access to clean needles can reduce the risk of abscesses and other infections associated with injection drug use. Additionally, harm reduction approaches can improve engagement in care by providing individuals with substance abuse disorders with non-judgmental and supportive services, such as counseling and peer support.

Moreover, harm reduction approaches can help to reduce the stigma associated with drug use and substance abuse disorders. Harm reduction approaches acknowledge that drug use is a complex issue and that individuals who use drugs may face significant challenges related to poverty, trauma, and mental health. By providing supportive services that acknowledge the complexity of drug use, harm reduction approaches can help to reduce the shame and stigma associated with substance abuse disorders.

However, there are several challenges to implementing harm reduction approaches. One of the primary challenges is the stigma associated with drug use, which can make it difficult to provide harm reduction services in some communities. Additionally, harm reduction approaches may be viewed by some as promoting drug use, rather than addressing the underlying issues related to substance abuse disorders.

While harm reduction approaches are important in addressing the immediate needs of individuals struggling with substance abuse disorders, they do not necessarily solve the root cause of the drug abuse issue. Harm reduction approaches focus on reducing harm associated with drug use, but they do not address the underlying factors that contribute to drug abuse, such as poverty, trauma, and mental health issues.

To address the root causes of drug use, it is important to provide individuals with substance abuse disorders with access to comprehensive and integrated care that includes both substance abuse treatment and mental health care. This approach, known as integrated care, aims to address both the mental health and substance abuse issues that contribute to drug use and homelessness.

Integrated care involves the coordination of mental health and substance abuse treatment to provide individuals with a holistic approach to care. This approach recognizes that mental health and substance abuse issues are often interconnected, and that addressing both issues is essential to improving outcomes for individuals with co-occurring disorders.

Integrated care can include a range of services, such as medication-assisted treatment for substance abuse disorders, counseling and therapy for mental health issues, and case management to help individuals access supportive services, such as housing and employment assistance. By providing individuals with a comprehensive approach to care, integrated care can improve outcomes and reduce the risk of relapse.

In addition to providing integrated care, it is also important to provide individuals with substance abuse disorders with access to rehabilitation treatment to help them overcome their addiction and achieve long-term recovery. Rehabilitation treatment can include a range of services, such as detoxification, medication-assisted treatment, counseling and therapy, and support groups.

Rehabilitation treatment can help individuals overcome their addiction and develop the skills and strategies they need to maintain their sobriety over the long-term. While harm reduction approaches can be important in addressing the immediate needs of individuals struggling with substance abuse disorders, they should be viewed as a stepping stone towards comprehensive care and rehabilitation treatment to achieve long-term recovery.

Conclusion

In conclusion, the drug use and homelessness crisis is a complex issue that requires a multifaceted approach. The lack of access to mental health services has contributed significantly to the crisis, leading to increased rates of substance abuse disorders, homelessness, and related health issues. The closure of mental health institutions through deinstitutionalization has also contributed to the lack of access to mental health services, leading to the displacement of many individuals with mental health disorders into the community, without adequate support.

To effectively address the crisis, there is a need for increased access to mental health services and integrated care. Integrated care, which involves the coordination of mental health and substance abuse treatment, can improve outcomes for individuals with co-occurring mental health and substance abuse disorders. This approach acknowledges the complexity of the issue and provides a comprehensive approach to treatment that addresses the root causes of drug use and homelessness.

Harm reduction approaches, such as providing access to clean needles or overdose prevention medication, are also critical in addressing the drug use crisis. These approaches can prevent overdose deaths and improve outcomes for individuals with substance abuse disorders by reducing the negative consequences associated with drug use. Additionally, harm reduction approaches can help to reduce the stigma associated with drug use and substance abuse disorders.

To achieve these goals, it is essential to support policies and initiatives that prioritize harm reduction, social justice, and community-based solutions. This includes funding for mental health services and integrated care, as well as harm reduction programs and services. It also requires a commitment to addressing the root causes of the drug use and homelessness crisis, such as poverty, trauma, and mental health.

In conclusion, the drug use and homelessness crisis is a complex issue that requires a multifaceted approach. By prioritizing increased access to mental health services, integrated care, and harm reduction approaches, we can work towards improving outcomes for individuals with substance abuse disorders and reducing the negative consequences associated with drug use. It is up to all of us to support policies and initiatives that promote social justice, community-based solutions, and a comprehensive approach to addressing the drug use and homelessness crisis.

The Impact of The Opioid Epidemic on the West Coast

The opioid epidemic is a public health crisis that has affected communities across the United States. In recent years, the West Coast has been hit particularly hard by the epidemic, with rising rates of prescription drug abuse and the spread of deadly synthetic opioids, such as fentanyl. This essay will explore the impact of the opioid epidemic on the West Coast, examining the causes of the crisis and its devastating effects on individuals, families, and communities. By understanding the scope and scale of the opioid epidemic on the West Coast, we can better address the root causes of the crisis and work towards effective solutions that prioritize harm reduction, social justice, and community-based initiatives.

The rise of prescription drug abuse

The rise of prescription drug abuse on the West Coast is a complex issue that has been shaped by a range of social, economic, and political factors. One of the primary drivers of the epidemic has been the overprescription of opioid painkillers by healthcare providers. In the early 2000s, pharmaceutical companies aggressively marketed prescription opioids as safe and effective treatments for chronic pain, leading to a surge in opioid prescriptions across the country. Many healthcare providers were not adequately trained in pain management or addiction, and they often prescribed opioids without fully understanding the risks of addiction and overdose.

The lack of access to alternative pain management treatments has also contributed to the rise of prescription drug abuse on the West Coast. Many individuals who experience chronic pain or injury have limited access to non-opioid pain management options, such as physical therapy, acupuncture, or cognitive-behavioral therapy. This has left many patients with few options other than to rely on prescription opioids for pain relief, which can quickly lead to addiction.

In addition to these systemic factors, the opioid epidemic has been fueled by a range of social and cultural factors that have contributed to the normalization of prescription drug abuse. For example, the widespread use of prescription opioids in popular culture and media has helped to create a false sense of safety and acceptability around these drugs. Additionally, the stigma associated with addiction and substance abuse has made it difficult for individuals to seek help for their addiction, which has contributed to the spread of the epidemic.

The opioid epidemic has had devastating consequences for individuals, families, and communities across the West Coast. High rates of opioid addiction and overdose have led to a range of negative outcomes, including job loss, financial instability, and homelessness. Additionally, the spread of opioid addiction has contributed to the breakdown of social networks and community cohesion, leading to increased rates of isolation and social dislocation.

To address the rise of prescription drug abuse on the West Coast, it is essential to address the root causes of the epidemic. This includes improving access to alternative pain management treatments, increasing education and training for healthcare providers, and implementing harm reduction strategies, such as providing access to overdose prevention medication and clean injection equipment. Additionally, addressing the social and cultural factors that contribute to the normalization of prescription drug abuse will be critical to reducing the impact of the epidemic on individuals, families, and communities across the West Coast.

The spread of fentanyl

Fentanyl is a synthetic opioid that is used medically to treat severe pain, such as in cancer patients. However, illicitly produced fentanyl has become a major contributor to the opioid epidemic on the West Coast and throughout the United States. Fentanyl is incredibly potent, with just a small amount capable of causing a fatal overdose. In fact, fentanyl is estimated to be 50 to 100 times more potent than morphine, and even a small amount can be lethal.

The spread of fentanyl on the West Coast has been driven by a number of factors, including its low cost and high potency. Fentanyl can be produced cheaply in illegal laboratories, and its potency means that a small amount can be used to create a large number of doses. As a result, fentanyl has become an attractive option for drug dealers looking to maximize their profits.

Another factor contributing to the spread of fentanyl is the fact that it is often mixed with other drugs, such as heroin or cocaine, without the user's knowledge. This can make it difficult for individuals to know what they are actually taking, and increase the risk of a fatal overdose. In addition, fentanyl can be difficult to detect using traditional drug testing methods, further complicating efforts to address the spread of the drug.

The potency of fentanyl also presents a challenge for first responders and medical professionals. Individuals who overdose on fentanyl may require higher doses of naloxone, an overdose reversal medication, than individuals who overdose on other opioids. This means that first responders and medical professionals may need to carry larger quantities of naloxone in order to effectively respond to overdoses involving fentanyl.

The spread of fentanyl on the West Coast has had devastating consequences for individuals, families, and communities. Fentanyl-related overdose deaths have risen dramatically in recent years, and many individuals who use opioids are unaware of the risks associated with fentanyl. In addition, the potency of fentanyl means that even individuals who have built up a tolerance to other opioids may be at risk of a fatal overdose.

Efforts to address the spread of fentanyl on the West Coast have focused on a number of strategies. These include increasing access to overdose reversal medications, such as naloxone, as well as improving drug testing methods to better detect the presence of fentanyl in illicit drugs. In addition, harm reduction strategies, such as providing access to clean needles and other supportive services, can help to reduce the risk of overdose and improve outcomes for individuals with substance abuse disorders.

Overall, the spread of fentanyl has significantly worsened the opioid epidemic on the West Coast and throughout the United States. Its potency and low cost have made it an attractive option for drug dealers, while its use in combination with other drugs has made it difficult for individuals to know what they are taking. Efforts to address the spread of fentanyl must focus on a range of strategies, including increasing access to overdose reversal medications and harm reduction services.

Demographics affected by the epidemic

The opioid epidemic on the West Coast has impacted various demographics, but some groups have been disproportionately affected. Young adults, particularly those aged 18 to 25, have been hit hard by the epidemic. This age group is more likely to misuse prescription opioids and to transition to heroin use. In addition, women have been affected at a higher rate than men, with a higher incidence of opioid-related deaths among women. The crisis has also had a significant impact on minority communities, with African Americans and Native Americans experiencing higher rates of opioid-related overdoses and deaths compared to other racial/ethnic groups.

Socioeconomic status is another factor that plays a role in the opioid epidemic. People living in poverty or with lower levels of education are more likely to experience chronic pain and may have limited access to alternative pain management treatments, making them more vulnerable to prescription drug abuse. These individuals may also face challenges accessing addiction treatment services, as they may not have insurance or the financial resources to pay for treatment.

The opioid epidemic has also affected people who are incarcerated or have a history of incarceration. Individuals who are incarcerated may have a higher likelihood of opioid use due to previous drug use or because of the high rates of chronic pain among prisoners. Additionally, people with a history of incarceration may face challenges accessing healthcare services, including addiction treatment, upon their release.

In summary, the opioid epidemic on the West Coast has affected a wide range of demographics, but certain groups are more vulnerable to its impact. Young adults, women, and minority communities have experienced higher rates of opioid-related overdoses and deaths. Socioeconomic factors, such as poverty and limited access to healthcare services, also play a role in the crisis. Additionally, people who are incarcerated or have a history of incarceration may face additional challenges in accessing addiction treatment services.

Impact on the healthcare system

The opioid epidemic has had a significant impact on the healthcare system on the West Coast. The increased use of prescription opioids and the spread of illicit drugs like fentanyl has resulted in a surge of overdoses and associated healthcare costs.

One of the primary impacts of the opioid epidemic on the healthcare system is the strain it has put on emergency services. Emergency rooms and paramedic services are often the first point of contact for individuals experiencing an overdose. This has led to a significant increase in demand for emergency services, which can overwhelm hospitals and first responders. The increased demand for emergency services can also result in longer wait times and delays in care for individuals with other health emergencies.

The opioid epidemic has also led to increased healthcare costs. The costs associated with treating opioid addiction, overdoses, and associated medical complications have put a significant strain on the healthcare system. The costs associated with emergency services, hospitalizations, and ongoing addiction treatment can be expensive and often fall on the healthcare system or insurance providers. This has resulted in increased healthcare costs for individuals and the broader healthcare system.

Moreover, the opioid epidemic has also had an impact on healthcare providers themselves. Providers are often on the front lines of the opioid epidemic, treating individuals with addiction and managing the associated medical complications. This can be emotionally and physically taxing, leading to burnout and other mental health issues among healthcare providers.

The opioid epidemic has also highlighted gaps in the healthcare system related to addiction treatment. Access to addiction treatment, including medication-assisted treatment, can be limited in some areas, particularly for individuals with limited financial resources or living in rural areas. This has resulted in significant disparities in access to care for individuals with addiction, exacerbating the impact of the opioid epidemic on vulnerable populations.

Additionally, the opioid epidemic has resulted in an increase in healthcare utilization for individuals with opioid addiction and associated medical conditions. This includes increased hospitalizations, emergency room visits, and primary care visits. Individuals with opioid addiction often have complex medical needs and may require ongoing medical care, leading to increased healthcare utilization and costs.

The impact on the healthcare system is not limited to the direct costs of treating opioid addiction and associated medical conditions. The opioid epidemic has also led to indirect costs, such as lost productivity and decreased quality of life. Individuals with opioid addiction may be unable to work or care for their families, resulting in lost wages and productivity. Additionally, the stigma associated with addiction can lead to social isolation and decreased quality of life.

The impact of the opioid epidemic on the healthcare system has prompted a response from policymakers, healthcare providers, and public health officials. Efforts to address the opioid epidemic include increased funding for addiction treatment and prevention programs, improved access to addiction treatment, and increased efforts to reduce overprescribing of opioids. Additionally, initiatives such as harm reduction programs and safe injection sites have been implemented in some areas to address the immediate risks associated with drug use and reduce the strain on emergency services.

In conclusion, the opioid epidemic has had a significant impact on the healthcare system on the West Coast. The increased use of prescription opioids and the spread of illicit drugs like fentanyl have resulted in increased healthcare costs, strain on emergency services, and gaps in addiction treatment. Addressing the opioid epidemic will require a comprehensive approach that includes increased funding for addiction treatment and prevention programs, improved access to care, and initiatives to reduce overprescribing and promote harm reduction.

Impact on law enforcement

The opioid epidemic has not only affected healthcare but also law enforcement on the West Coast. Law enforcement agencies have had to adapt to the changing nature of the drug crisis, which has increasingly shifted towards the abuse of prescription opioids and the spread of illicit drugs like fentanyl.

One of the primary roles of law enforcement in responding to the opioid epidemic has been to combat drug trafficking. Drug trafficking organizations are responsible for the distribution of illicit drugs like fentanyl and heroin, and law enforcement agencies have worked to disrupt these organizations through targeted investigations and arrests. This has been challenging, as drug trafficking organizations often operate across state and international borders.

In addition to traditional law enforcement efforts, there has also been a growing focus on harm reduction strategies. These strategies aim to reduce the negative consequences of drug use, including overdose deaths, without necessarily requiring individuals to stop using drugs altogether. Harm reduction strategies include initiatives such as distributing naloxone, a medication used to reverse opioid overdoses, and implementing syringe exchange programs to reduce the spread of infectious diseases like HIV and hepatitis C.

Law enforcement agencies have also been involved in efforts to increase access to addiction treatment. Many police departments have implemented diversion programs, which allow individuals with addiction to be diverted from the criminal justice system and into treatment programs. This approach recognizes addiction as a public health issue rather than a criminal issue, and aims to reduce recidivism and improve outcomes for individuals with addiction.

Overall, law enforcement agencies have played a critical role in responding to the opioid epidemic on the West Coast. However, there is growing recognition that traditional law enforcement approaches alone may not be sufficient to address the complex issues underlying the opioid crisis. Instead, a multifaceted approach that includes harm reduction strategies, addiction treatment, and community-based initiatives may be necessary to effectively address the opioid epidemic.
However, there have been criticisms of law enforcement's response to the opioid epidemic, particularly regarding their focus on drug trafficking rather than implementing harm reduction strategies. Critics argue that efforts to crack down on drug trafficking and impose harsh penalties on drug offenders have not effectively reduced drug use and have instead perpetuated the cycle of addiction and incarceration.

In response to these criticisms, some law enforcement agencies on the West Coast have started to shift their approach towards harm reduction. For example, some police departments have implemented diversion programs that allow individuals with addiction to receive treatment instead of facing criminal charges. Others have begun carrying naloxone, a medication that can reverse opioid overdoses, in order to quickly respond to overdose emergencies.

Overall, the opioid epidemic has had a significant impact on law enforcement on the West Coast. While efforts to combat drug trafficking remain a priority, there is increasing recognition of the importance of implementing harm reduction strategies and addressing the root causes of addiction in order to effectively address the opioid epidemic.

Impact on the criminal justice system

The opioid epidemic has had a significant impact on the criminal justice system on the West Coast. As the prevalence of opioid abuse has increased, so too have drug-related crimes and arrests. This has put a strain on the criminal justice system, with law enforcement and courts struggling to keep up with the volume of cases.

One of the primary impacts of the opioid epidemic on the criminal justice system has been the rise in drug-related crimes. Individuals with addiction may turn to crime to support their habit, such as theft or drug trafficking. This can lead to increased arrests and prosecution of drug-related offenses. The criminal justice system is also responsible for managing the incarceration and rehabilitation of individuals with addiction, which can be a significant burden on the system.

The opioid epidemic has also put a strain on law enforcement agencies, with officers responding to an increased number of drug-related calls. This has required additional resources and training for law enforcement to properly handle opioid-related cases. In some cases, law enforcement agencies have had to divert resources from other areas to address the opioid epidemic, potentially compromising public safety in other areas.

The criminal justice system has also struggled to provide appropriate care and support for individuals with addiction. Incarceration can exacerbate addiction and mental health issues, and many individuals do not receive adequate treatment for their addiction while in custody. This can lead to high rates of recidivism, with individuals cycling in and out of the criminal justice system.

The opioid epidemic has also highlighted issues of systemic inequality within the criminal justice system. Black and Hispanic individuals are disproportionately affected by drug-related arrests and incarceration, despite similar rates of drug use across racial and ethnic groups. This has raised concerns about racial bias within the criminal justice system and the need for reform.

The impact of the opioid epidemic on the criminal justice system has also extended to the courts. The rise in drug-related crimes has led to increased caseloads for courts, with judges struggling to manage the volume of cases. This can lead to delays in court proceedings and backlogs in the justice system. The cost of prosecuting drug-related offenses can also be high, putting a strain on already limited resources within the justice system.

In response to the opioid epidemic, some jurisdictions have implemented alternative programs for individuals with addiction, such as drug courts or diversion programs. These programs aim to provide treatment and support for individuals with addiction rather than incarceration. However, the availability and effectiveness of these programs can vary widely, and they may not be accessible to all individuals with addiction.

Overall, the impact of the opioid epidemic on the criminal justice system on the West Coast has been significant, with increased drug-related crimes and strain on law enforcement, courts, and correctional facilities. Addressing the opioid epidemic will require comprehensive solutions that address the underlying causes of addiction and provide support and treatment for individuals struggling with opioid use disorder.

Community response

The opioid epidemic has had a significant impact on communities on the West Coast, with many communities responding to the crisis through various initiatives and strategies aimed at addressing the root causes of opioid addiction and overdose.

One response to the opioid epidemic has been the implementation of harm reduction strategies. Harm reduction strategies aim to reduce the negative consequences of drug use, including overdose and the spread of infectious diseases like HIV and Hepatitis C. Examples of harm reduction strategies include the distribution of naloxone, a medication that can reverse an opioid overdose, and the implementation of safe injection sites, where individuals can use drugs under medical supervision.

Community-based solutions have also been a key response to the opioid epidemic. These solutions aim to address the root causes of opioid addiction and overdose, such as poverty, lack of access to healthcare, and social isolation. Examples of community-based solutions include the implementation of peer support programs, where individuals with lived experience of addiction provide support to others, and the creation of community recovery centers, where individuals can access addiction treatment and support services.

Advocacy efforts have also played a significant role in community responses to the opioid epidemic. Advocacy efforts aim to raise awareness of the opioid epidemic and promote policies and initiatives aimed at addressing the crisis. Examples of advocacy efforts include the lobbying of government officials for increased funding for addiction treatment and harm reduction strategies, and the creation of community coalitions and partnerships aimed at addressing the root causes of the opioid epidemic.

Additionally, many communities have taken a grassroots approach to addressing the opioid epidemic. This has involved individuals and community groups coming together to share their experiences with addiction and overdose, raise awareness of the issue, and advocate for change at the local level. These grassroots efforts have included everything from hosting community events and fundraisers to creating peer support groups and organizing neighborhood watch programs to combat drug-related crime.

In conclusion, communities on the West Coast have responded to the opioid epidemic in a variety of ways, including the implementation of harm reduction strategies, community-based solutions, and advocacy efforts. These responses aim to address the root causes of opioid addiction and overdose and to promote policies and initiatives aimed at addressing the crisis. While much work remains to be done, these community responses represent important steps in the fight against the opioid epidemic.

Policy solutions

There are various policy solutions that have been proposed to address the opioid epidemic on the West Coast. One approach is to increase access to addiction treatment, such as medication-assisted treatment (MAT) and counseling, particularly for underserved communities. MAT involves the use of medications, such as methadone, buprenorphine, and naltrexone, to manage withdrawal symptoms and cravings, while counseling helps individuals address the underlying factors contributing to their addiction. By improving access to addiction treatment, individuals struggling with opioid use disorder can receive the help they need to manage their addiction and reduce the risk of overdose.

Another proposed policy solution is to address the root causes of drug use, such as poverty, lack of access to healthcare, and trauma. Addressing these underlying issues requires a comprehensive approach that involves increasing access to healthcare, mental health services, and social services. Additionally, providing support for education and job training can help individuals attain economic stability and reduce the likelihood of turning to drugs as a means of coping.

Some policy solutions also involve harm reduction strategies, such as providing access to clean needles and overdose-reversing medications like naloxone. These interventions aim to reduce the risk of overdose and the spread of infectious diseases among individuals who use drugs.

Furthermore, policy solutions that focus on reducing the supply of illicit drugs include increased law enforcement efforts to disrupt drug trafficking and better regulation of prescription opioids to prevent overprescribing and diversion. Additionally, initiatives that promote responsible prescribing practices and patient education can help prevent the misuse of prescription opioids.

Finally, there are policy solutions that prioritize social justice, such as addressing racial and socioeconomic disparities in addiction treatment and reforming the criminal justice system to provide alternatives to incarceration for individuals with addiction. By prioritizing social justice, policy solutions can help address the systemic issues that contribute to the opioid epidemic and ensure that everyone has access to the support they need to manage their addiction and achieve recovery.

Conclusion

In conclusion, the opioid epidemic has had a devastating impact on the West Coast, resulting in widespread addiction, overdose, and associated health and social consequences. The rise of prescription drug abuse and the spread of fentanyl have contributed to the severity of the crisis, which has disproportionately affected certain demographics, including low-income individuals, people experiencing homelessness, and communities of color.

The opioid epidemic has also impacted the healthcare system, including emergency services, healthcare costs, and healthcare providers. The criminal justice system has also been overburdened by the epidemic, with a rise in drug-related crimes and mass incarceration of individuals with addiction. However, communities on the West Coast have responded with harm reduction strategies, community-based solutions, and advocacy efforts to address the crisis.

Policy solutions have also been proposed, including increasing access to addiction treatment, addressing the root causes of drug use, and implementing harm reduction strategies. Continued efforts are needed to address the opioid epidemic on the West Coast, with a focus on harm reduction, community-based solutions, and policy initiatives that prioritize access to addiction treatment. It is only through a multi-faceted approach that the West Coast can begin to address the opioid epidemic and its devastating impact on individuals, families, and communities.

The Rise of Fentanyl and Other Synthetic Opioids

The rise of fentanyl and other synthetic opioids has been one of the most significant developments in the ongoing drug crisis. Fentanyl, a synthetic opioid that is up to 100 times more potent than morphine, has been increasingly found in street drugs such as heroin and cocaine, leading to a surge in overdose deaths.

The widespread availability of fentanyl and other synthetic opioids has created a public health crisis in North America. The Centers for Disease Control and Prevention (CDC) reports that synthetic opioids were involved in over 60% of all opioid overdose deaths in the United States in 2020. Canada has also been grappling with a fentanyl crisis, with over 17,000 deaths attributed to opioid-related overdoses between 2016 and 2020.

The rise of synthetic opioids has been driven by various factors, including the illegal manufacture and distribution of these drugs, the high profitability of fentanyl for drug traffickers, and the challenges faced by individuals with opioid use disorders in accessing safe and effective treatment. Despite the dangers posed by these drugs, many people continue to use them, and the overdose crisis shows no signs of abating.

In light of the devastating impact of fentanyl and other synthetic opioids on individuals, families, and communities, there is a pressing need to understand the factors that have contributed to the rise of these drugs and to identify effective strategies for reducing their impact. In the following sections, we will explore some of the key issues related to the rise of synthetic opioids and their impact on the drug crisis.

Definition of synthetic opioids

Opioids are a class of drugs that are commonly prescribed for pain relief, but they are also widely abused. They produce effects that are similar to those of opium, a substance derived from the opium poppy. Opioids are categorized into two groups: natural opioids, which are derived from opium poppies, and synthetic opioids, which are chemically manufactured.

Synthetic opioids are opioid drugs that are synthesized chemically in a laboratory, rather than being derived from natural sources. Synthetic opioids are designed to mimic the effects of natural opioids, such as morphine and codeine, but they are much stronger and more potent. They are typically prescribed to treat severe pain, such as that experienced by cancer patients, but they can also be used recreationally. The most commonly abused synthetic opioids include fentanyl, tramadol, and methadone.

Synthetic opioids are different from natural opioids like heroin in several ways. First, synthetic opioids are typically much stronger and more potent than natural opioids. Fentanyl, for example, is up to 100 times more potent than morphine. This means that a much smaller dose of a synthetic opioid is needed to achieve the same effect as a larger dose of a natural opioid. Second, synthetic opioids are often manufactured in illegal laboratories, which means that they may be impure or contaminated with other substances, such as fentanyl analogues, which are even more potent and dangerous than fentanyl itself. Finally, synthetic opioids are often more difficult to detect than natural opioids, which makes them particularly dangerous.

Despite their potency and potential dangers, synthetic opioids are widely prescribed in the United States, particularly for the treatment of chronic pain. In recent years, there has been a significant increase in the use of synthetic opioids, which has contributed to the opioid epidemic. The rise of synthetic opioids has been particularly concerning because of their association with overdose deaths. Fentanyl, in particular, has been responsible for a large number of opioid-related deaths in recent years.

Overall, synthetic opioids are a significant contributor to the opioid crisis in the United States. While they can be effective for the treatment of pain when used appropriately, their potency and potential for abuse make them particularly dangerous. As such, there is a need for increased awareness and education around the use of synthetic opioids, as well as efforts to prevent their misuse and reduce the harm associated with their use.

The emergence of fentanyl

Fentanyl is a synthetic opioid that is many times more potent than morphine and heroin. It was first synthesized in the 1960s as a pain reliever and anesthetic, but it wasn't until the 1980s that fentanyl started being used in medical settings as a pain management medication. It is typically prescribed for patients with chronic pain or for pain management after surgery.

Fentanyl's potency is what sets it apart from other opioids. It is estimated to be 50-100 times stronger than morphine and 30-50 times stronger than heroin. This means that a small amount of fentanyl can have a powerful effect, and even a slight miscalculation in dosage can lead to an overdose. Because of its potency, fentanyl is often mixed with other drugs, such as heroin or cocaine, to increase their effects or stretch the supply. However, this also increases the risk of overdose as the user may not be aware of the presence of fentanyl in the drug they are using.

The emergence of fentanyl as a major synthetic opioid in the drug market is due in part to its potency and the ease of manufacturing. Fentanyl and its analogs can be produced in a laboratory setting with relative ease and at a low cost. This has made it an attractive alternative for drug dealers looking to increase their profit margins. Additionally, fentanyl and its analogs can be produced and shipped from overseas, particularly from China, making it difficult for law enforcement to track and intercept.

Overall, the emergence of fentanyl as a major synthetic opioid has significantly worsened the opioid epidemic. Its potency and ease of manufacturing have led to an increase in overdoses and deaths, and its presence in other drugs has made it difficult for users to know what they are consuming.

Contributing factors

The rise of synthetic opioids like fentanyl has been attributed to several factors that have contributed to the increased demand for stronger opioids and the availability of precursor chemicals. One of the main contributing factors is the ongoing opioid epidemic, which has led to a higher demand for potent opioids due to the development of tolerance among individuals with addiction.

Another contributing factor is the availability of precursor chemicals, which are necessary for the production of synthetic opioids like fentanyl. Fentanyl is produced from precursors that are primarily sourced from China and Mexico. In recent years, the availability of these precursors has increased, leading to a surge in fentanyl production and distribution.

Additionally, the profitability of fentanyl has made it an attractive option for drug traffickers. Fentanyl is cheaper to produce than other opioids and is highly potent, meaning that small amounts can be sold for significant profits. This has led to a proliferation of illicit fentanyl in the drug market, further contributing to the rise of synthetic opioids.

Furthermore, the over-prescription of opioids by healthcare providers has also contributed to the demand for synthetic opioids. Prescription opioids are often a gateway to addiction, and individuals who become addicted may turn to stronger opioids like fentanyl as their tolerance develops.

Lastly, the rise of the internet and online marketplaces has made it easier for individuals to access and purchase synthetic opioids. Illicit fentanyl and other synthetic opioids can be purchased on the dark web, allowing for a wider distribution network and making it more difficult for law enforcement to track and interdict the flow of drugs.

In summary, the rise of synthetic opioids like fentanyl can be attributed to several factors, including increased demand for potent opioids due to the opioid epidemic, the availability of precursor chemicals, the profitability of fentanyl for drug traffickers, over-prescription of opioids by healthcare providers, and the proliferation of online marketplaces for illicit drugs. These factors have contributed to the growth of the synthetic opioid market and have made it more difficult to address the ongoing drug crisis.

The impact of synthetic opioids on overdose deaths
The rise of synthetic opioids, particularly fentanyl, has had a devastating impact on the opioid crisis in the United States, and specifically on the West Coast. Synthetic opioids are responsible for a growing number of overdose deaths, surpassing natural opioids like heroin and prescription painkillers. This section will explore how synthetic opioids have contributed to the epidemic of overdose deaths, including the percentage of opioid overdose deaths that involve synthetic opioids.

To understand the impact of synthetic opioids on overdose deaths, it is important to first define what is meant by synthetic opioids. Synthetic opioids are man-made drugs that are designed to mimic the effects of natural opioids like morphine and heroin. These drugs are often more potent than their natural counterparts and can be easier and cheaper to produce, making them attractive to drug manufacturers and dealers. Fentanyl, for example, is a synthetic opioid that is 50-100 times more potent than morphine.

The impact of synthetic opioids on overdose deaths can be seen in the statistics. According to data from the Centers for Disease Control and Prevention (CDC), synthetic opioids were involved in 72.9% of opioid overdose deaths in 2019, up from 29.8% in 2013. This represents a significant shift in the opioid epidemic, as natural opioids like heroin and prescription painkillers were previously the primary drivers of overdose deaths.

The rise of synthetic opioids as a contributor to overdose deaths is due to a variety of factors. One factor is the increased demand for stronger opioids among drug users. As individuals develop tolerance to less potent opioids like heroin or prescription painkillers, they may seek out stronger drugs to achieve the same level of high. Synthetic opioids like fentanyl can provide a stronger high, making them an attractive option for drug users.

Another factor contributing to the rise of synthetic opioids is the availability of precursor chemicals. Fentanyl and other synthetic opioids can be produced using precursor chemicals that are often legally available for purchase. Criminal organizations have taken advantage of this by importing these chemicals and using them to produce synthetic opioids on a large scale. This has led to a flood of synthetic opioids on the black market, contributing to the increase in overdose deaths.

The potency of synthetic opioids like fentanyl is also a major factor in their contribution to overdose deaths. Due to the high potency of these drugs, individuals may inadvertently consume a lethal dose, leading to overdose and death. In addition, because fentanyl is often mixed with other drugs like heroin, cocaine, or methamphetamine, individuals may not be aware of the presence of fentanyl in their drug supply, increasing the risk of overdose.

The impact of synthetic opioids on overdose deaths has been particularly acute on the West Coast. States like California, Oregon, and Washington have seen significant increases in synthetic opioid-related overdose deaths in recent years. In fact, the West Coast has some of the highest rates of synthetic opioid-related overdose deaths in the country.

In response to the rise of synthetic opioids and their impact on overdose deaths, efforts have been made to increase access to overdose prevention strategies like naloxone, as well as to improve access to addiction treatment. Harm reduction strategies like syringe exchange programs and safe injection sites have also been implemented to reduce the risk of overdose among drug users.

Overall, the rise of synthetic opioids like fentanyl has had a significant impact on the opioid epidemic and overdose deaths in the United States, particularly on the West Coast. Addressing this issue will require a multifaceted approach, including efforts to increase access to overdose prevention and addiction treatment, as well as addressing the factors that contribute to the production and distribution of synthetic opioids.

Fentanyl analogs

Fentanyl analogs are synthetic opioids that are chemically similar to fentanyl but have slight structural differences. These analogs are often more potent than fentanyl, making them even more dangerous and contributing to the high number of overdose deaths in the opioid epidemic. The emergence of fentanyl analogs has added a new layer of complexity to the already devastating crisis.

Fentanyl analogs were first synthesized in the 1960s as part of research into potential new pain medications. However, they did not become widely known until the 21st century, when they started appearing on the illicit drug market. These analogs are often produced in clandestine laboratories in China and other countries and then smuggled into the United States.

One of the most concerning aspects of fentanyl analogs is their potency. Fentanyl itself is already many times stronger than heroin, and some analogs can be even more potent. Carfentanil, for example, is estimated to be 10,000 times stronger than morphine and 100 times stronger than fentanyl. This extreme potency means that even small amounts of these drugs can be deadly.

The emergence of fentanyl analogs has had a significant impact on the opioid epidemic. According to the National Institute on Drug Abuse, synthetic opioids like fentanyl and its analogs were involved in nearly 60% of opioid overdose deaths in the United States in 2019. In some regions, the percentage is even higher. For example, in some states on the East Coast, synthetic opioids were involved in over 70% of overdose deaths.

Fentanyl analogs are also contributing to the rapid increase in overdose deaths. In many cases, people who use opioids do not realize that they are taking a fentanyl analog instead of another drug, leading to unintentional overdose. Additionally, because fentanyl analogs are so potent, they require even more careful handling by medical professionals and emergency responders, which can put a strain on resources.

Another issue with fentanyl analogs is their ever-evolving nature. Because they are not regulated and can be synthesized with relatively simple chemical modifications, new analogs are constantly emerging. This can make it difficult for law enforcement and public health officials to stay ahead of the problem.

To address the issue of fentanyl analogs, a multi-pronged approach is needed. This includes efforts to increase awareness among opioid users, expand access to addiction treatment, and target the sources of illicit drug production and trafficking. In addition, innovative harm reduction strategies such as drug checking and overdose prevention sites may be helpful in reducing the harm caused by fentanyl analogs.

In conclusion, the emergence of fentanyl analogs has added a new layer of complexity to the already devastating opioid epidemic. These synthetic opioids are extremely potent and contribute to a high percentage of overdose deaths. Addressing the issue of fentanyl analogs will require a comprehensive approach that targets both the supply and demand for these drugs.

The spread of synthetic opioids

The rise of synthetic opioids, particularly fentanyl, has led to a new phase of the opioid epidemic that has spread across the United States and the world. While initially concentrated in certain regions, synthetic opioids have become a national and global issue, impacting communities that were previously not as affected by the opioid epidemic. In this section, we will explore the spread of synthetic opioids and their impact on various regions.

The spread of synthetic opioids is linked to the rise in production and trafficking of these drugs, often through the dark web and transnational criminal networks. Fentanyl and other synthetic opioids are produced primarily in China, but also in Mexico and other countries, and are often trafficked through various channels into the United States and other countries. These drugs can be mixed with other substances, making them difficult to detect and even more deadly.

In the United States, synthetic opioids have spread rapidly across the country. According to the Centers for Disease Control and Prevention (CDC), fentanyl was responsible for 36,509 overdose deaths in 2019, up from 19,413 in 2016. While the opioid epidemic initially hit states like West Virginia, Ohio, and Pennsylvania particularly hard, synthetic opioids have now spread to other regions, including the Northeast, Midwest, and Western states.

One example is California, where fentanyl overdose deaths increased by 614% between 2013 and 2019. According to the California Department of Public Health, fentanyl was responsible for 45% of all opioid overdose deaths in the state in 2019, up from 14% in 2016. This increase in fentanyl-related deaths has been particularly pronounced in Los Angeles County, where the number of fentanyl-related deaths increased by 68% in 2020 compared to the previous year.

The spread of synthetic opioids has also impacted Canada, particularly the province of British Columbia, which has seen a significant increase in fentanyl-related deaths. In 2016, there were 935 overdose deaths in British Columbia, with fentanyl detected in 67% of those cases. This trend has continued, with fentanyl-related deaths continuing to rise in the province and other parts of Canada.

In Europe, synthetic opioids have also become a major issue. In the United Kingdom, fentanyl-related deaths increased by 29% in 2019, and the drug has been implicated in a number of high-profile cases, including the death of musician Prince. In addition to fentanyl, other synthetic opioids like carfentanil and acetylfentanyl have also been detected in Europe, contributing to the rise in overdose deaths.

The spread of synthetic opioids is not limited to North America and Europe, as these drugs have also made their way into other parts of the world. In Australia, for example, fentanyl-related deaths increased by 1,000% between 2011 and 2018, with the drug being detected in a growing number of drug seizures. Similarly, in New

Zealand, fentanyl-related deaths have also increased, with the drug being detected in counterfeit prescription medication and other illicit substances.

The impact of synthetic opioids on communities across the globe has been devastating, with these drugs being responsible for a significant portion of overdose deaths. The ease with which synthetic opioids can be produced and trafficked, combined with their potency, has made them a particularly deadly force in the opioid epidemic. The spread of these drugs has also highlighted the need for international cooperation and collaboration to address the production and trafficking of synthetic opioids.

Efforts to address the spread of synthetic opioids have included increased law enforcement efforts to disrupt the production and trafficking of these drugs, as well as public health campaigns to raise awareness about the dangers of synthetic opioids and how to prevent overdoses. The development of overdose prevention strategies, such as the distribution of naloxone, has also been critical in reducing the number of opioid-related deaths.

In conclusion, the spread of synthetic opioids like fentanyl has had a significant impact on communities across the United States and the world. These drugs have contributed to a new phase of the opioid epidemic, with overdose deaths increasing in regions that were previously not as affected by the crisis. Addressing the spread of synthetic opioids requires a multi-faceted approach that includes increased law enforcement efforts, public health campaigns, and the development of overdose prevention strategies. It also requires international cooperation and collaboration to disrupt the production and trafficking of these deadly drugs.

Law enforcement and policy responses

The rise of synthetic opioids, particularly fentanyl, has posed a significant challenge to law enforcement and policymakers across the United States and the world. In this section, we will examine the responses of law enforcement and policymakers to the rise of synthetic opioids, including efforts to crack down on illegal drug trafficking and increase access to overdose reversal drugs.

Law enforcement agencies have responded to the rise of synthetic opioids with a variety of tactics aimed at disrupting drug trafficking and reducing overdose deaths. One strategy has been to target the production and distribution of fentanyl and other synthetic opioids in countries like China and Mexico, where much of the drug supply originates. In recent years, law enforcement agencies in the United States and Canada have worked closely with their counterparts in China to identify and shut down illicit fentanyl production facilities, as well as intercept shipments of fentanyl and other synthetic opioids before they reach their destinations.

Another strategy employed by law enforcement agencies has been to target domestic drug trafficking networks. This has involved increasing law enforcement resources to track and intercept shipments of fentanyl and other synthetic opioids at ports of entry, as well as increasing the number of drug investigations and arrests. In addition, law enforcement agencies have worked to disrupt drug trafficking networks through targeted operations, such as the takedown of the dark web marketplace AlphaBay in 2017, which was responsible for a significant portion of the illegal fentanyl trade.

In addition to law enforcement efforts, policymakers have also responded to the rise of synthetic opioids with a variety of policy initiatives aimed at reducing overdose deaths and increasing access to addiction treatment. One important policy initiative has been the expansion of access to naloxone, an overdose reversal drug that can quickly revive individuals experiencing an opioid overdose. In many states, naloxone is now available without a prescription and can be obtained at pharmacies, community health clinics, and other locations.

Policymakers have also focused on increasing access to addiction treatment for individuals struggling with opioid addiction. This has included expanding Medicaid coverage for addiction treatment services, increasing funding for substance abuse treatment programs, and supporting the development of new addiction treatment medications, such as buprenorphine and methadone. In addition, policymakers have worked to reduce the stigma associated with addiction and increase public awareness of the risks of synthetic opioids and other drugs.

Despite these efforts, the rise of synthetic opioids continues to pose significant challenges to law enforcement and policymakers. One major obstacle is the rapid rate at which new synthetic opioids are being developed, making it difficult for law enforcement agencies to keep up with changes in the drug market. In addition, the illegal drug trade is highly adaptable, and drug traffickers are constantly finding new ways to evade law enforcement efforts.

Another challenge is the complex nature of the opioid epidemic, which is driven by a range of social, economic, and health factors. In order to effectively address the opioid epidemic and the rise of synthetic opioids, it is necessary to take a comprehensive, multi-faceted approach that includes not only law enforcement efforts but also community-based solutions, public health interventions, and policy initiatives that address the root causes of drug use and addiction.

In conclusion, the rise of synthetic opioids has posed a significant challenge to law enforcement and policymakers across the United States and the world. Law enforcement agencies have responded to the rise of synthetic opioids with a variety of tactics aimed at disrupting drug trafficking and reducing overdose deaths, while policymakers have focused on increasing access to overdose reversal drugs and addiction treatment services. Despite these efforts, the rapid rate of new synthetic opioids being developed and the complex nature of the opioid epidemic continue to pose significant challenges to effectively addressing the crisis. A comprehensive, multi-faceted approach is necessary to address the root causes of drug use and addiction and reduce the harm caused by synthetic opioids and other drugs.

The impact of synthetic opioids on healthcare

The rise of synthetic opioids, particularly fentanyl, has had a significant impact on healthcare systems and providers. The increased potency of synthetic opioids has led to a surge in overdose deaths and hospitalizations, which has resulted in increased healthcare costs and a strain on healthcare resources.

One major impact of synthetic opioids on healthcare is the increase in emergency room visits and hospitalizations related to opioid overdoses. According to the Centers for Disease Control and Prevention (CDC), the rate of opioid overdose visits to emergency departments increased by 30% from July 2016 to September 2017. This increase has placed a significant burden on healthcare systems, particularly in regions where synthetic opioids have had a significant impact on overdose rates.

The cost of treating opioid overdoses has also increased significantly with the rise of synthetic opioids. A study by the National Institutes of Health found that the cost of treating opioid overdose patients in the United States increased from $58.6 million in 2005 to $1.94 billion in 2015. The increased use of naloxone, a medication used to reverse opioid overdoses, has also contributed to healthcare costs, as the price of naloxone has increased significantly in recent years.

The emotional toll of the opioid epidemic on healthcare workers is also significant. Healthcare providers, particularly those working in emergency departments and addiction treatment centers, are often on the front lines of the opioid epidemic, dealing with the consequences of overdose and addiction on a daily basis. The emotional toll of witnessing the devastating impact of the opioid epidemic can lead to burnout and mental health issues among healthcare workers.

In addition to the direct impact on healthcare providers and systems, the opioid epidemic has also had broader societal impacts on healthcare. The increased demand for addiction treatment and mental health services related to the opioid epidemic has placed a strain on healthcare resources, particularly in areas where access to healthcare is already limited. This has led to longer wait times for treatment and a shortage of healthcare providers in some areas.

The impact of synthetic opioids on healthcare also extends beyond the United States. In Canada, the rise in fentanyl-related deaths has led to increased demand for addiction treatment services, putting a strain on the country's healthcare system. In the United Kingdom, the National Health Service has also been impacted by the rise in fentanyl-related deaths, with a significant increase in emergency room visits related to opioid overdoses.

To address the impact of synthetic opioids on healthcare, there have been efforts to increase access to addiction treatment and mental health services, as well as to increase access to overdose reversal drugs like naloxone. In the United States, the federal government has allocated funding to support the expansion of addiction treatment and mental health services, as well as to increase access to naloxone. In Canada, the government has also invested in addiction treatment services and overdose prevention programs.

Efforts to address the impact of synthetic opioids on healthcare also include a focus on harm reduction strategies, such as providing safe injection sites and distributing clean needles. These strategies have been shown to reduce the transmission of blood-borne diseases and reduce the risk of overdose among people who use drugs.

In conclusion, the impact of synthetic opioids on healthcare has been significant, with increased healthcare costs, a strain on healthcare resources, and an emotional toll on healthcare providers. Efforts to address the impact of synthetic opioids on healthcare include increased access to addiction treatment and mental health services, increased access to overdose reversal drugs like naloxone, and a focus on harm reduction strategies.

Conclusion

The rise of synthetic opioids, particularly fentanyl, has had a devastating impact on individuals, families, and communities across the United States and the world. In this essay, we have explored various aspects of this issue, including the definition of synthetic opioids, the emergence of fentanyl, the contributing factors to their rise, the impact of synthetic opioids on overdose deaths, the emergence of fentanyl analogs, the spread of synthetic opioids, law enforcement and policy responses, and the impact of synthetic opioids on healthcare.

Synthetic opioids are man-made drugs that are chemically designed to mimic the effects of natural opioids like heroin and morphine. They are much more potent than natural opioids and can be much deadlier. Fentanyl is a particularly potent synthetic opioid that has emerged as a major contributor to the opioid epidemic. It is up to 100 times more potent than morphine and can be lethal in very small doses.

There are various factors that have contributed to the rise of synthetic opioids, including increased demand for stronger opioids, the availability of precursor chemicals, and the emergence of dark web markets and transnational criminal networks. The impact of synthetic opioids on overdose deaths has been particularly devastating, with synthetic opioids now responsible for the majority of opioid overdose deaths in the United States and other countries.

The emergence of fentanyl analogs, which are chemically similar to fentanyl but often even more potent, has added another layer of complexity to the opioid epidemic. Fentanyl analogs can be much more difficult to detect and treat than fentanyl, leading to even more overdose deaths.

The spread of synthetic opioids has been linked to the rise in production and trafficking of these drugs, often through transnational criminal networks. Synthetic opioids have spread rapidly across the United States, impacting communities that were previously not as affected by the opioid epidemic. In addition to the United States, synthetic opioids have also become a major issue in Canada and Europe.

Law enforcement and policymakers have responded to the rise of synthetic opioids through various efforts to crack down on illegal drug trafficking and increase access to overdose reversal drugs like naloxone. However, more needs to be done to address the root causes of the opioid epidemic and increase access to addiction treatment.

The impact of synthetic opioids on healthcare systems and providers has been significant, leading to increased healthcare costs and an emotional toll on healthcare workers. The high potency of synthetic opioids means that healthcare providers must take extra precautions when treating patients, which can be both time-consuming and emotionally challenging.

In conclusion, the rise of synthetic opioids has had a profound impact on individuals, families, and communities across the United States and the world. Addressing this issue requires a multi-faceted approach that includes reducing demand for these drugs, increasing access to addiction treatment, and cracking down on illegal drug trafficking. Healthcare providers and systems must also be prepared to respond to the unique challenges posed by synthetic opioids. Continued efforts are needed to address the rise of synthetic opioids and prevent further harm to individuals and communities affected by this crisis.

The Impact of Homelessness on Public Health

Homelessness is a pervasive issue that affects millions of people worldwide. It is a complex problem that is closely linked to poverty, mental illness, addiction, and lack of affordable housing. Homelessness not only impacts the individuals experiencing it, but also has significant implications for public health. Homeless individuals are at higher risk for a range of health issues, from infectious diseases to chronic conditions, and face significant barriers to accessing healthcare. In this essay, we will examine the impact of homelessness on public health, discussing how living on the streets can exacerbate health issues and spread disease. We will explore the prevalence of homelessness and the health disparities faced by homeless individuals, as well as the social and economic factors that contribute to homelessness. We will also discuss strategies for addressing homelessness and improving public health outcomes for this vulnerable population.

Homelessness and Mental Health

Homelessness and mental health are two issues that are closely intertwined, with a significant overlap between the homeless population and individuals living with mental illness. According to the National Alliance to End Homelessness, approximately 25% of the homeless population in the United States has a serious mental illness, compared to just 6% of the general population. Homelessness can exacerbate mental health issues, and conversely, mental illness can be a contributing factor to homelessness. In this section, we will explore the relationship between homelessness and mental health and the impact of homelessness on mental health.

Prevalence of Mental Illness among the Homeless Population:

As mentioned, the prevalence of mental illness among the homeless population is much higher than in the general population. The most common mental illnesses among the homeless population include depression, bipolar disorder, schizophrenia, and post-traumatic stress disorder (PTSD). The Substance Abuse and Mental Health Services Administration (SAMHSA) estimates that 30% of individuals experiencing homelessness have a serious mental illness, and 20-25% have co-occurring substance use disorders.

One factor that contributes to the high prevalence of mental illness among the homeless population is the lack of access to mental healthcare. Homeless individuals are less likely to have health insurance or access to mental healthcare services, which can prevent them from receiving necessary treatment for mental illness. Additionally, the stress and trauma associated with homelessness can exacerbate existing mental health issues or trigger the onset of new mental health problems.

Impact of Homelessness on Mental Health:

Living on the streets can have a significant impact on an individual's mental health. Homeless individuals are at a higher risk of experiencing trauma, violence, and victimization, which can lead to the development of mental health issues such as PTSD, depression, and anxiety. Additionally, the lack of stability and security that comes with homelessness can lead to chronic stress and exacerbate existing mental health issues.

Homeless individuals may also struggle with feelings of shame, guilt, and isolation, which can further worsen their mental health. The lack of privacy and personal space that comes with homelessness can make it difficult for individuals to maintain a sense of dignity and autonomy, which can contribute to feelings of hopelessness and despair.

Substance Use and Homelessness:

Substance use disorders are also common among the homeless population, and can further exacerbate mental health issues. The National Institute on Drug Abuse reports that homeless individuals are more likely to use drugs and alcohol than the general population, and are at a higher risk of overdosing. Substance use can also lead to other health problems, such as liver disease, heart disease, and infectious diseases like HIV/AIDS and hepatitis.

The relationship between substance use and homelessness is complex, and can be both a cause and a consequence of homelessness. Substance use can lead to financial instability, legal problems, and strained relationships, which can contribute to homelessness. On the other hand, the stress and trauma of homelessness can lead to substance use as a coping mechanism.

In conclusion, the relationship between homelessness and mental health is complex and multifaceted, with a high prevalence of mental illness among the homeless population and a significant impact of homelessness on mental health. Homeless individuals face numerous barriers to accessing mental healthcare, and living on the streets can exacerbate mental health issues and contribute to substance use disorders. Addressing the mental health needs of the homeless population is crucial for improving their overall health and well-being and helping them to transition out of homelessness.

Homelessness and Physical Health

Homelessness is a significant public health issue that impacts millions of people around the world. In addition to the social and economic consequences of homelessness, it also has a profound impact on physical health. Homeless individuals often face multiple health challenges, including higher rates of infectious diseases, chronic health conditions, and injuries. This section will examine the impact of homelessness on physical health, including the specific health risks faced by homeless individuals.

Increased Risk of Infectious Diseases:

Homeless individuals are at increased risk of infectious diseases due to a variety of factors, including poor living conditions and limited access to healthcare. Homeless shelters, which are often overcrowded and lack adequate sanitation facilities, can increase the risk of infectious diseases such as tuberculosis, influenza, and other respiratory infections. Homeless individuals are also at greater risk of contracting sexually transmitted infections due to their increased risk of sexual exploitation and the lack of access to sexual health services.

In addition to the increased risk of infectious diseases, homeless individuals are also more likely to experience poor nutrition, which can further compromise their immune systems. Homeless individuals often rely on food banks and other sources of free food, which may not provide a balanced diet with sufficient vitamins and minerals.

Chronic Health Conditions:

Homeless individuals also have higher rates of chronic health conditions, including diabetes, hypertension, and heart disease. These conditions are often exacerbated by poor living conditions, limited access to healthcare, and lack of access to healthy food. Homeless individuals may also be more likely to engage in risky health behaviors such as drug use and smoking, which can further increase the risk of chronic health conditions.

Injuries:

Homeless individuals are also at higher risk of injuries, both from accidents and violence. Homeless individuals are more likely to experience falls, fractures, and other injuries due to the lack of safe and stable housing. Homeless individuals are also at greater risk of violence, including physical assault and sexual violence. The risk of violence is particularly high for homeless women and LGBTQ individuals.

Access to Healthcare:

Access to healthcare is a significant challenge for homeless individuals. Homeless individuals may lack health insurance and may have limited access to healthcare services. Homeless individuals may also face stigma and discrimination from healthcare providers, which can make it more difficult to access care. Even when homeless individuals are able to access healthcare services, they may face additional barriers, such as transportation and the need to prioritize other basic needs such as food and shelter.

In conclusion, homelessness has a profound impact on physical health, including increased risks of infectious diseases, chronic health conditions, and injuries. Homeless individuals face multiple barriers to accessing healthcare, including lack of health insurance, limited access to healthcare services, and stigma and discrimination from healthcare providers. Addressing the physical health needs of homeless individuals requires a comprehensive approach that addresses both the social determinants of health and the unique health challenges faced by homeless individuals. This includes increasing access to stable and affordable housing, improving access to healthcare services, and addressing the social and economic factors that contribute to homelessness.

Substance Use and Homelessness

Substance Use and Homelessness: Discuss the relationship between substance use and homelessness, including the high prevalence of substance use disorders among homeless individuals and how substance use can exacerbate other health issues.

Homelessness and substance use are two issues that are closely intertwined. Homelessness can increase the risk of substance use, while substance use can also contribute to homelessness. According to the Substance Abuse and Mental Health Services Administration (SAMHSA), nearly one-third of homeless individuals in the United States have a substance use disorder. In this section, we will discuss the relationship between substance use and homelessness and the impact it has on the health of homeless individuals.

Prevalence of Substance Use Disorders Among Homeless Individuals

Homelessness is a risk factor for substance use disorders, and individuals experiencing homelessness are more likely to use substances than those who have stable housing. Substance use disorders are more prevalent among homeless individuals than the general population. According to SAMHSA, the rate of substance use disorders among homeless individuals is three to four times higher than the general population.

The most commonly used substances among homeless individuals are alcohol, cocaine, and opioids. The use of these substances can lead to a range of health problems, including liver disease, heart disease, and infectious diseases such as HIV and hepatitis.

Substance Use and Homelessness: A Vicious Cycle

Substance use can contribute to homelessness, and homelessness can increase the risk of substance use. Homeless individuals may turn to substance use as a way to cope with the stress and trauma of homelessness. Substance use can also be a way to escape from the harsh realities of living on the streets. Substance use can lead to poor decision-making and impulsive behavior, which can make it more difficult for individuals to find stable housing and employment.

On the other hand, homelessness can increase the risk of substance use by exposing individuals to high-risk environments and social networks that promote substance use. Homeless individuals may also lack access to healthcare, which can make it more difficult to receive treatment for substance use disorders.

Impact of Substance Use on Homeless Health

Substance use can exacerbate other health problems among homeless individuals. For example, individuals who use drugs or alcohol may be more likely to engage in risky sexual behaviors, which can increase the risk of sexually transmitted infections. Injection drug use can also increase the risk of infectious diseases such as HIV and hepatitis.

Substance use can also contribute to mental health issues among homeless individuals. Individuals who use substances may be more likely to experience depression, anxiety, and other mental health disorders. Substance use can also worsen existing mental health conditions.

In addition to the direct impact on health, substance use can also contribute to other issues that impact the health of homeless individuals. For example, substance use can lead to criminal behavior, which can result in incarceration and further exacerbate the risk of health problems.

Addressing Substance Use Among Homeless Individuals

Addressing substance use among homeless individuals is an important part of improving the health and well-being of this population. Treatment for substance use disorders can improve physical and mental health outcomes and increase the likelihood of finding stable housing and employment.

However, addressing substance use among homeless individuals can be challenging. Homeless individuals may face barriers to accessing healthcare, including lack of insurance, transportation, and other resources. Homeless individuals may also be hesitant to seek treatment due to stigma and fear of discrimination.

To address substance use among homeless individuals, it is important to provide comprehensive and accessible healthcare services that include substance use treatment. This may include outreach and engagement programs that meet homeless individuals where they are, such as in shelters or on the streets. It may also involve addressing the social determinants of health that contribute to substance use, such as poverty and lack of access to housing.

Conclusion

Substance use and homelessness are two complex issues that are closely intertwined. Substance use can contribute to homelessness, and homelessness can increase the risk of substance use. The high prevalence of substance use disorders among homeless individuals highlights the need for comprehensive healthcare services that include substance use treatment. Addressing substance use among homeless individuals can improve physical and mental health outcomes and increase the likelihood of finding stable housing and employment. To effectively address substance use among homeless individuals, it is important to also address the social determinants of health that contribute to substance use and homelessness, such as poverty and lack of access to housing.

Homelessness and HIV/AIDS

Homelessness and HIV/AIDS are two interrelated issues that have significant impacts on public health. Homeless individuals face increased risk for HIV/AIDS transmission and challenges in accessing testing and treatment. In this section, we will discuss the relationship between homelessness and HIV/AIDS and the challenges faced by homeless individuals in preventing and treating HIV/AIDS.

Prevalence of HIV/AIDS Among Homeless Individuals

Homelessness is a risk factor for HIV/AIDS transmission. According to the Centers for Disease Control and Prevention (CDC), homeless individuals are more likely to engage in behaviors that increase the risk of HIV transmission, such as injection drug use and unprotected sex. In addition, homeless individuals may have limited access to healthcare and HIV testing, which can result in undiagnosed and untreated HIV/AIDS.

The prevalence of HIV/AIDS among homeless individuals is higher than the general population. A study conducted by the National Alliance to End Homelessness found that the rate of HIV/AIDS among homeless individuals was three to nine times higher than the general population. Homeless individuals who are injection drug users are at even higher risk for HIV/AIDS transmission.

Challenges in Accessing HIV/AIDS Testing and Treatment

Homeless individuals face significant challenges in accessing HIV/AIDS testing and treatment. Homeless individuals may lack access to healthcare facilities that offer HIV testing and treatment, or may not have the resources to travel to these facilities. Homeless individuals may also face stigma and discrimination when seeking healthcare, which can deter them from accessing services.

In addition, homeless individuals may lack the stable housing necessary to access HIV/AIDS treatment. Many HIV/AIDS medications require refrigeration and must be taken at the same time every day. Homeless individuals may not have access to refrigeration or may not have a stable routine that allows them to take medication at the same time every day.

Homelessness also makes it more difficult to adhere to HIV/AIDS treatment. Homeless individuals may not have a safe place to store medication or may not be able to access medication if they are living in a different location each night. In addition, homeless individuals may be dealing with other issues, such as substance use or mental health disorders, which can make it more difficult to adhere to treatment.

Impact of Homelessness on HIV/AIDS Transmission

Homelessness increases the risk of HIV/AIDS transmission. Homeless individuals may engage in behaviors that increase the risk of HIV/AIDS transmission, such as injection drug use and unprotected sex. Homeless individuals may also lack access to healthcare and HIV testing, which can result in undiagnosed and untreated HIV/AIDS.

In addition, homelessness can contribute to the spread of HIV/AIDS by creating environments that promote high-risk behaviors. Homeless individuals may live in crowded and unsanitary conditions that increase the risk of infectious diseases. Homeless individuals may also be more likely to engage in survival sex, which can increase the risk of HIV/AIDS transmission.

Addressing HIV/AIDS Among Homeless Individuals

Addressing HIV/AIDS among homeless individuals requires a multifaceted approach. It is important to provide accessible HIV testing and treatment services that are tailored to the needs of homeless individuals. This may include outreach programs that bring HIV testing and treatment services to homeless individuals in their communities.

In addition, addressing homelessness is critical to preventing HIV/AIDS transmission. Providing stable housing and addressing the social determinants of health that contribute to homelessness, such as poverty and lack of access to healthcare, can reduce the risk of HIV/AIDS transmission among homeless individuals.

Conclusion

Homelessness and HIV/AIDS are two complex issues that have significant impacts on public health. Homeless individuals face increased risk for HIV/AIDS transmission and challenges in accessing testing and treatment. Addressing the social determinants of health that contribute to homelessness and providing accessible HIV testing and treatment services are key components of preventing and treating HIV/AIDS among homeless individuals.

Homelessness and Tuberculosis

Tuberculosis (TB) is a contagious bacterial infection that primarily affects the lungs but can also affect other parts of the body. It is spread through the air when an infected person coughs or sneezes. Homelessness is a risk factor for TB due to overcrowded and unsanitary living conditions, poor nutrition, and lack of access to healthcare. In this section, we will discuss the impact of homelessness on the spread of TB and the challenges faced by homeless individuals in accessing TB testing and treatment.

Increased Risk of TB Transmission among Homeless Individuals

Homelessness increases the risk of TB transmission due to the crowded and unsanitary living conditions in shelters and on the streets. Homeless individuals are also more likely to have weakened immune systems due to malnutrition, stress, and other health issues.

This makes them more susceptible to TB infection and more likely to develop active TB disease.

According to the Centers for Disease Control and Prevention (CDC), the TB rate among homeless individuals is approximately 10 times higher than the rate among the general population. Homeless individuals are also more likely to have drug-resistant TB, which can be more difficult to treat and can lead to longer hospital stays and higher healthcare costs.

Challenges Faced by Homeless Individuals in Accessing TB Testing and Treatment

Homeless individuals face numerous barriers to accessing TB testing and treatment. These include lack of access to healthcare, transportation, and stable housing. Homeless individuals may also be hesitant to seek healthcare services due to fear of discrimination, stigma, and lack of trust in healthcare providers.

TB testing and treatment require a long-term commitment to a treatment regimen that can be difficult for homeless individuals to adhere to. TB treatment can take several months to complete and requires daily medication, which can be challenging for homeless individuals who lack stable housing and may have difficulty keeping medications safe and accessible.

In addition to the challenges of accessing and adhering to treatment, homeless individuals with TB may also face isolation and quarantine. This can further exacerbate the challenges of homelessness, including difficulty finding employment and housing.

Addressing TB Among Homeless Individuals

Addressing TB among homeless individuals requires a comprehensive approach that addresses the underlying social determinants of health that contribute to TB transmission. This includes providing access to safe and affordable housing, nutritious food, and healthcare services.

TB testing and treatment should be integrated into existing healthcare services for homeless individuals, including outreach programs that bring healthcare services to shelters and other locations where homeless individuals congregate. Healthcare providers should also receive training on working with homeless individuals and addressing the unique challenges they face in accessing healthcare.

Conclusion

Homelessness is a risk factor for TB transmission and can make it difficult for homeless individuals to access TB testing and treatment. Addressing TB among homeless individuals requires a comprehensive approach that addresses the underlying social determinants of health that contribute to TB transmission. By providing access to healthcare services and addressing the challenges faced by homeless individuals, it is possible to reduce the impact of TB on this vulnerable population.

Homelessness and Hepatitis

Homelessness is a major risk factor for hepatitis, a viral infection that affects the liver. Hepatitis is highly transmissible and can spread easily in crowded, unsanitary conditions, making homeless individuals particularly vulnerable to infection. In this section, we will discuss the impact of homelessness on the spread of hepatitis, including the increased risk of transmission and the challenges faced by homeless individuals in accessing hepatitis testing and treatment.

Prevalence of Hepatitis Among Homeless Individuals

Studies have shown that the prevalence of hepatitis is higher among homeless individuals than the general population. According to the Centers for Disease Control and Prevention (CDC), the prevalence of hepatitis C among homeless individuals is estimated to be as high as 35%, compared to 1-2% in the general population. The prevalence of hepatitis B is also higher among homeless individuals.

Homeless individuals are at increased risk of hepatitis due to a variety of factors, including sharing needles or other injection equipment, engaging in high-risk sexual behaviors, and living in unsanitary conditions. Homeless individuals may also lack access to healthcare, which can make it more difficult to receive testing and treatment for hepatitis.

Challenges Faced by Homeless Individuals in Accessing Testing and Treatment

Homeless individuals face significant challenges in accessing hepatitis testing and treatment. Homeless individuals may lack access to healthcare facilities or may not have health insurance, making it difficult to access testing and treatment. Homeless individuals may also be hesitant to seek healthcare due to stigma or fear of discrimination.

Homeless individuals may also face challenges in adhering to treatment due to the unstable and unpredictable nature of homelessness. Treatment for hepatitis often requires regular medical appointments and adherence to medication regimens, which can be difficult for homeless individuals to maintain. Homeless individuals may also face challenges in storing medication and maintaining a healthy diet, which can be important for successful treatment.

Impact of Homelessness on Hepatitis Transmission

Homeless individuals are at increased risk of hepatitis transmission due to the living conditions commonly found among homeless populations. Homeless individuals may live in crowded shelters or on the streets, where unsanitary conditions can facilitate the spread of infectious diseases such as hepatitis. Homeless individuals may also engage in high-risk behaviors such as sharing needles or engaging in unprotected sex, which can increase the risk of hepatitis transmission.

Homeless individuals may also lack access to basic hygiene facilities, such as handwashing stations, which can help prevent the spread of hepatitis. Lack of access to clean water and sanitation facilities can also contribute to the spread of hepatitis.

Addressing Hepatitis Among Homeless Individuals

Addressing hepatitis among homeless individuals requires a comprehensive approach that addresses both the medical and social determinants of health that contribute to the spread of hepatitis. This may include outreach and education programs that provide information on the risk factors for hepatitis and the importance of testing and treatment.

It is also important to provide homeless individuals with access to healthcare services that include hepatitis testing and treatment. This may involve working with community-based organizations and healthcare providers to bring services directly to homeless individuals in shelters or on the streets.

Conclusion

Homelessness is a significant risk factor for hepatitis, and homeless individuals face significant challenges in accessing testing and treatment for this infectious disease. Addressing the spread of hepatitis among homeless populations requires a comprehensive approach that addresses the medical and social determinants of health that contribute to the spread of this disease. Providing homeless individuals with access to healthcare services and basic hygiene facilities is critical in preventing the spread of hepatitis and improving the health outcomes of homeless populations.

Homelessness and COVID-19

The COVID-19 pandemic has highlighted the vulnerabilities faced by homeless individuals and the impact of homelessness on the spread of infectious diseases. In this section, we will discuss the impact of homelessness on the spread of COVID-19 and the challenges faced by homeless individuals in accessing testing and treatment.

Increased Risk of Transmission

Homeless individuals are at an increased risk of contracting and transmitting COVID-19 due to their living conditions and lack of access to healthcare. Homeless individuals often live in overcrowded shelters or on the streets, which makes it difficult to practice social distancing and other preventive measures. In addition, homeless individuals often lack access to hygiene facilities, such as handwashing stations and bathrooms, which can increase the risk of transmission.

Homeless individuals also face barriers to accessing healthcare, which can delay diagnosis and treatment of COVID-19. Homeless individuals may lack insurance, transportation, and other resources that are necessary to access healthcare services.

Challenges in Accessing Testing

Homeless individuals face significant challenges in accessing COVID-19 testing. Homeless individuals may lack transportation to testing sites and may not have access to information about testing sites or the availability of testing. In addition, homeless individuals may be hesitant to seek testing due to fear of discrimination or lack of trust in the healthcare system.

To address these challenges, outreach and engagement programs that meet homeless individuals where they are, such as in shelters or on the streets, are necessary. Mobile testing units and testing sites in areas with high rates of homelessness can also increase access to testing.

Challenges in Accessing Treatment

Homeless individuals who are diagnosed with COVID-19 may face challenges in accessing treatment. Homeless individuals may lack access to quarantine or isolation facilities, which can increase the risk of transmission to others. Homeless individuals may also lack access to medications and other resources that are necessary to manage the symptoms of COVID-19.

To address these challenges, it is important to provide quarantine and isolation facilities for homeless individuals who have been diagnosed with COVID-19. In addition, healthcare services for homeless individuals should be comprehensive and accessible, including access to medications and other resources necessary to manage the symptoms of COVID-19.

Conclusion

Homelessness is a risk factor for the transmission of COVID-19 due to the living conditions and lack of access to healthcare faced by homeless individuals. Homeless individuals face significant challenges in accessing COVID-19 testing and treatment, which can delay diagnosis and treatment and increase the risk of transmission to others. Addressing these challenges requires comprehensive and accessible healthcare services for homeless individuals and outreach and engagement programs that meet homeless individuals where they are.

Addressing Homelessness and Public Health

Homelessness is a complex social issue that has a significant impact on public health. Homeless individuals face numerous health challenges, including increased risk of infectious diseases, chronic health conditions, and mental health disorders. Addressing homelessness and its impact on public health requires a multifaceted approach that involves a range of stakeholders, including policymakers, healthcare providers, social service providers, and community organizations.

One strategy for addressing homelessness and its impact on public health is the implementation of housing-first initiatives. Housing-first initiatives prioritize providing stable and permanent housing for homeless individuals as a first step toward addressing their other needs, including healthcare and employment. By providing stable housing, individuals are better able to address their health needs, such as managing chronic conditions or receiving treatment for mental health disorders.

Increased access to healthcare and social services is another strategy for addressing homelessness and its impact on public health. Homeless individuals often face barriers to accessing healthcare and social services, including lack of insurance, transportation, and other resources. Providing access to healthcare and social services can help homeless individuals address their health needs, receive treatment for chronic conditions, and access resources that can help them transition out of homelessness.

Harm reduction approaches are also an important strategy for addressing homelessness and its impact on public health. Harm reduction approaches seek to minimize the negative consequences associated with substance use and other high-risk behaviors, such as unprotected sex or injection drug use. For example, providing access to clean needles and condoms can help reduce the spread of infectious diseases, such as HIV and hepatitis, among homeless individuals who engage in these behaviors.

Another important strategy for addressing homelessness and its impact on public health is addressing the social determinants of health that contribute to homelessness. These include poverty, lack of affordable housing, and lack of access to healthcare and other resources. Addressing these social determinants of health can help prevent homelessness and improve health outcomes for homeless individuals.

Community engagement is also a key strategy for addressing homelessness and its impact on public health. Engaging with community organizations and stakeholders can help ensure that homeless individuals have access to the resources and support they need to address their health needs and transition out of homelessness. Community engagement can also help reduce stigma associated with homelessness and promote public awareness of the impact of homelessness on public health.

In conclusion, addressing homelessness and its impact on public health requires a multifaceted approach that involves a range of stakeholders and strategies. Housing-first initiatives, increased access to healthcare and social services, harm reduction approaches, addressing social determinants of health, and community engagement are all important strategies for addressing homelessness and improving public health outcomes for homeless individuals. By working together, we can help ensure that all individuals have access to the resources and support they need to achieve optimal health and well-being, regardless of their housing status.

Conclusion

In this essay, we have examined the relationship between homelessness and public health, including the increased risk of various health issues such as substance use disorders, HIV/AIDS, tuberculosis, hepatitis, and COVID-19 among homeless individuals. We also discussed the challenges faced by homeless individuals in accessing healthcare and social services, as well as the strategies to address the issue of homelessness and its impact on public health, such as housing-first initiatives, increased access to healthcare and social services, and harm reduction approaches.

It is clear that homelessness is a complex issue that requires a comprehensive and coordinated approach. Addressing the root causes of homelessness, such as poverty, lack of affordable housing, and structural inequalities, is crucial to reducing the impact of homelessness on public health. It is also important to provide homeless individuals with access to quality healthcare and social services, including substance use treatment, mental health services, and case management.

Continued efforts are needed to address the issue of homelessness and its impact on public health. This includes increased funding for housing and healthcare programs, as well as policies that prioritize the needs of homeless individuals. By taking a comprehensive and coordinated approach, we can work towards reducing the impact of homelessness on public health and improving the well-being of all individuals.

The Role of Housing Insecurity in Homelessness and Drug Use

Homelessness and drug use are two interrelated issues that have become a growing concern in many parts of the world. While the causes of homelessness are complex and multifaceted, housing insecurity is often cited as a key factor contributing to the crisis. The lack of affordable housing options has left many individuals and families struggling to make ends meet, with some forced to choose between paying for housing or other basic necessities like food and healthcare. This has created a vicious cycle where housing insecurity can lead to drug use and addiction, which in turn can lead to homelessness. In this essay, we will examine the link between housing insecurity, drug use, and homelessness, with a particular focus on how the lack of affordable housing options has contributed to this crisis. We will also explore potential solutions to this issue and the need for a comprehensive approach that addresses the root causes of homelessness and drug use.

The Scope of the Affordable Housing Crisis in the United States

The affordable housing crisis is a widespread issue that affects millions of people in the United States. The lack of affordable housing has contributed to a significant increase in housing insecurity, with many individuals and families struggling to find safe, stable, and affordable housing options. The scope of this crisis is staggering, with a significant portion of the population either homeless or at risk of homelessness.

According to a report by the National Low Income Housing Coalition, there is a shortage of over 7 million affordable and available rental homes for extremely low-income renters in the United States. Extremely low-income households are those earning 30% or less of the area median income. This means that millions of individuals and families are spending a large portion of their income on housing costs, leaving little to no room for other basic necessities such as food, healthcare, and education.

The lack of affordable housing has also led to a rise in homelessness, with an estimated 580,000 people experiencing homelessness on any given night in the United States. This includes individuals, families with children, and veterans. The homeless population is not limited to urban areas, with many rural and suburban communities also facing significant homelessness challenges.

The scope of the affordable housing crisis is further exacerbated by systemic issues such as racial and income inequality. Minorities and low-income individuals are disproportionately affected by the lack of affordable housing, with many facing additional barriers such as discrimination and lack of access to resources.

Overall, the affordable housing crisis is a complex issue that affects a large portion of the population and has far-reaching consequences on individual and public health. It is crucial to address this issue through policy changes and increased investment in affordable housing options.

The Link Between Housing Insecurity and Substance Use Disorders

The link between housing insecurity and substance use disorders has been extensively studied, and the evidence suggests that there is a strong relationship between the two. Housing insecurity refers to the lack of affordable and stable housing, which can lead to homelessness or precarious housing situations, such as living with friends or family or in temporary shelters. On the other hand, substance use disorders refer to the problematic use of drugs or alcohol that can lead to addiction and other negative consequences.

One of the main ways in which housing insecurity contributes to substance use disorders is through the stress and trauma that it causes. People who are struggling to find and maintain stable housing may experience chronic stress, anxiety, and uncertainty about their future. This can lead to depression and other mental health issues, which can increase the risk of substance use disorders. Additionally, the lack of stability and safety that comes with housing insecurity can also expose people to traumatic events such as violence, which can also increase the risk of substance use disorders.

Another way in which housing insecurity can lead to substance use disorders is through social isolation and marginalization. People who are homeless or living in precarious housing situations may face stigma and discrimination, which can lead to feelings of shame and social exclusion. This can lead to feelings of hopelessness and despair, which can increase the risk of substance use disorders as people turn to drugs or alcohol as a coping mechanism.

Moreover, the lack of affordable housing options and resources to help those in need also puts a strain on people's financial resources, which can lead to choices between paying rent or buying necessities like food and medication. This puts people in a vulnerable position where they might need to resort to risky coping strategies such as selling drugs, which could lead to the development of a substance use disorder. Homelessness and housing insecurity are also associated with higher rates of exposure to environmental toxins and infectious diseases, which can lead to poor physical health and chronic pain, both of which can increase the risk of substance use disorders.

It is essential to recognize the link between housing insecurity and substance use disorders to develop effective interventions to address both issues. Providing stable, affordable housing and support services can help to reduce the stress and trauma associated with housing insecurity, which can reduce the risk of substance use disorders. Access to resources like job training, health care, and mental health services can also help to improve people's financial security and overall well-being, reducing the risk of substance use disorders.

Furthermore, substance use disorder treatment programs should also recognize the impact of housing insecurity on their clients' recovery.

Treatment programs that provide stable housing and support services can help to address the underlying issues that may have contributed to the development of a substance use disorder, helping individuals achieve lasting recovery.

Overall, the link between housing insecurity and substance use disorders is a complex issue that requires a multifaceted approach. By recognizing and addressing the root causes of both problems, we can work towards creating more stable, healthy, and supportive communities for everyone.

The Connection Between Housing Insecurity and Homelessness
Housing insecurity is a major contributor to homelessness. When individuals or families cannot afford stable and safe housing, they are at risk of losing their homes and becoming homeless. This can happen for a variety of reasons, including rising rent prices, job loss, medical bills, or other unforeseen circumstances. When housing insecurity becomes chronic, it can lead to homelessness, which can have devastating consequences for individuals and communities.

Homelessness is a complex issue that affects millions of people in the United States. According to the National Alliance to End Homelessness, over half a million people were experiencing homelessness on a single night in 2020, and over 1.4 million people accessed homeless services during the year. Homelessness can have a profound impact on individuals and families, including physical and mental health problems, increased risk of violence and trauma, and limited access to basic needs such as food, water, and sanitation.

The connection between housing insecurity and homelessness is multifaceted. For many people, housing insecurity is a precursor to homelessness. When individuals cannot afford stable housing, they may turn to temporary solutions such as couch surfing, staying with friends or family, or living in unsafe or overcrowded conditions. These temporary solutions may not be sustainable, and individuals may eventually find themselves without a place to live.

In addition, the lack of affordable housing options exacerbates the issue of homelessness. When affordable housing is not available, individuals may be forced to choose between paying for housing or other basic needs such as food and medical care. In some cases, individuals may choose to prioritize other needs, leaving them unable to pay rent or mortgage payments and at risk of eviction or foreclosure. Once they lose their housing, it can be difficult to find affordable housing options, especially in areas with high rent prices and low vacancy rates.

Homelessness can also be a result of systemic issues such as racism, discrimination, and poverty. People from marginalized communities, such as people of color and LGBTQ individuals, are more likely to experience homelessness due to these systemic factors. Additionally, people living in poverty are more likely to experience housing insecurity and are at higher risk of becoming homeless.

Once an individual experiences homelessness, it can be difficult to find stable housing. Homeless individuals face numerous challenges in accessing affordable housing, including discrimination from landlords, lack of access to financial resources, and limited availability of affordable housing units. Homeless individuals also face mental and physical health challenges that can make it difficult to maintain stable housing.

In conclusion, the link between housing insecurity and homelessness is a complex issue that requires a comprehensive approach to address. Increasing the availability of affordable housing, providing financial assistance to those in need, and addressing systemic issues such as poverty and discrimination can all help to prevent homelessness. For those who are already experiencing homelessness, access to supportive services such as mental health care and addiction treatment can help them find stable housing and improve their overall well-being.

The Role of Housing Assistance Programs in Preventing Homelessness and Drug Use

Housing assistance programs play a crucial role in preventing homelessness and drug use by providing stable and affordable housing to individuals and families who are at risk of becoming homeless. These programs can include a range of services, such as rental assistance, transitional housing, and permanent supportive housing, and are typically administered by government agencies, non-profit organizations, or a combination of both.

One of the main ways that housing assistance programs prevent homelessness is by providing affordable housing options for low-income individuals and families. This can include rental subsidies that make it easier for people to afford housing in high-cost areas, as well as programs that help families become homeowners. By providing stable and affordable housing, these programs can help to prevent families from falling into homelessness due to a lack of affordable housing options.

In addition to preventing homelessness, housing assistance programs can also play a key role in preventing drug use by providing a stable and supportive living environment. Many individuals who struggle with drug addiction also face housing instability, which can make it difficult for them to access the resources and support they need to recover. By providing stable and affordable housing, housing assistance programs can help to remove this barrier and make it easier for individuals to access treatment and support services.

One example of a housing assistance program that has been successful in preventing homelessness and drug use is the Housing First model. This model prioritizes providing individuals experiencing homelessness with permanent housing, without requiring them to meet certain criteria such as being sober or completing treatment first. By providing housing first, individuals are able to stabilize their living situation and are better able to access the resources and support they need to address their substance use disorders.

Another effective housing assistance program is the Supportive Housing program, which provides individuals with long-term housing support services, such as case management, counseling, and other supportive services, to help them maintain their housing stability and improve their overall well-being. This program has been particularly effective in serving individuals with chronic substance use disorders and mental health issues, who often face significant barriers to accessing stable housing.

Overall, housing assistance programs play a critical role in preventing homelessness and drug use by providing stable and affordable housing options, as well as supportive services that help individuals maintain their housing stability and address their substance use disorders. These programs can have a significant impact on reducing the number of individuals experiencing homelessness and substance use disorders, and should continue to be a priority for policymakers and advocates.

Innovative Approaches to Providing Stable Housing for Homeless Individuals with Substance Use Disorders

In recent years, there has been an increasing recognition of the need for innovative approaches to providing stable housing for homeless individuals with substance use disorders. Traditional housing models, such as shelters and transitional housing programs, have proven to be inadequate in addressing the complex needs of this population. However, there are several innovative approaches that have emerged in recent years that show promise in providing stable housing for homeless individuals with substance use disorders.

One such approach is Housing First, which prioritizes providing individuals with permanent housing as quickly as possible, without requiring them to meet preconditions such as sobriety or participation in treatment programs. This approach recognizes that stable housing is a critical foundation for recovery and that individuals are more likely to engage in treatment and other services when they have a stable place to live. Housing First programs provide supportive services to help individuals maintain their housing, such as case management, peer support, and access to mental health and substance use treatment.

Another approach is the use of scattered-site housing, which provides individuals with individual apartments in various locations throughout a city or region. This approach allows individuals to live independently while still receiving supportive services, such as case management and access to treatment. Scattered-site housing can also help to reduce the concentration of poverty and homelessness in a particular area, which can have positive effects on both individuals and communities.

Community Land Trusts (CLTs) are another innovative approach to providing stable housing for homeless individuals with substance use disorders. CLTs are nonprofit organizations that acquire and hold land and buildings for the benefit of the community. They provide affordable homeownership opportunities for low-income families and individuals, including those who have experienced homelessness or are in recovery from substance use disorders. CLTs can provide long-term stability and affordability for individuals and families, while also building community wealth and promoting social equity.

Finally, tiny homes and other small-scale housing options have emerged as a promising approach to providing stable housing for homeless individuals with substance use disorders. These small homes can be built quickly and inexpensively, providing a cost-effective solution to homelessness. They also promote self-sufficiency and independence, which can be important for individuals in recovery. Tiny homes can be located on individual lots or as part of a community, providing opportunities for social support and community building.

While there is no one-size-fits-all solution to providing stable housing for homeless individuals with substance use disorders, these innovative approaches offer new and promising options for addressing this complex issue. By providing stable housing and supportive services, we can help individuals to break the cycle of homelessness and addiction, and build a better future for themselves and their communities.

Challenges Faced by Homeless Individuals with Substance Use Disorders in Accessing Housing and Support Services

Homeless individuals with substance use disorders often face multiple challenges in accessing housing and support services. One of the primary challenges is the lack of affordable and stable housing options. Many of these individuals do not have the financial resources to secure housing and may face discrimination from landlords due to their history of substance use or homelessness.

In addition, homeless individuals with substance use disorders may also face challenges in accessing support services such as mental health treatment, medical care, and addiction treatment. These services can be expensive, and many homeless individuals do not have health insurance or the financial means to pay for them. This can lead to a lack of access to necessary medical care and addiction treatment, which can exacerbate substance use disorders and lead to further housing instability.

Another challenge faced by homeless individuals with substance use disorders is the stigma surrounding addiction and homelessness. Many individuals in society view substance use disorders as a personal choice or a moral failing rather than a medical condition. This can lead to discrimination and a lack of support for homeless individuals with substance use disorders, further exacerbating their housing instability.

Finally, homeless individuals with substance use disorders may also face legal and criminal justice system barriers to accessing housing and support services. These individuals may have criminal records or face legal consequences related to their substance use, which can make it difficult to secure housing and access necessary support services.

Overall, the challenges faced by homeless individuals with substance use disorders in accessing housing and support services are complex and multifaceted. Addressing these challenges will require a coordinated effort from government agencies, non-profit organizations, and the broader community to provide affordable and stable housing options, increase access to necessary support services, reduce stigma surrounding addiction and homelessness, and address legal and criminal justice system barriers.

Conclusion

In conclusion, the issues of housing insecurity, drug use, and homelessness are interconnected and require comprehensive solutions. The lack of affordable housing and inadequate support services contribute to substance use disorders and homelessness. Homeless individuals with substance use disorders face numerous challenges, including stigma, limited access to support services, and difficulty accessing stable housing. Innovative approaches to housing, such as the Housing First model and harm reduction programs, show promise in providing stable housing for homeless individuals with substance use disorders.

Housing assistance programs are crucial in preventing homelessness and drug use, but more needs to be done to ensure that they are accessible and effective. Policy changes, such as increased funding for affordable housing and expanded access to healthcare and social services, are necessary to address these issues. Additionally, addressing the root causes of housing insecurity, such as income inequality and the racial wealth gap, is essential in creating long-term solutions.

It is clear that homelessness and substance use disorders are complex issues that require a coordinated and comprehensive approach. Addressing the underlying causes of housing insecurity and providing accessible and effective support services are essential steps in ending the cycle of homelessness and drug use. With a commitment to innovative solutions and a focus on equity and social justice, we can work towards creating a society where everyone has access to safe and stable housing and the support they need to thrive.

The Challenges of Addiction Treatment on the West Coast

The West Coast of the United States has been hit hard by the opioid epidemic, with overdose rates soaring in recent years. While addiction treatment is available, there are many challenges to accessing care and limitations to current treatment options. This essay will explore the challenges of providing addiction treatment on the West Coast, including barriers to accessing care and the limitations of current treatment options. It will also emphasize the need for effective treatment options and the importance of addressing these challenges in order to combat the devastating impact of addiction in the region.

Barriers to accessing addiction treatment

Barriers to accessing addiction treatment are a significant challenge for individuals struggling with substance use disorders on the West Coast of the United States. These barriers can take many forms and can prevent people from getting the care they need to overcome addiction.

One of the most significant barriers to accessing addiction treatment is financial. Many people on the West Coast cannot afford the cost of treatment, which can be prohibitively expensive. Even with insurance coverage, co-pays and deductibles can be too high for many individuals to manage. Additionally, not all insurance plans cover addiction treatment, leaving some people with few options for care.

Geographic barriers also pose a significant challenge for those seeking addiction treatment on the West Coast. Many rural areas lack the resources and infrastructure necessary to provide comprehensive addiction treatment services. In addition, transportation can be a significant issue for people who live in areas without reliable public transit or who cannot afford the cost of private transportation to treatment facilities.

Social barriers can also prevent individuals from accessing addiction treatment. The stigma surrounding addiction can make it difficult for people to seek care without fear of judgment or discrimination. Family and social pressures can also prevent people from seeking treatment, particularly if their loved ones do not understand the nature of addiction or the importance of seeking professional care.

Another significant barrier is the shortage of addiction treatment providers on the West Coast. There are not enough trained professionals to meet the demand for care, particularly in rural and low-income areas. This shortage can lead to long wait times for treatment, which can be particularly challenging for individuals struggling with addiction.

Finally, the current legal and regulatory environment in some parts of the West Coast can also be a barrier to accessing addiction treatment. For example, in some states, laws governing addiction treatment can be restrictive or confusing, making it difficult for individuals to access care. Additionally, regulations governing the prescription of medication-assisted treatment (MAT) can limit the availability of this effective form of treatment.

In conclusion, barriers to accessing addiction treatment are a significant challenge for individuals struggling with substance use disorders on the West Coast of the United States. These barriers can take many forms, including financial, geographic, social, and regulatory challenges. Addressing these barriers will require a comprehensive approach that includes increased funding for addiction treatment, the expansion of addiction treatment services in rural and low-income areas, and the elimination of legal and regulatory barriers that limit access to care.

Limited availability of treatment resources

The shortage of addiction treatment resources is a significant challenge faced by those seeking addiction treatment on the West

Coast. There is a limited number of healthcare professionals and treatment centers that specialize in addiction treatment, which means that many individuals who need treatment are unable to access it.

One of the primary reasons for the shortage of addiction treatment resources is the lack of funding for addiction treatment programs. Many addiction treatment centers rely on funding from government sources, such as Medicaid, but the amount of funding provided is often insufficient to meet the demand for treatment. Additionally, private insurance plans may not cover the full cost of addiction treatment, making it difficult for those without adequate financial resources to access care.

Another factor contributing to the limited availability of treatment resources is the shortage of healthcare professionals trained in addiction treatment. There is a significant shortage of addiction medicine physicians, psychiatrists, and therapists in many areas of the West Coast. The shortage of healthcare professionals trained in addiction treatment can result in long wait times for appointments and limited access to specialized care.

Furthermore, there is a shortage of inpatient addiction treatment centers, particularly for those who require intensive treatment for substance use disorders. This can result in long waiting lists for treatment and limited availability of inpatient beds for those who need them.

The shortage of addiction treatment resources has a significant impact on the ability of healthcare professionals to provide adequate care to those who need it. Without access to treatment, individuals struggling with addiction are at a higher risk of overdose, hospitalization, and other negative health outcomes.

To address this challenge, there needs to be a significant investment in addiction treatment resources, including funding for treatment programs, training for healthcare professionals, and the development of new treatment options. Additionally, policies that improve access to affordable and comprehensive health insurance coverage for addiction treatment can help reduce financial barriers to care.

Stigma and discrimination

Stigma and discrimination are significant barriers to addiction treatment for individuals on the West Coast. Stigma can be defined as negative attitudes and beliefs held by society towards individuals with substance use disorders, while discrimination is the unfair treatment of these individuals due to their condition. These negative attitudes can manifest in a variety of ways, including social exclusion, shaming, and blame.

The stigma surrounding addiction can make it difficult for individuals to seek treatment, as they may fear being judged or labeled as weak or morally deficient. This can lead to feelings of shame and guilt, which may further exacerbate their addiction. Additionally, those who do seek treatment may face discrimination from healthcare providers, employers, and others due to their substance use disorder. This can lead to a lack of access to resources and support, as well as difficulty in finding employment or stable housing.

The stigma and discrimination surrounding addiction can also impact the quality of care provided by healthcare professionals. Providers may hold negative attitudes towards individuals with substance use disorders, leading to biases in their treatment approach. This can result in inadequate or inappropriate treatment, further perpetuating the cycle of addiction.

Addressing stigma and discrimination is crucial in ensuring that individuals on the West Coast have access to effective addiction treatment. Education and awareness campaigns can help to challenge negative attitudes and beliefs, while destigmatizing substance use disorders. Additionally, healthcare professionals can be trained in cultural competence and sensitivity, ensuring that they provide high-quality care to all individuals, regardless of their background or condition.

Overall, the impact of stigma and discrimination on addiction treatment cannot be overstated. By addressing these issues, individuals on the West Coast can be provided with the care and support they need to overcome their addiction and live healthy, fulfilling lives.

Lack of insurance coverage

The lack of insurance coverage for addiction treatment is a significant barrier for individuals seeking care on the West Coast. Many insurance companies do not cover the full cost of addiction treatment, leaving patients to pay for expensive out-of-pocket expenses. The high costs of addiction treatment can be prohibitive, making it difficult for individuals without insurance coverage to access the care they need.

However, some insurance companies do provide coverage for addiction treatment. For example, the Affordable Care Act (ACA) requires insurance companies to cover substance use disorder treatment as an essential health benefit. This means that insurance companies are required to cover the cost of addiction treatment, including both inpatient and outpatient care. Medicaid also covers addiction treatment for eligible individuals.

Despite these requirements, not all insurance plans offer comprehensive coverage for addiction treatment. Some plans may place restrictions on the type or length of treatment covered, making it difficult for patients to access the care they need. In addition, the costs associated with insurance premiums and deductibles can still be a significant financial burden for patients.

The lack of insurance coverage for addiction treatment can lead to a range of negative outcomes for individuals on the West Coast. It can prevent people from seeking care in the first place, leading to increased rates of overdose and other health complications. It can also result in financial hardship for patients and their families, as they are forced to pay for costly treatments out-of-pocket.

To address this issue, there have been calls for increased insurance coverage for addiction treatment. Some advocacy groups are pushing for reforms to insurance policies to ensure that all individuals have access to comprehensive addiction treatment coverage. In addition, some states have implemented their own policies to expand access to addiction treatment, such as Medicaid expansion and requirements for insurance companies to cover certain types of addiction treatment.

In conclusion, the lack of insurance coverage for addiction treatment is a significant barrier to care for individuals on the West Coast. While some insurance companies do provide coverage, it is often limited, leaving many patients to pay out-of-pocket expenses. More needs to be done to ensure that all individuals have access to comprehensive addiction treatment coverage, to improve health outcomes and reduce the financial burden on patients and their families.

Limited treatment options

The challenges of addiction treatment on the West Coast are compounded by the limited treatment options available. Despite the growing need for effective and evidence-based addiction treatment, there is a shortage of available treatment options that meet the needs of individuals with substance use disorders.

One of the main challenges is the lack of evidence-based treatment options. Many addiction treatment programs still rely on outdated and ineffective approaches such as detoxification and 12-step programs. These methods may work for some individuals, but they do not address the complex needs of many individuals with substance use disorders. In addition, these programs often fail to provide the long-term support and care that individuals need to achieve and maintain recovery.

Furthermore, addiction treatment programs on the West Coast often lack personalized care options. Substance use disorders are complex and affect individuals differently. Therefore, it is essential that addiction treatment options are tailored to the individual's specific needs. This includes providing personalized treatment plans, individual therapy, and access to a range of evidence-based treatment modalities such as medication-assisted treatment (MAT), cognitive-behavioral therapy (CBT), and dialectical behavior therapy (DBT).

Another factor that limits treatment options is the lack of funding for addiction treatment programs. Many individuals seeking addiction treatment do not have the financial resources to access care, and public funding for addiction treatment programs is often limited. This can result in long waitlists for treatment, with many individuals unable to access care when they need it.

The limited treatment options for substance use disorders can also lead to a lack of continuity of care. This can occur when individuals are unable to access the same level of care consistently or when they move from one treatment program to another. A lack of continuity of care can negatively impact an individual's recovery, as it disrupts the treatment process and can result in a loss of progress.

Overall, the limited treatment options for substance use disorders highlight the urgent need for increased funding and support for addiction treatment programs on the West Coast. It is essential that policymakers and healthcare providers work together to develop evidence-based treatment options that are tailored to the needs of individuals with substance use disorders. By doing so, we can help individuals achieve and maintain recovery and improve the overall health and well-being of our communities.

Overcrowding in treatment centers

Overcrowding in addiction treatment centers is a significant challenge faced by those seeking care on the West Coast. The high demand for treatment combined with the limited availability of resources leads to overcrowding in treatment centers. As a result, many individuals are unable to access the care they need, which can have detrimental effects on their health and well-being.

One of the main reasons for overcrowding in treatment centers is the opioid epidemic, which has significantly increased the demand for addiction treatment. According to the National Institute on Drug Abuse, approximately 2.1 million people in the United States had an opioid use disorder in 2019. This has placed a significant strain on the already limited treatment resources available on the West Coast.

Another factor contributing to overcrowding in treatment centers is the lack of alternative treatment options. Many individuals with substance use disorders require long-term care, but the limited availability of outpatient treatment programs and aftercare resources means that they often end up seeking treatment in overcrowded inpatient facilities.

Overcrowding in treatment centers can also have negative effects on the quality of care provided. Treatment centers that are overcrowded may have limited resources to provide individualized care, which can impact the effectiveness of treatment. Additionally, the increased demand for care can result in longer wait times for treatment, which can lead to individuals giving up on seeking care altogether.

To address the issue of overcrowding in addiction treatment centers, it is essential to increase the availability of treatment resources. This can include expanding access to outpatient treatment programs and increasing funding for aftercare resources. Additionally, implementing evidence-based practices, such as medication-assisted treatment, can help reduce the demand for inpatient treatment and alleviate overcrowding in treatment centers.

In conclusion, overcrowding in addiction treatment centers is a significant challenge faced by those seeking care on the West Coast. The high demand for treatment combined with the limited availability of resources has resulted in many individuals being unable to access the care they need. To address this issue, it is essential to increase the availability of treatment resources and implement evidence-based practices to reduce the demand for inpatient treatment.

Co-occurring mental health disorders

Co-occurring mental health disorders are common among individuals with substance use disorders and can significantly impact their ability to seek and receive effective addiction treatment on the

West Coast. According to the Substance Abuse and Mental Health Services Administration (SAMHSA), approximately 7.9 million adults in the United States have co-occurring mental health and substance use disorders.

Individuals with co-occurring disorders often require integrated treatment that addresses both their substance use disorder and mental health disorder simultaneously. However, many addiction treatment programs on the West Coast may not have the resources or expertise to provide this type of integrated care, resulting in incomplete or ineffective treatment.

Moreover, mental health disorders can contribute to the development of substance use disorders and vice versa. For example, individuals with depression or anxiety may turn to drugs or alcohol as a way to cope with their symptoms, while substance abuse can exacerbate underlying mental health conditions.

The prevalence of co-occurring mental health disorders underscores the need for a comprehensive and integrated approach to addiction treatment on the West Coast. This can include a combination of medication-assisted treatment, behavioral therapies, and other evidence-based practices that address both the substance use disorder and mental health disorder.

Moreover, healthcare providers and addiction treatment centers should also work to reduce the stigma surrounding mental health and substance use disorders, as many individuals may be hesitant to seek treatment due to fear of discrimination or judgement. By providing integrated and stigma-free care, individuals with co-occurring disorders can receive the support they need to overcome addiction and improve their overall health and well-being.

Treatment retention and completion rates

Treatment retention and completion rates are significant challenges in addiction treatment on the West Coast. Research shows that the longer a person stays in treatment, the greater the likelihood of achieving lasting recovery from substance use disorders. However, many individuals struggle to remain in treatment due to various factors.

One significant barrier to treatment retention is the high rate of relapse. Addiction is a chronic disease, and relapse is a common occurrence. When individuals experience setbacks, they may become discouraged and drop out of treatment altogether.

Another factor that contributes to low retention rates is the lack of engagement in treatment. Many individuals may feel disconnected from the treatment process and not fully invested in their recovery. This may be due to various reasons, such as dissatisfaction with the treatment program or not feeling understood by the treatment team.

Additionally, the stigma surrounding addiction can also impact treatment retention rates. Many individuals may feel shame or embarrassment about their addiction and avoid seeking treatment or drop out of treatment early due to fear of being judged or labeled as "addicts."

Moreover, treatment completion rates can be low due to financial constraints. Many individuals may not have the financial resources to complete their treatment program or may have to leave treatment early to attend to other responsibilities such as work or family obligations.

To address these challenges, addiction treatment centers on the West Coast may need to adopt new strategies to increase treatment retention and completion rates. These may include more personalized treatment plans tailored to individual needs, greater engagement of patients in the treatment process, and increased support for individuals who experience setbacks or relapse.

Furthermore, integrating mental health treatment into addiction treatment can also improve retention rates. Many individuals with substance use disorders also have co-occurring mental health disorders, and treating both conditions simultaneously can lead to better treatment outcomes.

In conclusion, improving treatment retention and completion rates is essential in addressing the challenges of addiction treatment on the West Coast. By implementing personalized, evidence-based treatment plans and providing support and resources for individuals in treatment, addiction treatment centers can help more individuals achieve lasting recovery from substance use disorders.

Conclusion

The challenges of addiction treatment on the West Coast are complex and multifaceted. Barriers to accessing care, limited availability of treatment resources, stigma and discrimination, lack of insurance coverage, limited treatment options, overcrowding in treatment centers, and co-occurring mental health disorders all contribute to the difficulties faced by individuals seeking addiction treatment. Additionally, retention and completion rates for treatment programs pose a significant challenge.

Despite these challenges, there are opportunities to address them through policy changes and innovative approaches to care. Policies that expand insurance coverage for addiction treatment, increase funding for treatment centers and healthcare professionals, and reduce stigma and discrimination towards individuals with substance use disorders are critical for improving access to care. Innovative approaches to care, such as telehealth and peer support programs, can also help expand access to care and improve treatment outcomes.

It is essential to address the challenges of addiction treatment on the West Coast to improve the health and well-being of individuals struggling with substance use disorders. By implementing comprehensive solutions that address the root causes of these challenges, we can work towards a future where addiction treatment is accessible, affordable, and effective for all who need it.

The Impact of the COVID-19 Pandemic on The Crisis

The COVID-19 pandemic has brought a multitude of challenges to communities worldwide, and vulnerable populations such as those experiencing homelessness and substance use disorders have been particularly affected. This introduction aims to explore the impact of the pandemic on the drug and homelessness crisis, which has created new challenges and exacerbated existing issues.

In this discussion, we will examine the ways in which the pandemic has affected individuals experiencing homelessness and those with substance use disorders, including increased rates of COVID-19 transmission, a lack of access to essential resources, and disruptions to existing support systems. We will also look at how the pandemic has further complicated the already complex issues of homelessness and substance use disorders, including the need for increased mental health and addiction treatment services.

Moreover, we will explore the policy responses to the pandemic, including the allocation of funding and resources to support vulnerable populations and the implementation of new public health measures. Finally, we will address the long-term implications of the pandemic on the drug and homelessness crisis, including the need for innovative solutions to ensure that individuals experiencing homelessness and substance use disorders have access to essential services, safe housing, and adequate healthcare.

Overall, this discussion aims to provide a comprehensive understanding of the impact of the COVID-19 pandemic on the drug and homelessness crisis, highlighting the urgent need for continued support and advocacy for vulnerable populations during these challenging times.

Economic impact

The COVID-19 pandemic has had a significant impact on the global economy, leading to widespread job loss, reduced income, and increased poverty. This economic fallout has been particularly devastating for individuals who were already struggling with substance use disorders and housing insecurity. The closure of businesses, layoffs, and reduced work hours have left many people unable to afford basic necessities such as rent, food, and healthcare. As a result, some individuals may have turned to drugs as a coping mechanism, while others may have been forced into homelessness.

The economic impact of the pandemic has been especially pronounced in the United States, where millions of people lost their jobs in the early months of the pandemic. According to the Bureau of Labor Statistics, the national unemployment rate reached 14.8% in April 2020, the highest level since the Great Depression. This unemployment crisis disproportionately affected low-income individuals and people of color, who were already more likely to experience poverty and housing insecurity.

The economic downturn also resulted in reduced funding for addiction treatment programs and support services, which has further compounded the challenges faced by individuals with substance use disorders. Treatment programs have had to reduce staff or even close their doors due to financial strain, leaving many people without access to the care they need. In addition, the pandemic has made it difficult for individuals to access resources such as food banks, shelters, and medical care, which are critical for people experiencing homelessness.

Overall, the economic impact of the COVID-19 pandemic has been a major contributing factor to the drug and homelessness crisis, exacerbating existing issues and creating new challenges.

Housing insecurity

The COVID-19 pandemic has had a significant impact on housing insecurity, which in turn has had a negative effect on drug use and addiction. The pandemic has led to widespread economic disruption and increased unemployment, making it difficult for many individuals to afford rent or mortgage payments. This has resulted in increased rates of eviction and foreclosure, leaving many people without stable housing.

The lack of stable housing has been linked to higher rates of substance use disorders, as individuals experiencing housing insecurity may turn to drugs or alcohol as a coping mechanism. With the pandemic exacerbating housing insecurity, there has been a corresponding increase in drug use and addiction.

Additionally, the pandemic has made it more difficult for individuals experiencing homelessness to access necessary services and resources, including addiction treatment. Many shelters and treatment centers have had to reduce capacity or close altogether to comply with social distancing guidelines, leaving individuals without access to the care they need.

The pandemic has also resulted in an increase in unsheltered homelessness, as individuals who previously relied on temporary accommodations such as couch-surfing or staying with friends are now finding themselves without any stable housing options. This has led to more individuals living on the streets, in encampments, or in their vehicles.

Overall, the pandemic has worsened the issue of housing insecurity and homelessness, which has, in turn, impacted drug use and addiction rates. Addressing the issue of housing insecurity and homelessness will be critical to mitigating the negative effects of the pandemic on drug use and addiction. This will require a comprehensive approach that addresses both the immediate needs of individuals experiencing housing insecurity and the underlying systemic issues that contribute to the problem.

Treatment access

The COVID-19 pandemic has posed significant challenges for individuals seeking addiction treatment. The closure of treatment facilities, limitations on in-person care, and the shift to virtual care have all had a significant impact on access to care. For those who rely on in-person treatment, the pandemic has made it difficult to receive the care they need. Many addiction treatment centers have had to close their doors, reduce their capacity, or transition to virtual care, making it harder for individuals to access the necessary care.

Virtual care, while offering a solution to the lack of in-person care, has also presented its own set of challenges. Not everyone has access to reliable internet or the technology necessary to participate in virtual care, particularly in low-income communities. Moreover, virtual care may not be the preferred option for everyone seeking addiction treatment, as some individuals may prefer the in-person support and connection that treatment centers offer.

The pandemic has also led to a shortage of healthcare professionals and staff in addiction treatment centers, making it even more difficult to access care. Healthcare professionals may have been redeployed to COVID-19 units, or may have fallen ill themselves, leading to staff shortages in addiction treatment centers.

The pandemic has highlighted the need for more innovative and accessible addiction treatment options, particularly those that can be delivered virtually. As the pandemic continues, it is important to address the challenges of treatment access to ensure that individuals with substance use disorders have access to the care they need.

Mental health

The COVID-19 pandemic has had a significant impact on mental health worldwide, with many individuals experiencing heightened levels of stress, anxiety, and depression. This has been attributed to a range of factors, including social isolation, financial insecurity, and fear of the virus. These mental health challenges have been particularly acute for individuals who were already struggling with substance use disorders and/or homelessness.

The pandemic has disrupted access to mental health care, with many clinics and treatment centers either closing or transitioning to virtual care. This has created significant barriers for individuals who rely on these services to manage their mental health and substance use.

Moreover, the closure of public spaces, such as libraries and community centers, has eliminated safe spaces for homeless individuals, exacerbating the issue of social isolation and contributing to poor mental health outcomes.

Research has shown that mental health disorders are closely linked to substance use disorders, with individuals with mental health conditions being at higher risk of developing substance use disorders and vice versa. The pandemic has likely increased this risk due to the added stress and anxiety caused by the pandemic, as well as the disruption of social support networks.

Moreover, the pandemic has led to an increase in substance use, with individuals turning to drugs and alcohol as a coping mechanism. This has been attributed to a range of factors, including increased stress and boredom, decreased access to treatment, and reduced social support. The pandemic has also disrupted the drug supply chain, leading to an increase in drug-related deaths due to the use of contaminated substances.

In summary, the pandemic has had a significant impact on mental health and substance use, with individuals who were already struggling with these issues being particularly vulnerable. The disruption of mental health care, the elimination of safe spaces for homeless individuals, and the increase in substance use have all contributed to the drug and homelessness crisis. It is important for policymakers and healthcare providers to prioritize mental health and substance use treatment during and after the pandemic to mitigate the long-term impacts on individuals and communities.

Overdose rates

The COVID-19 pandemic has had a significant impact on the drug and homelessness crisis, with overdose rates being one of the most pressing issues. According to the Centers for Disease Control and Prevention (CDC), drug overdose deaths increased by 29.4% in the United States from 2019 to 2020, reaching a record high of 93,331 deaths. This increase is the largest in a single year since the CDC started tracking overdose deaths in 1999. The pandemic has contributed to this increase in several ways.

First, social isolation has been a significant factor in the rise of overdose rates. Many people with substance use disorders have been cut off from their support systems and treatment programs due to lockdowns and social distancing measures. This has left them more vulnerable to relapse and overdose. Additionally, the closure of businesses and public spaces has led to a decrease in the availability of clean syringes and other harm reduction supplies, which can increase the risk of overdose.

Second, reduced access to treatment has also been a significant contributor to the increase in overdose rates. The closure of many treatment facilities and limitations on in-person care have made it challenging for people to access the care they need. While some providers have shifted to virtual care, this may not be effective for all patients, particularly those with more severe substance use disorders.

Finally, the pandemic has created a great deal of stress and uncertainty, which can exacerbate substance use and increase the risk of overdose. Many people have lost their jobs, experienced financial difficulties, and struggled with mental health issues as a result of the pandemic. These stressors can trigger substance use and make it more challenging for people to stay in recovery.

Overall, the increase in overdose rates during the pandemic highlights the urgent need for effective addiction treatment and harm reduction strategies. It also underscores the need for policies that address the root causes of substance use, such as economic inequality and social isolation.

Homelessness

The COVID-19 pandemic has had a significant impact on homelessness, exacerbating an already critical issue. With the closure of businesses and loss of jobs, many individuals have found themselves without a stable income or housing. In addition, social distancing measures and the need to limit the spread of the virus have created challenges in providing shelter for those experiencing homelessness.

One significant challenge has been the closure of homeless shelters and other traditional forms of emergency housing. Many shelters have had to reduce their capacity or close altogether due to health and safety concerns. This has forced many individuals to sleep on the streets or in other unsafe and unsanitary conditions, increasing their vulnerability to COVID-19 and other health risks.

Another challenge has been the need for social distancing and the limitations this has placed on the availability of temporary housing. Hotels and motels have been used in some areas to provide temporary housing for those experiencing homelessness during the pandemic, but the cost and availability of such accommodations have been limited.

These challenges have had a significant impact on the mental health and well-being of those experiencing homelessness. The stress and uncertainty of not having a stable place to live, coupled with the fear of contracting COVID-19, have led to increased rates of depression, anxiety, and substance use.

Addressing the issue of homelessness during the pandemic will require innovative solutions and increased resources. This could include the expansion of programs that provide affordable housing and rental assistance, as well as the development of safe and secure temporary housing options. Additionally, providing increased access to mental health and substance use treatment for those experiencing homelessness can help address the underlying issues that contribute to homelessness and drug use.

Harm reduction

The COVID-19 pandemic has had a significant impact on the provision of harm reduction services to individuals with substance use disorders. Harm reduction services aim to reduce the harms associated with drug use, including overdose and the transmission of infectious diseases such as HIV and hepatitis C. These services include syringe exchange programs, overdose prevention education and training, and access to naloxone, a medication used to reverse opioid overdose.

The pandemic has created new challenges for harm reduction services, including the need for social distancing, reduced access to healthcare facilities, and the closure of public spaces where individuals may have accessed harm reduction services. In addition, many harm reduction services rely on peer outreach and face-to-face interactions, which have been severely curtailed due to social distancing requirements and lockdown measures.

One of the major impacts of the pandemic on harm reduction services has been the disruption of syringe exchange programs. These programs provide individuals with clean needles and syringes to reduce the transmission of blood-borne infections such as HIV and hepatitis C. However, with the closure of many public spaces and the reduction of face-to-face interactions, the availability of syringe exchange programs has been significantly reduced. This has increased the risk of HIV and hepatitis C transmission among people who inject drugs.

Another challenge facing harm reduction services during the pandemic has been the increased risk of overdose. The closure of treatment centers and the reduction in face-to-face interactions have limited access to harm reduction services such as overdose prevention education and naloxone distribution. This has increased the risk of fatal overdose among individuals with substance use disorders.

Furthermore, the pandemic has created new challenges for harm reduction services to reach vulnerable populations such as homeless individuals and those who live in remote areas. These populations often have limited access to healthcare facilities and rely on harm reduction services for access to naloxone and other harm reduction tools.

To address the challenges facing harm reduction services during the pandemic, innovative approaches have been developed. These include the use of telemedicine to provide harm reduction services remotely, the distribution of harm reduction supplies through mail or delivery services, and the development of mobile harm reduction clinics to reach underserved populations.

In conclusion, the COVID-19 pandemic has created significant challenges for harm reduction services, which have been essential in reducing the harms associated with drug use. The disruption of these services has increased the risk of fatal overdose and transmission of blood-borne infections among individuals with substance use disorders. Innovative approaches are needed to ensure that harm reduction services continue to reach vulnerable populations during the pandemic and beyond.

Policy responses

The COVID-19 pandemic has had a significant impact on the drug and homelessness crisis, exacerbating existing issues and creating new challenges. As a result, policymakers have had to implement various responses to mitigate the effects of the pandemic on these issues. This section will examine the policy responses to the drug and homelessness crisis during the pandemic, including emergency funding, eviction moratoriums, and initiatives to expand treatment access.

One of the most critical policy responses to the pandemic's impact on the drug and homelessness crisis has been emergency funding. Governments at all levels have provided additional funding to support homelessness and addiction services during the pandemic. For example, in the United States, the CARES Act allocated $4 billion in emergency funding for homelessness services, and the American Rescue Plan Act included an additional $5 billion for homelessness assistance. These funds have helped support homelessness services such as emergency shelter, outreach programs, and rental assistance.

In addition to emergency funding, policymakers have implemented eviction moratoriums to prevent individuals from losing their homes during the pandemic. These moratoriums have been critical in preventing a surge in homelessness due to pandemic-related job loss and economic insecurity. The moratoriums have provided a temporary reprieve for renters who are unable to make rent payments due to pandemic-related financial hardship.

Finally, policymakers have implemented initiatives to expand treatment access during the pandemic. For example, many treatment centers have shifted to virtual care to ensure individuals can continue to receive care while practicing social distancing. Governments have also implemented policies to increase access to telemedicine and other virtual care services, which has helped individuals access treatment despite the pandemic's challenges.

Overall, the policy responses to the drug and homelessness crisis during the pandemic have been critical in mitigating the pandemic's impact on these issues. However, the pandemic has exposed significant gaps in the availability of resources to address these issues, which must be addressed in the long term to prevent a resurgence of the crisis once the pandemic subsides.

Conclusion

The COVID-19 pandemic has had a significant impact on the ongoing drug and homelessness crisis, exacerbating existing issues and creating new challenges. In this conclusion, we will summarize the key points discussed in this analysis.

The economic consequences of the pandemic, including job loss, reduced income, and increased poverty, have contributed to the drug and homelessness crisis. The closure of businesses and limited access to social services have made it difficult for people to find employment, maintain housing, and access treatment.

The pandemic has also worsened the issue of housing insecurity, with increased evictions, foreclosures, and homelessness. This has led to a rise in drug use, as individuals turn to substances to cope with the stress and instability of their living situations.

Access to addiction treatment has been limited during the pandemic, with the closure of treatment facilities and the shift to virtual care. This has created challenges for individuals seeking help for their substance use disorders.

The pandemic has also had a significant impact on mental health, with increased anxiety, depression, and substance use. This has contributed to the drug and homelessness crisis, as individuals struggle to cope with the added stress and uncertainty of the pandemic.

The increase in overdose rates during the pandemic is a concerning trend, with social isolation, reduced access to treatment, and increased stress all contributing factors.

The pandemic has made it difficult to address homelessness, with the closure of shelters and the need for social distancing measures. This has impacted drug use among homeless populations.

Providing harm reduction services during the pandemic has also been challenging, with the need for social distancing and reduced access to services creating barriers for individuals seeking help.

Policy responses to the drug and homelessness crisis during the pandemic have included emergency funding, eviction moratoriums, and initiatives to expand treatment access. These efforts are essential to addressing the immediate needs of those impacted by the pandemic.

In conclusion, the COVID-19 pandemic has had a significant impact on the ongoing drug and homelessness crisis, exacerbating existing issues and creating new challenges. Continued efforts are needed to address these issues, including the importance of addressing the root causes of these issues. The pandemic has highlighted the need for a comprehensive and coordinated approach to addressing the complex issues of drug use and homelessness.

The Role of Race and Ethnicity in Drug Use and Homelessness

The drug and homelessness crisis in the United States affects individuals of all races and ethnicities, but some groups are disproportionately impacted. Studies have shown that people of color are more likely to experience homelessness and struggle with substance use disorders compared to their white counterparts. The root causes of these disparities are complex and multifaceted, and understanding the role of race and ethnicity in the drug and homelessness crisis is crucial to developing effective solutions.

In this discussion, we will examine the various ways in which race and ethnicity impact drug use and homelessness. We will explore the historical and systemic factors that contribute to these disparities, the barriers faced by people of color in accessing treatment and support services, and the ways in which racism and discrimination impact the health outcomes of individuals struggling with drug use and homelessness.

Overall, this discussion aims to shed light on the inequities in the drug and homelessness crisis and provide a foundation for developing more inclusive and equitable solutions to these complex issues.

Historical context

Historically, race and ethnicity have played a significant role in shaping drug policies and access to housing in the United States. The origins of the war on drugs can be traced back to the early 20th century when drug use was associated with particular racial and ethnic groups. For example, opium use was linked to Chinese immigrants, and cocaine use was associated with African Americans in the South. This led to the passage of the first federal drug law in 1914, the Harrison Narcotics Tax Act, which was primarily aimed at controlling the distribution of opium and cocaine.

Over the following decades, drug policies continued to be shaped by racial and ethnic biases. In the 1960s and 1970s, drug use became more widespread, particularly among young people and anti-war activists. The government's response was to declare a "War on Drugs," which was largely focused on criminalizing drug use and targeting communities of color. This was exemplified by the passage of strict drug sentencing laws, such as the Anti-Drug Abuse Act of 1986, which established mandatory minimum sentences for drug offenses.

Access to housing has also been impacted by race and ethnicity. Discrimination in housing has been documented since the early 20th century, with African Americans and other people of color experiencing discrimination in both rental and home ownership markets. Racial segregation has also played a role in access to affordable housing, with minority communities often located in neighborhoods with fewer resources and higher rates of poverty.

Understanding this historical context is important for recognizing how race and ethnicity have played a role in shaping drug policies and access to housing, and how these factors continue to impact the drug and homelessness crisis today.

Disproportionate impact

People of color in the United States are disproportionately impacted by drug use and homelessness. Studies have consistently shown that African Americans, Latinos, Native Americans, and other people of color are more likely to experience drug-related arrests, incarceration, and health consequences than their white counterparts.

One of the major factors contributing to this disparity is systemic racism. For example, drug policies and law enforcement practices have historically targeted communities of color. The War on Drugs, initiated in the 1980s, disproportionately impacted communities of color through mandatory minimum sentencing, three-strikes laws, and aggressive policing in low-income neighborhoods. These policies resulted in mass incarceration, broken families, and a cycle of poverty that perpetuated drug use and homelessness.

Additionally, people of color are more likely to experience poverty and housing insecurity, which increases their risk of experiencing homelessness and drug use. Inequities in the criminal justice system, educational system, and employment opportunities also contribute to these disparities. For example, individuals with criminal records, which disproportionately affect people of color, face significant barriers to employment and housing, which can lead to further financial instability and increased risk of drug use and homelessness.

The COVID-19 pandemic has only exacerbated these disparities. Communities of color have been disproportionately impacted by the economic and health consequences of the pandemic, including job loss and increased illness rates. This has led to further housing insecurity and financial instability, which can increase the risk of drug use and homelessness.

It is important to acknowledge and address the disproportionate impact of drug use and homelessness on people of color. This requires a comprehensive approach that includes policy changes, funding for social services, and addressing systemic racism in all aspects of society.

Systemic racism

Systemic racism has played a significant role in perpetuating the cycle of drug use and homelessness among communities of color. Discrimination in housing, healthcare, and criminal justice has created barriers to resources and opportunities that would support individuals in these communities and address the underlying causes of drug use and homelessness.

Housing discrimination has been a longstanding issue for communities of color. Discriminatory practices such as redlining and racial steering have limited access to safe and affordable housing for people of color, particularly Black Americans. This lack of access to stable housing has been linked to higher rates of homelessness and increased vulnerability to substance use disorders. According to the Substance Abuse and Mental Health Services Administration (SAMHSA), people experiencing homelessness are more likely to use drugs than the general population, and they are at increased risk of overdose and other health complications due to the lack of access to healthcare and social services.

Discrimination in healthcare also contributes to the cycle of drug use and homelessness. People of color have historically faced disparities in healthcare access and quality, leading to higher rates of chronic illnesses and mental health conditions. These disparities can make it more challenging to access appropriate treatment for substance use disorders and mental health conditions, increasing the risk of homelessness and relapse.

Additionally, the criminal justice system has been shown to disproportionately impact communities of color, particularly Black Americans. The war on drugs, for example, has led to the disproportionate criminalization and incarceration of people of color for non-violent drug offenses. This has disrupted families and communities, creating barriers to education, employment, and housing, which can increase the risk of homelessness and substance use disorders. Moreover, incarceration can exacerbate substance use disorders and mental health conditions due to the trauma and stress associated with being incarcerated.

The disproportionate impact of drug use and homelessness on communities of color highlights the need for systemic change to address underlying issues related to discrimination and inequality. This includes changes to housing policies that address discrimination and provide affordable and safe housing options for people of color, increasing access to healthcare and mental health services, and reforming the criminal justice system to address systemic racism and mass incarceration.

Furthermore, addressing systemic racism requires a shift in societal attitudes and values towards communities of color. Addressing implicit biases, increasing cultural competency, and engaging in anti-racism work can help to promote equity and inclusion and reduce disparities in drug use and homelessness.

In conclusion, systemic racism plays a significant role in perpetuating the cycle of drug use and homelessness among communities of color. Addressing these issues requires systemic change that addresses discrimination and promotes equity and inclusion. By taking a comprehensive and inclusive approach to drug and homelessness policy, we can help to create a more just and equitable society for all.

Trauma and mental health

Trauma and mental health issues have long been linked to substance use disorders and homelessness, with individuals who experience traumatic events or mental health conditions being more likely to turn to drugs and become homeless. Unfortunately, people of color are disproportionately impacted by trauma and mental health issues, which in turn increases their risk of experiencing drug use and homelessness.

One of the main reasons for this disparity is the ongoing impact of systemic racism and discrimination. People of color are more likely to experience discrimination and oppression, which can lead to experiences of trauma and mental health issues. For example, individuals who have experienced racial discrimination may develop PTSD or depression as a result of the trauma. Additionally, systemic racism can lead to ongoing stress and anxiety, which can also contribute to the development of mental health conditions.

Studies have shown that people of color are more likely to experience traumatic events, such as violence and poverty, which can contribute to the development of mental health conditions. In fact, a study published in the Journal of Traumatic Stress found that African Americans are more likely to experience trauma than white Americans, with higher rates of exposure to violence, crime, and poverty.

These experiences of trauma and mental health issues can then contribute to drug use and homelessness. For example, individuals who experience PTSD may turn to drugs to self-medicate and cope with their symptoms, while those who experience depression or anxiety may become homeless as a result of their inability to cope with daily life.

Unfortunately, people of color also face barriers to accessing mental health care and treatment for substance use disorders, which can exacerbate the impact of trauma and mental health issues. For example, people of color are less likely to have health insurance and access to mental health services, and may face stigma and discrimination when seeking care.

To address the impact of trauma and mental health issues on drug use and homelessness among communities of color, it is important to address systemic racism and discrimination. This includes increasing access to mental health care and substance use disorder treatment for people of color, as well as addressing the underlying social determinants of health, such as poverty and discrimination. Additionally, it is important to increase awareness and education about trauma and mental health in communities of color, and to provide culturally sensitive and appropriate care for individuals who may be experiencing these issues.

Stigma and discrimination

Stigma and discrimination play a significant role in the drug and homelessness crisis, particularly for people of color. The negative perceptions and assumptions about drug use and homelessness can create significant barriers to accessing housing, employment, and healthcare services, further exacerbating the issues. The stigma attached to drug use and homelessness is often rooted in racism and stereotypes about people of color, perpetuating systemic injustices.

Historically, drug policies have been used to criminalize communities of color, leading to disproportionate rates of incarceration and social exclusion. The War on Drugs, initiated in the 1970s, targeted low-income communities of color and led to harsher sentencing for drug offenses. These policies contributed to a cycle of poverty and criminalization, further stigmatizing people of color who use drugs or experience homelessness.

The impact of stigma and discrimination can be seen in the lack of access to affordable housing and healthcare services for people of color. Discrimination in housing can result in increased levels of homelessness, as people of color are often denied access to affordable housing due to discriminatory practices. Inadequate access to healthcare services also leads to poorer health outcomes and increased risk of substance use, particularly for those who experience trauma and mental health issues.

For people of color who use drugs or experience homelessness, stigma can also result in increased levels of harassment and violence. Police brutality and other forms of discrimination can further traumatize individuals and create further distrust of law enforcement and social service providers.

The impact of stigma and discrimination on people of color who use drugs or experience homelessness cannot be overstated. Addressing these issues requires a multifaceted approach that includes education, policy changes, and cultural shifts. It is essential to recognize the ways in which stigma and discrimination are rooted in systemic racism and work to dismantle these systems of oppression.

In addition, there must be increased access to affordable housing and healthcare services, as well as harm reduction programs that prioritize the health and safety of all individuals. Education campaigns can also help combat stigma and promote a more compassionate understanding of drug use and homelessness.

Overall, addressing the impact of stigma and discrimination on people of color who use drugs or experience homelessness requires a systemic approach that prioritizes equity and justice. By recognizing and addressing these issues, we can work towards creating a more just and compassionate society for all.

Policing and criminalization

The role of policing and criminalization in perpetuating disparities among communities of color who experience drug use and homelessness has been a long-standing issue in the United States. Historically, drug policies have disproportionately targeted communities of color, leading to overrepresentation in the criminal justice system and a lack of access to essential resources, such as housing and healthcare.

One of the main issues with policing and criminalization is the way in which drug use and homelessness are criminalized, rather than being treated as public health issues. This approach often leads to criminal charges and incarceration, which can further exacerbate poverty and homelessness. Moreover, it can lead to the disruption of social networks, loss of employment opportunities, and the destruction of families, all of which can contribute to drug use and homelessness.

Communities of color are disproportionately affected by policing and criminalization. For instance, African Americans are four times more likely to be arrested for drug offenses than Whites, despite similar rates of drug use. This disparity is even more pronounced for Hispanic and Latino communities. Research has shown that these disparities in drug-related arrests and sentencing are not due to differences in drug use or sales, but rather due to systemic racism.

Policing and criminalization also affect people experiencing homelessness. Homeless individuals are often subject to police harassment and criminalization of acts of survival, such as sleeping in public spaces. This can lead to cycles of arrests, fines, and imprisonment, which further entrenches individuals in homelessness.

Moreover, policing and criminalization often lead to the over-policing of low-income communities of color, which can result in a distrust of law enforcement and reluctance to seek help or report crimes. This can be particularly damaging in cases of overdose or violence, where individuals may be hesitant to seek help due to fear of police involvement.

In recent years, there has been a growing movement to decriminalize drug use and homelessness and to shift towards a public health approach. This approach emphasizes harm reduction, access to healthcare and housing, and community-based interventions. Such initiatives have shown success in reducing the negative consequences of drug use and homelessness while also addressing the underlying factors that contribute to these issues.

In conclusion, the role of policing and criminalization in perpetuating disparities among communities of color who experience drug use and homelessness is a complex issue that requires a multifaceted approach. Addressing systemic racism, providing access to housing and healthcare, and implementing harm reduction strategies are all critical steps in reducing these disparities and ensuring equitable outcomes for all.

Access to treatment and services

Access to addiction treatment and housing services for people of color is a complex issue that is influenced by various factors, including systemic racism, cultural differences, and language barriers. These challenges have contributed to significant disparities in access to services and treatment outcomes among communities of color.

One major barrier to accessing addiction treatment and housing services is the lack of culturally appropriate services. Many programs and services may not be tailored to the specific needs and preferences of people of color, leading to a disconnect between providers and the communities they serve. This can result in lower rates of engagement and treatment retention, as well as reduced trust in healthcare providers.

Language barriers are another significant challenge that can impede access to services. Limited English proficiency can make it difficult for people of color to access information about addiction treatment and housing services, communicate with providers, and participate in treatment programs. This can lead to reduced access to care and a lack of understanding of treatment options and recommendations.

Systemic racism also plays a role in limiting access to addiction treatment and housing services for people of color. Historical and ongoing discrimination in housing, healthcare, and criminal justice can lead to mistrust of systems and providers, and create barriers to accessing services. The criminalization of drug use and homelessness, for example, has led to increased policing and incarceration of people of color, rather than providing them with access to treatment and supportive housing services.

Additionally, there may be a lack of financial resources to access addiction treatment and housing services for people of color, particularly for those who may be experiencing poverty and low-income. This can be exacerbated by systemic inequalities in education and employment opportunities that limit financial stability.

Efforts to improve access to addiction treatment and housing services for people of color must address these barriers and take into account the unique needs and preferences of these communities. This includes expanding the availability of culturally appropriate services and language access, addressing systemic racism in housing, healthcare, and criminal justice systems, and increasing resources for those experiencing poverty and low-income. Addressing these barriers is essential to reducing disparities in addiction treatment and housing outcomes among communities of color.

Solutions and interventions

The drug and homelessness crisis is a complex issue that disproportionately affects communities of color. Addressing this issue requires a comprehensive approach that considers the unique challenges faced by these communities. In this section, we will examine some promising solutions and interventions that can help address the role of race and ethnicity in the drug and homelessness crisis.

One promising strategy is harm reduction, which is an approach that focuses on reducing the negative consequences of drug use rather than eliminating drug use altogether. Harm reduction strategies include providing clean needles to prevent the spread of infectious diseases, offering overdose prevention services, and providing access to medication-assisted treatment (MAT) for opioid use disorder. These strategies can be particularly effective for communities of color, who may face stigma and discrimination when seeking treatment. By providing non-judgmental, compassionate care, harm reduction programs can help reduce the barriers to accessing treatment and support for people of color who use drugs.

Another important strategy is trauma-informed care. Trauma is a common experience among people who use drugs or experience homelessness, and it can have a profound impact on their mental and physical health. Trauma-informed care involves recognizing the impact of trauma on individuals and providing care that is sensitive to their needs. This approach can help build trust between healthcare providers and people of color who have experienced trauma, which can be an important first step in accessing treatment and services.

Community-based initiatives can also be effective in addressing the drug and homelessness crisis among communities of color. These initiatives involve working with community members to develop solutions that are tailored to the unique needs of their community. For example, a community-based initiative might involve partnering with a local faith-based organization to provide housing and support services for people who are experiencing homelessness. By working with community members and taking a holistic approach to care, these initiatives can help address the root causes of the drug and homelessness crisis.

Finally, it is important to ensure that addiction treatment and housing services are culturally appropriate and accessible to people of color. This can involve providing services in languages other than English, hiring staff who reflect the diversity of the community, and providing services that are sensitive to the unique needs and experiences of people of color. By taking these steps, we can help ensure that people of color have access to the care and support they need to overcome the drug and homelessness crisis.

In conclusion, addressing the role of race and ethnicity in the drug and homelessness crisis requires a comprehensive approach that considers the unique challenges faced by communities of color. Promising solutions and interventions include harm reduction strategies, trauma-informed care, community-based initiatives, and culturally appropriate services. By working together to implement these strategies, we can help build healthier, more resilient communities that are better equipped to address the drug and homelessness crisis.

Conclusion

In conclusion, examining the role of race and ethnicity in the drug and homelessness crisis is crucial to understanding and addressing the disparities that exist among communities of color. From a historical perspective, systemic racism has played a significant role in shaping drug policies and access to housing, perpetuating the cycle of drug use and homelessness. Furthermore, people of color are disproportionately impacted by drug use and homelessness due to various factors, including trauma and mental health issues, stigma and discrimination, and barriers to accessing treatment and services.

Policing and criminalization of drug use and homelessness have also contributed to the disparities among communities of color. In addressing these issues, it is important to implement promising solutions and interventions, including harm reduction strategies, trauma-informed care, and community-based initiatives that are culturally appropriate and sensitive to the needs of diverse communities.

In moving forward, it is essential to continue efforts to address the root causes of the drug and homelessness crisis among communities of color, including systemic racism and providing equitable access to housing, healthcare, and services. Through a comprehensive and holistic approach, it is possible to create more just and equitable systems that prioritize the well-being of all individuals and communities.

The impact of immigration policies on the crisis

Immigration policies have a significant impact on various aspects of society, including drug use and homelessness. The drug and homelessness crisis in the United States is a complex issue that affects individuals from all walks of life, including immigrants. This topic is of great importance because immigration policies can either exacerbate or mitigate the crisis. Therefore, it is essential to examine the impact of immigration policies on the drug and homelessness crisis, particularly for immigrant communities.

This paper will provide an overview of the impact of immigration policies on the drug and homelessness crisis. The following sections will discuss the ways in which immigration policies affect drug use and homelessness, and explore the challenges faced by immigrants in accessing housing and healthcare services. Additionally, the paper will discuss the role of stigma and discrimination towards immigrants and its impact on drug use and homelessness. Finally, the paper will highlight promising interventions and policy solutions aimed at mitigating the impact of immigration policies on the drug and homelessness crisis.

Overall, this paper emphasizes the need for a comprehensive approach to addressing the drug and homelessness crisis, one that takes into account the impact of immigration policies on these issues. By examining the intersection of immigration policies and the drug and homelessness crisis, we can identify strategies to mitigate the impact on immigrant communities and ensure equitable access to housing, healthcare, and services.

Historical context

Immigration policies in the United States have a long and complex history, with varying degrees of openness and restrictionism towards immigrants. Throughout this history, immigrants have faced numerous challenges accessing housing, healthcare, and addiction treatment. This historical context is important to understanding the impact of current immigration policies on the drug and homelessness crisis.

The United States has a long history of immigration, with waves of immigrants from various regions and backgrounds coming to the country seeking new opportunities. However, this history is also marked by periods of exclusion and discrimination against certain groups of immigrants. The Chinese Exclusion Act of 1882, for example, prohibited Chinese laborers from immigrating to the US, and subsequent legislation continued to restrict immigration from certain regions and countries.

In the early 20th century, the US implemented a quota system that limited the number of immigrants from certain countries, with a preference given to immigrants from Western Europe. This policy remained in place until the Immigration and Nationality Act of 1965, which abolished the quota system and opened up immigration to people from all over the world. However, the 1965 Act also created a preference for immigrants with family members already in the US, which has disproportionately benefited certain groups of immigrants.

Throughout this history, immigrants have faced barriers accessing housing, healthcare, and addiction treatment. Discrimination and prejudice against immigrant communities has often made it difficult for them to find affordable housing and access to healthcare. Immigrants also face additional barriers to accessing addiction treatment, including fear of deportation and language barriers.

Additionally, current immigration policies have created new challenges for immigrant communities. The Trump administration's "public charge" rule, for example, made it more difficult for immigrants to obtain green cards and citizenship if they accessed certain public benefits, including healthcare and housing assistance. This policy created fear and confusion among immigrant communities, which may have discouraged them from accessing needed services.

Overall, the historical context of immigration policies in the US underscores the ways in which immigrant communities have been systematically excluded and discriminated against in access to housing, healthcare, and addiction treatment. This history is important to consider when examining the impact of current immigration policies on the drug and homelessness crisis.

Barriers to services

Immigrants often face numerous challenges when it comes to accessing housing, healthcare, and addiction treatment services. Immigration policies in the US have created significant barriers for immigrants, making it difficult for them to receive the care they need. These policies disproportionately affect undocumented immigrants, who are often excluded from many public programs.

One significant barrier for immigrants is the fear of deportation. Many undocumented immigrants are hesitant to access healthcare or addiction treatment services because they fear that their information will be shared with immigration authorities. This fear can also prevent them from seeking housing services, as they may be afraid to provide personal information to housing providers.

Language barriers also present a significant obstacle for immigrant communities. Many immigrants speak languages other than English, and there may not be sufficient interpretation or translation services available to them. This can make it challenging for them to understand their rights, navigate the healthcare system, or communicate their needs to housing providers.

Additionally, lack of documentation can prevent immigrants from accessing healthcare or addiction treatment services. Some programs require proof of citizenship or legal residency, which can exclude undocumented immigrants from receiving care. This can lead to a lack of treatment for addiction or other health issues, further exacerbating the drug and homelessness crisis among immigrant communities.

Overall, these barriers make it difficult for immigrant communities to access the care they need and contribute to the disproportionate impact of the drug and homelessness crisis on these communities. Efforts to address these barriers, such as providing language services, expanding eligibility for public programs, and creating safe spaces for immigrants to access services without fear of deportation, are crucial in ensuring that all individuals have access to the care they need.

Increased vulnerability

The impact of immigration policies on the drug and homelessness crisis extends beyond the barriers to accessing housing, healthcare, and addiction treatment services. These policies have also increased the vulnerability of immigrant communities to drug use and homelessness.

Immigrants, especially those who are undocumented, often face economic instability due to limited job opportunities and low wages. This economic vulnerability can lead to poverty, which in turn can increase the risk of homelessness and drug use. For example, a study found that undocumented immigrants are more likely to experience housing instability and overcrowding than documented immigrants and US-born individuals, increasing their risk of homelessness and associated health problems.

Additionally, immigration policies can contribute to social isolation for immigrant communities. The fear of deportation or discrimination may prevent them from seeking out social services or community resources. This isolation can lead to increased stress and mental health issues, which in turn can contribute to drug use and homelessness.

Furthermore, immigrant communities may also be targeted by drug trafficking organizations due to their vulnerability and lack of access to legal protection. The stress of living in fear of deportation or being targeted by drug traffickers can contribute to mental health issues and increase the risk of substance abuse.

In summary, immigration policies can increase the vulnerability of immigrant communities to drug use and homelessness by contributing to economic instability, social isolation, and targeting by drug traffickers. It is important to address these systemic issues to prevent and address the root causes of the crisis.

Criminalization

The criminalization of undocumented immigrants is a highly controversial issue in the United States, with far-reaching implications for drug use and homelessness. The policies that criminalize undocumented immigrants often result in their being detained and deported, creating a climate of fear and mistrust that can make it difficult for them to access housing, healthcare, and addiction treatment services.

The criminalization of undocumented immigrants contributes to the cycle of poverty and homelessness in several ways. For example, undocumented immigrants may be afraid to seek out affordable housing options or other social services, for fear of being detected and deported. They may also be reluctant to seek out addiction treatment services, for fear that their status as undocumented immigrants will be discovered.

In addition to these direct impacts, the criminalization of undocumented immigrants has broader implications for drug use and homelessness. For example, it can lead to increased economic instability and social isolation, both of which are factors that can contribute to drug use and homelessness. It can also make it more difficult for undocumented immigrants to access employment, education, and other resources that could help them build stable, secure lives.

Furthermore, the criminalization of undocumented immigrants often results in their being detained and deported, which can lead to family separation and trauma. This can have long-term impacts on mental health, further contributing to the cycle of poverty and homelessness.

Overall, the criminalization of undocumented immigrants is a complex issue with far-reaching implications for drug use and homelessness. It creates barriers to accessing housing, healthcare, and addiction treatment services, and contributes to the cycle of poverty and homelessness by creating economic instability, social isolation, and trauma. To address the impact of immigration policies on the drug and homelessness crisis, it is necessary to look beyond just the criminalization of undocumented immigrants and examine the broader societal factors that contribute to these issues.

Access to healthcare

The impact of immigration policies on access to healthcare for immigrant communities is a complex issue. The lack of insurance and limited access to mental health services are just two of the challenges that immigrants face in accessing healthcare. This is particularly true for undocumented immigrants, who often face significant barriers to receiving medical care.

One of the most significant challenges that immigrants face in accessing healthcare is the lack of insurance. Many immigrants are unable to afford private health insurance and are not eligible for public insurance programs such as Medicaid or Medicare. Undocumented immigrants are not eligible for these programs and often do not qualify for coverage under the Affordable Care Act.

Language barriers can also be a significant obstacle to accessing healthcare for immigrants. Many immigrants do not speak English fluently, which can make it difficult to communicate with healthcare providers and understand medical information. This can lead to misunderstandings and misdiagnoses, which can have serious consequences for the health of the individual.

Immigrants also face limited access to mental health services. This is due in part to the shortage of mental health professionals in many communities, but also to the stigma attached to mental illness in some cultures. Immigrants may be reluctant to seek treatment for mental health issues due to cultural beliefs or fear of being labeled as "crazy" or "mentally ill."

Immigration policies can also impact access to healthcare for immigrants. For example, policies that restrict access to healthcare for undocumented immigrants can have a negative impact on the health of the entire community. Undocumented immigrants who are unable to receive medical care are more likely to spread infectious diseases and may delay seeking care until their condition becomes more serious and more difficult and expensive to treat.

Additionally, immigration policies that target certain groups of immigrants, such as those from Muslim-majority countries, can have a chilling effect on healthcare access for these individuals. They may be afraid to seek medical care due to fear of discrimination or harassment.

In conclusion, the impact of immigration policies on access to healthcare for immigrant communities is significant. The lack of insurance, language barriers, limited access to mental health services, and policies that restrict access to healthcare all contribute to this challenge. Addressing these issues is critical to improving the health and well-being of immigrant communities and reducing the impact of the drug and homelessness crisis on these vulnerable populations.

Family separation

Family separation policies in the United States have had a devastating impact on immigrant communities. These policies, implemented under the Trump administration, resulted in the separation of thousands of children from their parents at the U.S.-Mexico border. This trauma has had lasting effects on the mental health of both children and parents, and has been shown to contribute to substance abuse and addiction.

The trauma of family separation can lead to a range of mental health issues, including anxiety, depression, post-traumatic stress disorder (PTSD), and other psychological distress. Children who are separated from their parents may experience feelings of abandonment and fear, while parents may suffer from guilt and grief.

In some cases, the trauma of family separation has led to suicidal ideation among both children and parents.

Studies have shown that traumatic experiences, such as family separation, can contribute to substance abuse and addiction. Immigrants who have experienced trauma may turn to drugs and alcohol as a coping mechanism, and the stress of navigating the immigration system can exacerbate these issues. Furthermore, the lack of access to mental health services due to immigration policies can make it even harder for immigrants to address their substance abuse and mental health issues.

In addition to the psychological impact, family separation policies can also have a practical impact on housing and homelessness. Immigrants who are separated from their families may be left without a support system, making it harder for them to access stable housing or other resources. In some cases, families have been forced to turn to homelessness as a result of family separation policies.

It is important to note that family separation policies are not unique to the Trump administration, and have been a part of U.S. immigration policy for decades. However, the scale and impact of the Trump administration's policies have brought renewed attention to this issue.

Efforts to reunite families and provide mental health services to those impacted by family separation are ongoing, but much work remains to be done. Policies that prioritize family reunification and provide access to mental health services for immigrants are critical to addressing the impact of family separation on the drug and homelessness crisis among immigrant communities.

Supportive policies and programs

The impact of immigration policies on the drug and homelessness crisis among immigrant communities cannot be addressed without considering the role of supportive policies and programs. Initiatives that provide access to healthcare, legal protections, and social services are crucial in addressing the unique needs of immigrant populations. In this section, we will examine the role of supportive policies and programs in addressing the drug and homelessness crisis among immigrant communities.

One of the most critical supportive policies for immigrant communities is access to healthcare. Immigrants face significant barriers to accessing healthcare due to their immigration status, language barriers, and lack of insurance. The Affordable Care Act (ACA) has helped to increase access to healthcare for many immigrants, but undocumented immigrants remain largely excluded from the benefits of the ACA. Therefore, it is important to provide access to affordable healthcare for all immigrants, regardless of their status.

Another important policy is providing legal protections for immigrants. Immigrants who are at risk of deportation are less likely to access healthcare and social services, and more likely to experience poverty and homelessness. Providing legal protections, such as DACA (Deferred Action for Childhood Arrivals) and TPS (Temporary Protected Status), can help to alleviate the fear of deportation and provide stability for immigrant families.

Furthermore, culturally and linguistically appropriate services are essential in addressing the unique needs of immigrant communities. Programs that provide language support, cultural competency training for service providers, and community-based initiatives can help to reduce the barriers that immigrant communities face in accessing services.

Addressing the root causes of drug use and homelessness among immigrant communities also requires a comprehensive approach that includes addressing social determinants of health such as poverty, housing insecurity, and discrimination. For example, affordable housing programs that prioritize immigrant families can provide stable housing and reduce the risk of homelessness.

In addition, community-based initiatives that address the social and economic needs of immigrant families can help to promote resilience and prevent substance use disorders. These initiatives can include mentorship programs, job training and placement, and education and training on financial literacy.

Overall, supportive policies and programs that address the unique needs of immigrant communities are crucial in addressing the drug and homelessness crisis among immigrant populations. These policies and programs must be culturally appropriate, linguistically accessible, and take into account the impact of immigration policies on immigrant communities. Addressing the root causes of these issues requires a comprehensive approach that includes providing legal protections, access to healthcare, affordable housing, and community-based initiatives. By providing support and addressing the unique needs of immigrant communities, we can help to prevent and reduce substance use disorders and homelessness.

Conclusion

In conclusion, the impact of immigration policies on the drug and homelessness crisis among immigrant communities is significant and multifaceted. Historical policies have created barriers to accessing housing, healthcare, and addiction treatment services, which have increased the vulnerability of immigrant communities to drug use and homelessness. Fear of deportation, language barriers, and lack of documentation have made it difficult for immigrants to access the support they need. Additionally, criminalization of undocumented immigrants contributes to the cycle of poverty and homelessness, and family separation policies have further worsened the situation, leading to mental health issues and substance abuse.

However, there are also supportive policies and programs that can address the crisis. Providing access to healthcare and legal protections for immigrants can help reduce barriers and create opportunities for recovery. Community-based initiatives that provide culturally appropriate services and focus on harm reduction strategies can also help improve outcomes.

It is crucial to recognize and address the impact of immigration policies on the drug and homelessness crisis among immigrant communities. Continued efforts must be made to provide equitable access to services and legal protections, and to create more supportive policies and programs that meet the needs of these vulnerable populations. By doing so, we can work towards addressing the root causes of the crisis and improving outcomes for all.

The Rise of "Tent Cities" and other forms of Homelessness on the West Coast

The rise of "tent cities" and other forms of homelessness on the West Coast of the United States has become a pressing issue in recent years. Homelessness has increased dramatically in cities such as Los Angeles, San Francisco, and Seattle, leading to the emergence of makeshift encampments and "tent cities" as a response to the lack of affordable housing. This trend has not only highlighted the housing crisis in these cities but has also raised questions about the government's ability to address this issue. In this essay, we will discuss the rise of "tent cities" and other forms of homelessness on the West Coast, exploring the underlying causes, impact on individuals and communities, and potential solutions.

Historical context

Homelessness has been a longstanding issue in the United States, with varying degrees of visibility and political attention over the decades. The issue has been exacerbated by factors such as the lack of affordable housing, economic inequality, and limited access to social services. In recent years, the West Coast has seen a notable increase in the number of homeless individuals and the emergence of "tent cities" as a response to the lack of affordable housing.

The history of homelessness in the US can be traced back to the Great Depression of the 1930s, which saw a significant increase in the number of people who were unable to secure stable housing. The federal government responded with the New Deal programs, which aimed to create jobs and provide assistance to those in need. However, this did not fully resolve the issue of homelessness, and the problem persisted through subsequent decades.

In the 1980s, the Reagan administration implemented significant cuts to federal housing and social service programs, which further exacerbated homelessness across the country. The homeless population grew significantly during this time, with many people forced to live on the streets or in temporary shelters. While some cities responded by investing in affordable housing and social services, others implemented harsh measures to criminalize homelessness, such as anti-camping ordinances and aggressive policing.

In the 1990s, the federal government responded with the creation of the Interagency Council on Homelessness and the implementation of the McKinney-Vento Homeless Assistance Act, which provided funding for homeless services and support. However, these efforts have not been enough to fully address the issue of homelessness, particularly in regions with high housing costs and limited affordable options.

In recent years, the West Coast has seen a notable increase in the number of homeless individuals, with many people forced to live in encampments, including "tent cities." The lack of affordable housing has been a major contributing factor to this rise, with many individuals unable to secure stable housing due to rising rents and limited supply. The high cost of living in cities like San Francisco, Los Angeles, and Seattle has made it increasingly difficult for low-income individuals to make ends meet, leading to a growing number of people experiencing homelessness.

The emergence of "tent cities" is a response to the lack of affordable housing and inadequate shelter options. These encampments often consist of makeshift shelters constructed from tarps, tents, and other materials, and may be located in public parks, sidewalks, or other areas. While some cities have attempted to dismantle these encampments, others have allowed them to persist as a temporary solution to the homelessness crisis.

Overall, the history of homelessness in the United States has been marked by a lack of political will and inadequate support for affordable housing and social services. The rise of "tent cities" on the West Coast is a reflection of these broader issues, and highlights the urgent need for comprehensive solutions to address homelessness and provide stable, affordable housing for all.

Homelessness and mental health

Homelessness and mental health are deeply interconnected, and the lack of affordable housing exacerbates mental health issues, leading to the emergence of "tent cities" on the West Coast. According to the National Alliance to End Homelessness, nearly one-third of people experiencing homelessness have a serious mental illness, such as schizophrenia, bipolar disorder, or major depression. The National Institute of Mental Health reports that people experiencing homelessness are at increased risk of mental health disorders, including anxiety, depression, and post-traumatic stress disorder (PTSD).

The relationship between homelessness and mental health issues is cyclical. Homelessness can cause or worsen mental health problems, such as anxiety and depression. On the other hand, mental health issues can lead to homelessness, as people with mental illnesses may struggle to maintain employment or relationships and may be unable to pay for housing.

The lack of affordable housing exacerbates the situation, as people with mental health issues are more likely to be living in poverty and unable to afford stable housing. Homelessness, in turn, can further exacerbate mental health issues and make it more challenging to access mental health services. The lack of access to mental health services also contributes to the rise of "tent cities" as people are unable to receive the support they need to address their mental health needs.

The issue is particularly prevalent on the West Coast, where housing prices are skyrocketing, and the cost of living is high. In cities like San Francisco, Los Angeles, and Seattle, the homeless population has surged, leading to the emergence of "tent cities" as people resort to living in makeshift shelters in public spaces. These "tent cities" often lack basic sanitation facilities, putting people at risk of illness and disease. Furthermore, the cramped living conditions can exacerbate mental health issues, leading to a cycle of homelessness and poor mental health outcomes.

To address the rise of "tent cities" on the West Coast, it is essential to recognize the link between homelessness and mental health issues. Providing affordable and stable housing options is crucial to breaking the cycle of homelessness and improving mental health outcomes. Additionally, access to mental health services is crucial to ensuring that people experiencing homelessness can address their mental health needs and get back on their feet. It is crucial to prioritize mental health care for people experiencing homelessness to help them recover and reintegrate into society. Without addressing mental health concerns, the "tent cities" on the West Coast will continue to persist and may even worsen.

Drug use and homelessness

The rise of "tent cities" and other forms of homelessness on the West Coast has been influenced by many factors, one of which is drug use. It is not uncommon to see drug use among the homeless population, and it has been linked to the lack of access to drug addiction treatment and affordable housing.

Drug addiction can be a contributing factor to homelessness as individuals may lose their jobs, homes, and relationships due to their addiction. The lack of resources and support systems often leaves them with limited options for seeking help, leading them to turn to the streets and ultimately contribute to the rise of "tent cities."

Drug addiction and homelessness often form a vicious cycle where homelessness can lead to drug addiction, and drug addiction can lead to homelessness. People who experience homelessness are more likely to use drugs to cope with the stress and trauma of their situation, and drug addiction can make it challenging to find and maintain stable housing.

Furthermore, drug addiction can exacerbate mental health issues, making it even more challenging for people to find their way out of homelessness. Drug use can contribute to feelings of depression, anxiety, and hopelessness, which can further hinder efforts to secure employment and stable housing.

In response to the rise of "tent cities" and the issues of drug addiction and homelessness, harm reduction strategies have been developed to help address the challenges faced by this population. These strategies aim to reduce the negative consequences associated with drug use, such as overdose and the spread of infectious diseases, by providing access to clean needles, overdose prevention medications, and other resources.

However, it is essential to recognize that harm reduction strategies alone are not enough to address the root causes of drug addiction and homelessness. More comprehensive approaches are needed to provide access to affordable housing, mental health services, and addiction treatment to help individuals break the cycle of homelessness and drug addiction.

Addressing the underlying causes of drug addiction and homelessness requires a multifaceted approach that addresses social and economic factors, including poverty, unemployment, and inadequate access to healthcare. It is also essential to address systemic issues such as racism and discrimination that contribute to the disproportionate representation of people of color in the homeless and drug-addicted population.

In conclusion, the relationship between drug addiction and homelessness is complex and multifaceted, and it has contributed to the rise of "tent cities" on the West Coast. Addressing this issue requires a comprehensive approach that prioritizes the provision of affordable housing, mental health services, and addiction treatment, as well as addressing the underlying social and economic factors that contribute to homelessness and drug addiction.

The impact of COVID-19

The COVID-19 pandemic has had a significant impact on homelessness on the West Coast, exacerbating an already dire situation and leading to the growth of "tent cities" and other forms of encampments. The pandemic has affected the availability of resources and services for people experiencing homelessness, such as shelters, food banks, and healthcare facilities, leading to an increase in the number of individuals living on the streets.

The pandemic has also resulted in a surge in unemployment and economic instability, further contributing to the rise of homelessness. As many people lost their jobs or had their hours reduced due to lockdowns and business closures, they were unable to pay their rent or mortgages, leading to eviction and homelessness.

In addition to economic factors, the pandemic has also had a direct impact on the physical and mental health of individuals experiencing homelessness. Homeless encampments, including "tent cities," have become hotspots for the spread of COVID-19, as they often lack access to sanitation facilities and adequate healthcare. Individuals experiencing homelessness are also more vulnerable to the virus due to pre-existing health conditions and a lack of access to healthcare.

To address the impact of COVID-19 on homelessness, many cities and organizations have implemented temporary measures such as providing emergency shelter and housing to individuals experiencing homelessness, as well as increasing sanitation facilities in encampments. However, these measures have been insufficient to fully address the scope of the problem, and there is a need for more long-term solutions.

The pandemic has highlighted the urgent need for affordable housing and comprehensive healthcare for all individuals, including those experiencing homelessness. It has also underscored the need for a more comprehensive approach to homelessness, one that addresses the root causes of the issue, such as economic instability, mental health, and substance abuse.

In summary, the COVID-19 pandemic has had a profound impact on homelessness on the West Coast, leading to the growth of "tent cities" and other forms of encampments. The pandemic has highlighted the need for comprehensive solutions to homelessness, including access to affordable housing, healthcare, and mental health services. It is essential that policymakers and communities continue to work towards addressing the root causes of homelessness to ensure that all individuals have access to safe and stable housing.

Challenges facing "tent cities"

The rise of "tent cities" and other forms of homelessness on the West Coast has brought about a new set of challenges for individuals experiencing homelessness and the communities surrounding them. As these encampments continue to grow, there are several challenges that need to be addressed in order to ensure the safety and well-being of all involved.

One major challenge facing "tent cities" is access to healthcare. People experiencing homelessness often have limited access to medical care and are at greater risk for health complications due to their living conditions. The lack of access to healthcare can lead to untreated medical conditions and exacerbate mental health issues, which can further contribute to homelessness. In addition, during the COVID-19 pandemic, access to healthcare has become even more critical as the virus poses a significant threat to individuals experiencing homelessness.

Another challenge facing "tent cities" is sanitation. Without access to proper facilities, individuals experiencing homelessness may be forced to use nearby alleys or streets as restrooms, which can create health hazards for both the homeless population and the surrounding community. Furthermore, a lack of proper sanitation facilities can contribute to the spread of infectious diseases, including COVID-19.

Safety concerns also pose a challenge for "tent cities." Individuals experiencing homelessness are often vulnerable to crime and violence, and "tent cities" can become targets for theft, assault, and other criminal activities. In addition, "tent cities" can be at risk of fires, as many encampments use open flames for cooking and heating.

Moreover, the residents of the surrounding communities may view "tent cities" as a threat to their safety and property values. This can lead to tension between the homeless population and the surrounding community, which can further exacerbate the challenges faced by those living in "tent cities."

In conclusion, the challenges facing "tent cities" and other forms of homelessness on the West Coast are numerous and complex. Addressing these challenges will require a coordinated effort from government agencies, community organizations, and the homeless population themselves. By providing access to healthcare, sanitation facilities, and addressing safety concerns, we can work towards a solution that supports the well-being of everyone involved.

Responses and solutions

The rise of "tent cities" and other forms of homelessness on the West Coast is a complex issue that requires a multifaceted approach. The lack of affordable housing is a key factor in the emergence of these encampments, but there are also other factors at play, such as mental health issues and drug addiction.

Homelessness is not a new phenomenon in the United States, but it has become more visible in recent years due to the growing number of people living in "tent cities" and other forms of encampments. Homelessness has been a persistent problem in the US since the 1980s, with a significant increase in the number of people experiencing homelessness in the late 2000s due to the Great Recession.

The West Coast has been particularly affected by the homelessness crisis, with cities such as Los Angeles, San Francisco, and Seattle seeing a significant increase in the number of people living on the streets. The lack of affordable housing is a key factor in the rise of "tent cities," as many people are unable to afford rent or are forced out of their homes due to rising housing costs.

In addition to the lack of affordable housing, mental health issues are also a significant factor in the rise of "tent cities." Many people experiencing homelessness also struggle with mental health issues, which can make it difficult for them to find stable housing or hold down a job.

Drug addiction is another factor that has contributed to the rise of "tent cities." Many people experiencing homelessness struggle with addiction, which can make it difficult for them to access resources or seek help. The COVID-19 pandemic has also had a significant impact on homelessness, with many people losing their jobs or being unable to afford rent due to the economic downturn.

The challenges facing "tent cities" are numerous, including access to healthcare, sanitation, and safety concerns. Many people living in "tent cities" do not have access to basic healthcare services, and the lack of sanitation can lead to the spread of disease. Safety is also a concern, as people living in "tent cities" are often vulnerable to violence and other forms of abuse.

To address the rise of "tent cities," a variety of solutions have been proposed. Increasing affordable housing is one of the most important steps that can be taken to address homelessness. Expanding access to healthcare and mental health services is also critical, as many people experiencing homelessness struggle with mental health issues or addiction.

Harm reduction strategies, such as providing clean needles and safe injection sites, can also help to address drug addiction among people experiencing homelessness. These strategies can help to reduce the spread of disease and prevent overdose deaths.

In conclusion, the rise of "tent cities" and other forms of homelessness on the West Coast is a complex issue that requires a multifaceted approach. Addressing the lack of affordable housing, providing access to healthcare and mental health services, and implementing harm reduction strategies are all important steps that can be taken to address the homelessness crisis. It is essential that we continue to work towards finding sustainable solutions to this pressing issue.

Conclusion

In conclusion, the rise of "tent cities" and other forms of homelessness on the West Coast is a complex issue with deep-rooted causes. The historical context of homelessness in the United States, coupled with mental health issues, drug addiction, and the impact of the COVID-19 pandemic, has led to the growth of these encampments. However, it is important to note that these encampments are symptomatic of larger issues related to affordable housing, poverty, and systemic inequalities.

Furthermore, the challenges facing "tent cities" are numerous, including access to healthcare, sanitation, and safety concerns. While there have been responses and solutions proposed to address the issue, such as increasing affordable housing, expanding access to healthcare and mental health services, and harm reduction strategies, these efforts must be continued and expanded upon.

In order to truly address the root causes of homelessness on the West Coast, there needs to be a concerted effort to provide equitable access to housing, healthcare, and other services for all individuals. This requires addressing systemic inequalities and policies that perpetuate poverty and homelessness. By working towards these goals, we can create a society that values the basic needs and rights of all its members, and ensure that no one is left without a safe and stable place to call home.

The Role of The Tech Industry in Exacerbating the Crisis

The rise of the tech industry in cities across the United States has brought significant economic growth and development. However, this growth has also led to rising housing costs and gentrification, exacerbating the drug and homelessness crisis in many urban areas. This has highlighted the need to examine the role of the tech industry in contributing to this crisis. In this discussion, we will explore how the tech industry has driven the rising housing costs and gentrification, contributing to the drug and homelessness crisis in cities across the United States. We will examine the impact on low-income communities, the displacement of residents, and the role of local and state government policies in regulating the tech industry.

Gentrification and rising housing costs

The tech industry has been hailed for driving innovation and creating high-paying jobs, but it has also played a significant role in the housing crisis that has led to the rise in homelessness on the West Coast. The influx of tech workers in cities such as San Francisco and Seattle has led to gentrification, a process in which low-income residents are pushed out of their neighborhoods as property values rise. As a result, many people have been left without access to affordable housing, leading to a rise in homelessness.

One of the key drivers of gentrification is the rising cost of housing, which has become increasingly unaffordable for many low-income residents. The tech industry has played a significant role in driving up these costs, as tech workers often earn high salaries and are able to pay premium prices for housing. This has put immense pressure on housing markets in cities with a high concentration of tech companies, leading to skyrocketing prices that have made it difficult for many residents to afford to stay in their homes.

In addition to driving up housing prices, the tech industry has also contributed to the displacement of low-income residents through the process of gentrification. As neighborhoods become more desirable to young, affluent tech workers, landlords and property owners often seek to capitalize on this trend by raising rents or converting affordable housing into high-end apartments. This can lead to the displacement of long-time residents who are unable to afford the higher rents or mortgages that come with the changes.

The impact of gentrification on homelessness is significant. As low-income residents are pushed out of their neighborhoods, many are left with few options for affordable housing. This can lead to overcrowding, unsafe living conditions, or even homelessness. In some cases, entire communities have been displaced, with residents forced to leave their homes and seek shelter elsewhere.

The tech industry has also played a role in exacerbating the homelessness crisis by contributing to the shortage of affordable housing. Many tech companies have been criticized for their lack of investment in affordable housing initiatives, instead focusing on building luxurious campuses and expanding their business operations. This has left little room for investment in affordable housing initiatives that could help alleviate the homelessness crisis.

In summary, the tech industry has played a significant role in exacerbating the housing crisis and the resulting rise in homelessness on the West Coast. By driving up housing prices and contributing to gentrification, the industry has made it difficult for low-income residents to access affordable housing, leading to overcrowding, displacement, and homelessness. Addressing this crisis will require the tech industry to take a more active role in investing in affordable housing initiatives, as well as working with local governments and community organizations to find solutions that benefit everyone.

Tech industry employment practices

The employment practices of the tech industry have been a major contributing factor to income inequality and the rising cost of living in cities where the industry has a strong presence. The industry's reliance on contract workers and low-wage jobs has made it difficult for many workers to afford housing and access healthcare, leading to an increase in homelessness and the drug crisis.

One major issue with tech industry employment practices is the use of contract workers. These workers are often hired on a temporary or project basis, without the benefits and job security of full-time employees. This means they often have unstable income and struggle to afford basic necessities like housing and healthcare. In cities where the cost of living is high, such as San Francisco and Seattle, this can lead to homelessness and reliance on drugs as a coping mechanism.

Additionally, the tech industry has been criticized for creating low-wage jobs that do not provide a living wage in cities where the cost of living is high. Many tech companies have moved their operations to cities like San Francisco and Seattle, where the cost of living is high and the demand for workers is strong. However, many of these jobs do not pay enough to allow workers to afford housing and healthcare without experiencing financial hardship.

This is especially true for workers in non-technical roles, such as customer service and administrative positions, who are often paid significantly less than their technical counterparts. This has contributed to income inequality in cities with a strong tech industry presence, making it difficult for low-income workers to find affordable housing and access healthcare.

Furthermore, the tech industry has also been criticized for its lack of diversity, with many companies struggling to hire and retain workers from underrepresented communities. This lack of diversity can exacerbate income inequality and make it more difficult for workers from underrepresented communities to access well-paying jobs in the tech industry.

In conclusion, the employment practices of the tech industry have played a significant role in exacerbating the drug and homelessness crisis. The industry's reliance on contract workers and low-wage jobs has contributed to income inequality and made it difficult for many workers to afford housing and access healthcare. In order to address this crisis, the tech industry must take steps to provide more stable and well-paying jobs, as well as increase diversity in hiring and retainment.

Impact of tech industry on small businesses

The rapid growth of the tech industry has had a profound impact on the economies of cities where it has become concentrated, such as San Francisco and Seattle. While the industry has brought new jobs and wealth to these cities, it has also had significant negative impacts, including on small businesses.

As the tech industry has grown, so too has the demand for real estate in areas where tech companies have set up shop. This has driven up the cost of rent and property, making it difficult for small businesses to remain in the area. Many have been priced out of their neighborhoods or forced to close altogether, leading to a loss of community and exacerbating the drug and homelessness crisis.

One way that the tech industry has contributed to the displacement of small businesses is by offering high salaries to their employees, which has led to an influx of highly paid workers to the area. This has created a situation where the cost of living in these cities has become unaffordable for many residents who are not employed in the tech industry. This has resulted in a loss of diversity and culture in these neighborhoods, further eroding the sense of community and contributing to the drug and homelessness crisis.

Additionally, the tech industry has also contributed to the displacement of small businesses by investing in large, high-end development projects, which often do not prioritize the needs of the surrounding community. These projects can lead to the displacement of local businesses and residents, further exacerbating the drug and homelessness crisis.

Overall, the impact of the tech industry on small businesses has been significant, with the displacement of long-time residents and small businesses leading to a loss of community and exacerbating the drug and homelessness crisis. It is important for the tech industry to acknowledge its role in this process and work towards solutions that prioritize the needs of the entire community, rather than just those employed in the industry.

Responses to the tech industry's role

The tech industry has played a significant role in exacerbating the drug and homelessness crisis, particularly in cities like San Francisco and Seattle. This has led to a range of responses from various stakeholders, including corporate leaders, community organizers, and policymakers.

One response has been a push for greater corporate responsibility from tech companies. Some advocates argue that these companies should take more proactive steps to address the issues their presence has caused, such as investing in affordable housing or providing direct support for homeless individuals. Some companies, such as Salesforce, have responded by making substantial donations to organizations that work to address the crisis.

Another response has been the implementation of community benefits agreements (CBAs). These are contracts negotiated between community organizations and developers, which outline specific commitments the developer will make in exchange for community support for their projects. CBAs have been used in a number of cities to ensure that new development projects benefit the community and do not contribute to displacement or gentrification.

Policymakers have also proposed a range of solutions to address the tech industry's role in the crisis. One example is the creation of affordable housing mandates for new development projects. In San Francisco, for instance, developers are required to either set aside a certain percentage of new units as affordable housing or pay a fee that goes toward the creation of affordable housing elsewhere in the city.

Other proposed policy solutions include increased investment in public transportation, which could help alleviate some of the pressures on housing markets, and stronger protections for small businesses and long-term residents. Overall, there is a recognition that addressing the root causes of the drug and homelessness crisis will require collaboration across a range of stakeholders and sectors, and that solutions will need to be tailored to the unique needs of each community.

Conclusion

In conclusion, the role of the tech industry in exacerbating the drug and homelessness crisis cannot be ignored. The industry's impact on rising housing costs and gentrification, employment practices, and displacement of small businesses have all contributed to the crisis. The tech industry has a responsibility to be accountable for its actions and work towards solutions that address the root causes of the issue.

Efforts to hold the tech industry accountable can include corporate responsibility, community benefits agreements, and policy solutions. Additionally, there is a need for continued efforts to address income inequality and provide equitable access to housing and healthcare for all residents, regardless of their socioeconomic status.

It is essential to recognize the interconnectedness of these issues and work towards comprehensive solutions that address the complex and systemic problems that have led to the drug and homelessness crisis. By working together and taking collective responsibility, we can make progress towards creating more just and equitable communities where everyone has access to the resources they need to thrive.

The Political and Policy Responses to the Crisis

The drug and homelessness crisis is a major social issue that affects communities across the United States. With rising housing costs, income inequality, and limited access to healthcare and mental health services, many individuals and families are struggling to make ends meet and find stable housing. This crisis requires a coordinated effort from government leaders and policymakers to address the root causes and provide effective solutions. In this context, this essay examines the political and policy responses to the drug and homelessness crisis, including the role of different levels of government and the effectiveness of their responses.

Federal government response

The role of the federal government in responding to the drug and homelessness crisis has been critical in providing funding for housing and healthcare programs. The federal government allocates funding through various agencies, such as the Department of Housing and Urban Development (HUD) and the Department of Health and Human Services (HHS), to support programs aimed at addressing homelessness and drug addiction.

HUD's Continuum of Care (CoC) program provides funding for local communities to support the development of affordable housing and services for people experiencing homelessness. In addition, the HHS Substance Abuse and Mental Health Services Administration (SAMHSA) provides funding for substance abuse treatment and mental health services for people experiencing addiction and homelessness.

While these programs have been successful in providing much-needed support, the funding allocated to these programs is often inadequate to address the scale of the crisis. The federal government has also been criticized for not adequately prioritizing funding for homelessness and drug addiction programs in their budget allocations.

Furthermore, political polarization and partisan gridlock in Congress have hindered efforts to provide more comprehensive solutions to the drug and homelessness crisis. While there have been some bipartisan efforts to address the crisis, many proposals have been stalled or blocked due to political disagreements.

Overall, while the federal government has played a critical role in providing funding for housing and healthcare programs, there is a need for more sustained and comprehensive solutions to address the scale of the drug and homelessness crisis.

State government response

State governments have played a significant role in addressing the drug and homelessness crisis. Many states have implemented policies and programs to address the issue, recognizing that homelessness is a complex issue that requires a comprehensive response.

One example of a state-level response is California's "Homeless Emergency Aid Program" (HEAP), which provides funding to cities and counties to address homelessness. The program has provided over $1 billion in funding since its inception in 2018, and has supported a variety of services, including emergency housing, rental assistance, and mental health services. Additionally, California's "Project Roomkey" initiative has helped to house thousands of homeless individuals in hotels and motels during the COVID-19 pandemic.

Other states have also implemented policies and programs to address the issue. For example, Washington State has implemented a "Housing and Essential Needs" program, which provides rental assistance and other support services to individuals who are unable to work due to a physical or mental disability. Oregon has implemented a "Housing First" approach, which prioritizes providing housing to individuals experiencing homelessness as a first step towards stabilization and recovery.

Despite these efforts, there are still significant challenges facing state governments in addressing the drug and homelessness crisis. Funding for housing and healthcare programs remains a significant issue, as does the need for coordination and collaboration between state agencies and local governments. Additionally, there is a need for ongoing evaluation and improvement of state-level policies and programs to ensure their effectiveness and impact on the issue.

It is also important to note that state-level responses to the drug and homelessness crisis are often impacted by federal policies and funding. For example, the federal government's recent elimination of the "Stable Housing Initiative," which provided funding for affordable housing for low-income individuals, could have a significant impact on state-level efforts to address the issue.

Overall, while state governments have implemented a variety of policies and programs to address the drug and homelessness crisis, there is still much work to be done to ensure that all individuals have access to safe and affordable housing and healthcare. Ongoing evaluation and improvement of state-level responses, as well as increased federal funding and support, will be critical in addressing this complex issue.

Local government response

The drug and homelessness crisis is often most visible at the local level, where people experiencing homelessness may be seen living in tents or makeshift encampments on the streets. As such, local governments have been at the forefront of developing policies and programs to address the issue.

One key policy area is the regulation of encampments. Some cities have implemented policies allowing for the creation of sanctioned encampments or safe parking programs where people experiencing homelessness can live temporarily. Other cities have taken a more punitive approach, banning encampments and aggressively enforcing laws related to loitering, sleeping in public, and other activities associated with homelessness. However, studies have shown that such policies often do little to actually address the root causes of homelessness and may even exacerbate the problem by pushing people into more hidden or unsafe locations.

Housing is another important policy area at the local level. Some cities have implemented programs to provide affordable or supportive housing for people experiencing homelessness, while others have focused on preventing homelessness through rental assistance programs or legal assistance for tenants facing eviction. However, the effectiveness of these programs may be limited by the availability of funding and the high cost of housing in many urban areas.

Social services are also a critical component of local responses to the drug and homelessness crisis. Cities may offer a range of services, including mental health and addiction treatment, job training, and access to healthcare. However, these services may be inadequate or insufficiently coordinated, making it difficult for people experiencing homelessness to access the support they need.

Overall, the effectiveness of local government responses to the drug and homelessness crisis can vary widely depending on a range of factors, including funding availability, political will, and the specific needs of the local community. However, it is clear that local governments have a crucial role to play in addressing the issue and developing solutions that are responsive to the needs of their communities.

Funding and budgetary issues

The issue of funding and budgetary constraints has been a significant challenge in addressing the drug and homelessness crisis. While there have been efforts at the federal, state, and local levels to allocate funding towards homelessness and housing programs, the need still outstrips the available resources.

At the federal level, funding for homelessness and housing programs has been inconsistent and subject to political and economic pressures. For example, the 2018 federal budget proposed significant cuts to affordable housing programs, including a $1.3 billion cut to the Department of Housing and Urban Development's (HUD) public housing capital fund. However, in response to pressure from advocates and policymakers, the final budget included a $4.6 billion increase in funding for HUD programs, including $2.6 billion for homeless assistance grants.

State governments also face challenges in securing funding for homelessness and housing programs, particularly in times of budget constraints. For example, in California, the state budget for fiscal year 2020-2021 included $1 billion in funding for homelessness and housing programs, but this was significantly less than the $2.4 billion proposed in Governor Gavin Newsom's initial budget due to the economic impacts of the COVID-19 pandemic.

At the local level, cities and counties face competing priorities for limited resources, and the costs of addressing the drug and homelessness crisis can be substantial. For example, San Francisco spent $364 million on homelessness services in 2020, but this was still not enough to address the scale of the crisis in the city.

In addition to securing funding, budgetary issues also impact the allocation of resources and the effectiveness of programs. For example, in some cases, funding may be allocated towards emergency shelter services, rather than longer-term housing solutions, which can be more effective in addressing homelessness.

Addressing funding and budgetary issues will require a sustained commitment from all levels of government, as well as innovative approaches to securing and allocating resources. This may include exploring public-private partnerships, advocating for increased federal funding, and implementing policies to support affordable housing development.

Public-private partnerships

Public-private partnerships can play a crucial role in addressing the drug and homelessness crisis by combining the resources and expertise of government and private sector organizations. These partnerships can take many forms, such as collaborations between local governments and non-profit organizations, or partnerships between private businesses and social service providers.

One example of a successful public-private partnership is the Partnership for Permanent Housing in Los Angeles County. This partnership brings together local government, non-profit organizations, and private sector partners to provide housing and support services to homeless individuals and families. The partnership has helped to reduce homelessness in the county by over 50% since 2011.

Another example is the "Built for Zero" initiative, which is a collaboration between the federal government and communities across the country to end chronic and veteran homelessness. This partnership uses data-driven strategies to identify and target resources to the most vulnerable populations, and has helped to reduce chronic homelessness by over 90% in participating communities.

However, public-private partnerships also face challenges, including differences in priorities and values between government and private sector partners, potential conflicts of interest, and issues related to accountability and transparency. It is important for these partnerships to have clear goals, transparent decision-making processes, and mechanisms for monitoring and evaluating progress towards these goals.

Overall, public-private partnerships have the potential to be a powerful tool in addressing the drug and homelessness crisis, but it is important for these partnerships to be carefully structured and managed to ensure their effectiveness and accountability.

Housing policies

Housing policies are an essential part of addressing the drug and homelessness crisis. Permanent supportive housing (PSH) is a model that provides long-term, affordable housing with supportive services for individuals experiencing chronic homelessness, often due to disabilities or mental health conditions. PSH has been found to be effective in reducing homelessness and improving health outcomes for residents.

Affordable housing policies aim to increase the supply of affordable housing units in areas where rising housing costs have contributed to homelessness. These policies may include incentives for developers to build affordable housing units or mandates requiring a certain percentage of new developments to be designated as affordable.

Housing first is another model that prioritizes providing individuals experiencing homelessness with immediate access to permanent housing, without requiring participation in treatment or sobriety programs first. This approach has been found to be effective in reducing homelessness and improving health outcomes, as stable housing provides a foundation for individuals to address other challenges they may be facing.

While these policies have shown promise in reducing homelessness, they face challenges related to funding, community opposition, and political will. In addition, the effectiveness of these policies may be limited by other factors, such as limited access to healthcare and social services.

Efforts to address the drug and homelessness crisis through housing policies must be accompanied by comprehensive services and support to ensure individuals are able to maintain stable housing and address the root causes of their homelessness. This includes access to healthcare, mental health services, substance abuse treatment, and employment and educational opportunities.

Healthcare policies

The drug and homelessness crisis is often accompanied by a range of health issues, including addiction, mental illness, and physical health problems. As such, healthcare policies are an important aspect of the overall response to the crisis.

One critical component of healthcare policies aimed at addressing the crisis is ensuring access to addiction treatment. This can include medication-assisted treatment (MAT) for opioid addiction, as well as behavioral therapies and support services to help individuals overcome addiction. Many cities and states have implemented programs to expand access to addiction treatment, including through partnerships with healthcare providers and community-based organizations. However, challenges remain in terms of ensuring access to treatment for all who need it, particularly in areas with limited healthcare resources.

In addition to addiction treatment, mental health services are also critical for addressing the drug and homelessness crisis. Many individuals experiencing homelessness also struggle with mental illness, including conditions such as schizophrenia, bipolar disorder, and depression. Providing access to mental health services can be a challenge, particularly given the shortage of mental health providers in many areas. However, some cities and states have implemented innovative programs to expand access to mental health care for homeless individuals, including through telemedicine and mobile clinics.

Finally, ensuring access to primary care is also important for addressing the overall health needs of homeless individuals. Many individuals experiencing homelessness face significant barriers to accessing healthcare, including lack of insurance, limited transportation options, and a lack of healthcare providers in their area. Some cities and states have implemented programs to expand access to primary care for homeless individuals, including through mobile clinics and partnerships with community health centers.

Overall, healthcare policies aimed at addressing the drug and homelessness crisis are critical for ensuring that individuals experiencing homelessness receive the care they need to overcome addiction, manage mental illness, and address their overall health needs. While challenges remain in terms of ensuring access to care for all who need it, innovative programs and partnerships offer hope for improving healthcare outcomes for homeless individuals.

Criminal justice policies

The criminal justice system has played a significant role in the drug and homelessness crisis, as policies related to drug offenses and homelessness have often criminalized those who are experiencing these issues. Many jurisdictions have implemented policies focused on enforcement, such as increased policing of drug activity and criminalization of behaviors associated with homelessness, such as panhandling and sleeping in public spaces. These policies have been criticized for exacerbating the crisis by further marginalizing and stigmatizing individuals who are already struggling with addiction and homelessness.

However, there have also been efforts to shift towards more compassionate and evidence-based policies, such as harm reduction approaches and diversion programs. Harm reduction approaches aim to reduce the harms associated with drug use, such as overdose and the spread of infectious diseases, by providing access to sterile injection equipment, naloxone, and other resources. Diversion programs focus on providing individuals with alternatives to incarceration, such as treatment and supportive services, and have been shown to be more effective than traditional criminal justice responses in addressing addiction and homelessness.

Additionally, there have been efforts to repeal or reform laws that criminalize homelessness, such as laws prohibiting sleeping in public spaces or panhandling. These efforts aim to reduce the barriers that prevent individuals from accessing housing and supportive services and to reduce the stigma associated with experiencing homelessness.

Overall, while criminal justice policies have historically contributed to the drug and homelessness crisis, there have been efforts to shift towards more compassionate and effective approaches. The effectiveness of these policies, however, will depend on continued political and social support and adequate funding to implement them.

Conclusion

The drug and homelessness crisis is a complex issue that requires political and policy responses at all levels of government. This paper has examined the political and policy responses to the crisis, including the role of the federal government, state governments, and local governments. Funding and budgetary issues, public-private partnerships, housing policies, healthcare policies, and criminal justice policies have all been discussed.

While progress has been made in addressing the drug and homelessness crisis, there is still much work to be done. Continued funding and collaboration across all levels of government, as well as effective public-private partnerships, will be necessary to address the root causes of the crisis and provide sustainable solutions. Evidence-based policies, such as permanent supportive housing and access to addiction treatment and mental health services, will also be crucial in addressing the crisis.

It is important that policymakers prioritize addressing the drug and homelessness crisis and take a comprehensive approach that considers the interconnected nature of the issue. By working together and implementing evidence-based policies, we can make progress towards ending the drug and homelessness crisis and ensuring that all individuals have access to safe and stable housing and healthcare.

The Role of the Media in Shaping Perceptions of the Crisis

The drug and homelessness crisis is a complex issue that affects communities across the world. While there are many factors that contribute to the crisis, the role of the media in shaping public perceptions cannot be overlooked. Media coverage can impact policy decisions and public attitudes towards those impacted by the crisis. Therefore, it is important to examine the role of the media in shaping perceptions of the drug and homelessness crisis. This paper will explore how media coverage can influence public attitudes, how media outlets choose to report on the crisis, and the ethical considerations that should be taken into account when reporting on the crisis.

Media coverage and public attitudes

Media coverage of the drug and homelessness crisis can have a significant impact on public attitudes towards those impacted. In some cases, media coverage can reinforce harmful stereotypes and stigmatization of people experiencing homelessness or struggling with addiction, leading to victim-blaming attitudes and a lack of empathy for those in need. For example, media coverage that focuses on the criminalization of homelessness or drug use can contribute to the idea that individuals experiencing these issues are to blame for their circumstances, rather than considering the root causes of these problems, such as systemic poverty and lack of access to resources.

On the other hand, media coverage that highlights the complexities and struggles of those impacted by the drug and homelessness crisis can help to raise awareness and generate empathy for individuals and families who are experiencing these challenges. Such coverage can help to break down stereotypes and encourage a more nuanced understanding of the issue.

It is important to note that media coverage can also influence policy decisions related to the drug and homelessness crisis. When media coverage emphasizes the need for policy solutions, it can help to mobilize public support for policy changes that address the root causes of the issue, such as affordable housing and access to healthcare. Conversely, media coverage that reinforces negative stereotypes can make it more difficult to advocate for policy changes and garner public support for effective solutions.

Framing and bias in media coverage

Media outlets play a crucial role in framing the drug and homelessness crisis, which can have a significant impact on public attitudes and policy decisions. The framing of the crisis can shape how the public perceives those impacted, as well as the potential solutions that are considered.

There are several ways in which media outlets can frame their coverage of the crisis. One common frame is the "blame frame," which focuses on individual responsibility for addiction and homelessness. This frame can contribute to stigmatization and victim-blaming, and may detract from broader systemic issues that contribute to the crisis.

Another common frame is the "policy frame," which focuses on the government's response to the crisis, including funding and policy decisions. This frame may be more likely to highlight systemic issues and potential solutions, but can also be biased depending on the outlet's political leanings.

It is also important to consider bias in media coverage of the crisis. Media outlets may have implicit biases towards certain populations impacted by the crisis, such as people of color, those experiencing homelessness, or those struggling with addiction. This can impact the way these groups are portrayed in media coverage, and can perpetuate stereotypes and stigmatization.

Overall, understanding the framing and potential biases in media coverage of the drug and homelessness crisis is crucial for recognizing the impact of media on public attitudes and policy decisions.

Media coverage and policy decisions

Media coverage plays a crucial role in shaping policy decisions related to the drug and homelessness crisis. News coverage of the crisis can bring attention to the issue and generate public support for policy solutions. However, media coverage can also have negative effects on policy decisions.

For example, some studies have shown that media coverage of drug-related crime can contribute to "moral panic," leading to harsher criminal justice policies and increased funding for law enforcement at the expense of social services and public health initiatives. Media coverage can also perpetuate stereotypes and stigmatization of those impacted by the crisis, leading to policies that further marginalize and harm vulnerable populations.

On the other hand, media coverage can also highlight evidence-based solutions and encourage policymakers to prioritize funding for effective programs. In recent years, media coverage of the housing-first approach to homelessness, which prioritizes providing permanent housing to individuals experiencing homelessness, has contributed to increased support for this approach among policymakers.

Overall, the relationship between media coverage and policy decisions is complex, with both positive and negative impacts. It is important for media outlets to prioritize balanced and accurate coverage of the drug and homelessness crisis and for policymakers to consider a range of perspectives and evidence-based solutions when making policy decisions.

Media coverage and public opinion

Media coverage of the drug and homelessness crisis can play a significant role in shaping public opinion and determining the level of public support for policy solutions. News outlets have the power to highlight or downplay certain aspects of the crisis, as well as frame the issue in a way that influences public perception.

For example, media coverage that focuses on the criminalization of drug use and homelessness may lead to public perceptions that these issues are solely the result of individual behavior and moral failings, rather than systemic issues that require comprehensive policy solutions. This, in turn, can result in decreased public support for policies aimed at addressing the root causes of the crisis, such as systemic inequality, lack of affordable housing, and limited access to healthcare and addiction treatment.

On the other hand, media coverage that emphasizes the human impact of the crisis, including the experiences of individuals and families affected by drug use and homelessness, can lead to increased empathy and understanding among the public. This, in turn, can lead to increased support for policies aimed at providing housing, healthcare, and other social services to those in need.

It is important to note that media coverage alone cannot be solely responsible for shaping public opinion on the drug and homelessness crisis. Other factors such as personal experiences, political ideologies, and social networks also play a significant role in shaping public attitudes. Nonetheless, media coverage remains a powerful tool for shaping public perceptions and influencing policy decisions.

The role of social media

The role of social media in shaping public perceptions of the drug and homelessness crisis has become increasingly important in recent years. Social media platforms provide a space for individuals to share information, opinions, and personal experiences related to the issue, which can impact public attitudes towards those impacted by the crisis.

One potential downside of social media is the spread of misinformation and fake news, which can perpetuate stigmatizing and inaccurate narratives about drug use and homelessness. Additionally, social media algorithms can create echo chambers, where users are only exposed to viewpoints that align with their existing beliefs, further exacerbating existing biases and misconceptions.

However, social media can also be a powerful tool for raising awareness and promoting advocacy efforts related to the drug and homelessness crisis. Social media campaigns and hashtags, such as #housingforall or #endhomelessness, can mobilize public support and pressure policymakers to take action. Social media also provides a platform for those impacted by the crisis to share their stories and experiences, which can help to humanize the issue and challenge stigmatizing stereotypes.

Overall, the role of social media in shaping public perceptions of the drug and homelessness crisis is complex and multifaceted, and requires ongoing attention and critical analysis.

Examples of media coverage

There have been numerous examples of media coverage of the drug and homelessness crisis that have influenced public perceptions and policy decisions. For instance, media coverage often portrays individuals experiencing homelessness as dangerous and undesirable, perpetuating harmful stigmatization and victim-blaming attitudes. This negative portrayal can lead to public support for policies that criminalize homelessness, such as anti-camping ordinances, instead of policies that provide supportive services and affordable housing.

In contrast, media coverage that highlights the systemic factors contributing to the drug and homelessness crisis, such as income inequality and lack of affordable housing, can shape public opinion in favor of policy solutions that address these root causes. This type of coverage can also increase public support for policies that provide harm reduction services, such as syringe exchange programs and safe consumption sites, and evidence-based treatment options for individuals struggling with addiction.

Furthermore, media coverage has the potential to impact political priorities and funding decisions. For example, coverage of the opioid epidemic in recent years has increased public and political attention to the issue, leading to increased funding for addiction treatment programs and harm reduction services. Similarly, media coverage of the rising homelessness rates in many cities has led to increased political will and funding for housing programs.

Social media also plays a role in shaping public perceptions of the drug and homelessness crisis. Social media platforms can amplify certain narratives and contribute to the spread of misinformation, which can perpetuate harmful stereotypes and attitudes towards those impacted by the crisis. Additionally, social media can fuel polarized and divisive public discourse, making it more difficult to build consensus and support for policy solutions.

It is important to note that media coverage of the drug and homelessness crisis is not monolithic and can vary depending on the media outlet and individual journalist. However, media outlets have a responsibility to accurately and ethically report on the crisis, avoid harmful stereotypes, and highlight the root causes and potential policy solutions. Additionally, media consumers have a responsibility to critically evaluate the information they receive and seek out diverse perspectives and sources.

Overall, the role of the media in shaping perceptions of the drug and homelessness crisis is significant and underscores the importance of accurate and ethical reporting. Media coverage has the potential to influence public attitudes, policy decisions, and funding priorities, highlighting the need for responsible and inclusive coverage of this complex issue.

Alternative media perspectives

Alternative media perspectives on the drug and homelessness crisis can provide a valuable counterbalance to mainstream media narratives, challenging stigmatizing stereotypes and promoting more equitable policy solutions. Alternative media can include independent media outlets, community-based media, and grassroots media campaigns. These media outlets often have a closer connection to the communities affected by the drug and homelessness crisis and are more likely to prioritize perspectives and voices that are often excluded from mainstream media coverage.

One example of alternative media coverage is the Street Roots newspaper, a weekly publication in Portland, Oregon, that covers issues related to poverty and homelessness. Street Roots features in-depth reporting on the challenges faced by individuals experiencing homelessness and provides a platform for their stories and perspectives. The newspaper also advocates for policy solutions aimed at addressing the root causes of homelessness, such as affordable housing and access to healthcare. By providing a more nuanced and compassionate perspective on homelessness, Street Roots challenges mainstream media narratives that often stigmatize individuals experiencing homelessness.

Another example of alternative media coverage is the documentary film "The Homestretch," which follows the lives of three homeless youth in Chicago. The film provides a close-up look at the challenges faced by young people experiencing homelessness, including lack of access to education and healthcare, family dysfunction, and trauma. The film also highlights the resilience and resourcefulness of these young people and their determination to overcome the barriers to stable housing. "The Homestretch" has been used as an advocacy tool to promote policy solutions that address the root causes of homelessness, such as affordable housing and support for young people who are aging out of the foster care system.

Grassroots media campaigns, such as the Voices of Community Activists and Leaders (VOCAL-NY), have also emerged as a powerful force in shaping public opinion and policy solutions related to the drug and homelessness crisis. VOCAL-NY is a grassroots organization that advocates for policies to end the drug overdose crisis and provides support to people who use drugs. The organization uses a range of media tactics, including social media campaigns, street art, and video testimonials, to raise awareness about the impact of the drug crisis on individuals and communities. By elevating the voices of people who use drugs and challenging stigmatizing stereotypes, VOCAL-NY has been successful in promoting policies aimed at harm reduction, such as syringe exchange programs and access to overdose prevention medication.

Alternative media perspectives on the drug and homelessness crisis have the potential to challenge mainstream media narratives, promote more equitable policy solutions, and elevate the voices of those most affected by the crisis. These perspectives provide a counterbalance to stigmatizing stereotypes and highlight the complexity and diversity of experiences among those impacted by the crisis. By amplifying the voices of those who are often excluded from mainstream media coverage, alternative media can play an important role in shaping public opinion and policy decisions related to the drug and homelessness crisis.

Media and advocacy

Media plays a significant role in advocacy efforts aimed at addressing the drug and homelessness crisis. Media outlets, including traditional and alternative media, can elevate the voices of those impacted by the crisis and provide a platform for advocates to promote policy solutions. Through effective media advocacy, advocates can engage with the public, policymakers, and other stakeholders to raise awareness of the issue and drive action.

One key way in which media can support advocacy efforts is by providing a platform for those impacted by the crisis to share their stories. Personal narratives can be a powerful tool for raising awareness and humanizing complex issues. Through interviews, feature stories, and other forms of media coverage, media outlets can give voice to those who are often marginalized and overlooked. For example, a news story about a homeless family struggling to access healthcare can help to illustrate the impact of policy decisions on real people, generating public support for solutions that address the root causes of the crisis.

Media can also be used to promote specific policy solutions. Advocacy groups can work with journalists and media outlets to place op-eds, letters to the editor, and other content that promotes policy solutions and calls for action. By framing policy solutions in a way that resonates with the public, advocates can generate public support and increase pressure on policymakers to act.

In addition to traditional media outlets, social media can also be a powerful tool for advocacy. Advocacy groups can use social media platforms to share stories, raise awareness, and mobilize supporters. Social media can also be used to engage with policymakers and hold them accountable for addressing the crisis. For example, by using hashtags and tagging elected officials, advocates can create a sense of urgency and generate public pressure for action.

However, it is important to note that media advocacy is not without its challenges. One potential concern is the potential for media coverage to perpetuate negative stereotypes and stigmatize those impacted by the crisis. Advocates must be mindful of how their messaging is framed and work to ensure that media coverage accurately reflects the complexities of the issue.

Another potential challenge is the limited resources of advocacy organizations, which may make it difficult to compete with larger organizations and special interest groups for media coverage. Advocates must be strategic in their media outreach efforts, targeting outlets that are likely to be receptive to their message and working to build relationships with reporters and editors.

In conclusion, media plays a critical role in advocacy efforts aimed at addressing the drug and homelessness crisis. By elevating the voices of those impacted by the crisis, promoting policy solutions, and engaging with the public and policymakers, advocates can generate support for solutions that address the root causes of the crisis. While there are challenges associated with media advocacy, the potential benefits of effective media engagement make it a key strategy for advocates working to address this pressing social issue.

Media and advocacy

Media plays an important role in advocacy efforts aimed at addressing the drug and homelessness crisis. Advocacy organizations and community groups can use media coverage to raise awareness of the issue, promote their policy solutions, and elevate the voices of those impacted by the crisis. Media coverage can also provide a platform for those who have experienced homelessness or substance use disorder to share their stories and advocate for change.

One way in which media can support advocacy efforts is by highlighting the personal stories of those impacted by the crisis. By sharing these stories, media outlets can help humanize the issue and illustrate the real-world consequences of inadequate policy solutions. This can be especially powerful when those sharing their stories are members of marginalized communities who are often underrepresented in media coverage.

Media coverage can also help to promote policy solutions by bringing attention to successful programs and initiatives. When media outlets report on effective programs that have reduced homelessness or improved access to addiction treatment, they can help to build public support for these solutions and encourage policymakers to take action.

Furthermore, media can serve as a watchdog for accountability and transparency in policy implementation. By reporting on the use of public funding for homelessness and drug crisis response, the media can inform the public and hold officials accountable for their actions. This can help to ensure that resources are being used effectively and efficiently to address the crisis.

However, it is important to note that not all media coverage is positive or helpful for advocacy efforts. Some media outlets may perpetuate harmful stereotypes or stigmatizing narratives that undermine efforts to address the crisis. Additionally, media coverage can sometimes oversimplify complex issues, leaving out important context or contributing to a narrow understanding of the problem.

Advocacy organizations can work to address these challenges by engaging with media outlets and providing them with accurate and nuanced information about the crisis. By building relationships with journalists and media organizations, advocates can help to ensure that media coverage is informed by the perspectives of those impacted by the crisis and promotes equitable policy solutions.

Overall, the role of media in advocacy efforts aimed at addressing the drug and homelessness crisis is multifaceted. Media coverage can both help to promote policy solutions and raise awareness of the issue, but it can also perpetuate harmful stereotypes and oversimplify complex problems. By working to build relationships with media organizations and promote accurate and nuanced coverage, advocates can help to ensure that media plays a positive role in addressing the crisis.

Conclusion

In conclusion, media coverage plays a crucial role in shaping public perceptions of the drug and homelessness crisis. It can impact public attitudes towards those impacted, shape policy decisions, and influence public opinion on policy solutions. Media framing and bias can further exacerbate stigmatization and victim-blaming of those impacted. Social media also plays a significant role in shaping public perceptions and discourse around the issue.

However, media coverage is not monolithic, and alternative perspectives and advocacy efforts have the potential to challenge mainstream narratives and promote more equitable policy solutions. Advocacy groups can utilize media to elevate the voices of those impacted and raise awareness of evidence-based policy solutions. By critically engaging with media coverage and amplifying diverse perspectives, we can work towards a more informed and equitable public discourse on the drug and homelessness crisis.

Ultimately, addressing the drug and homelessness crisis will require a multifaceted approach that includes not only media coverage but also policy solutions that are evidence-based, collaborative, and prioritize the needs of those impacted. With continued critical engagement and a commitment to equitable policy solutions, we can work towards addressing this pressing issue and building more just and   equitable   communities.

Innovative Approaches to Addressing the Crisis

The drug and homelessness crisis continues to be a major public health and social issue in many parts of the world, with devastating impacts on individuals, families, and communities. Despite the efforts of governments, non-profits, and other stakeholders, the crisis persists, and traditional approaches to addressing it have often fallen short. In this context, it is increasingly important to explore innovative approaches that can address the root causes of the crisis and support those impacted. This paper will examine some of the most promising innovative approaches to addressing the drug and homelessness crisis, with a focus on models that have shown success in promoting recovery, stability, and well-being.

Housing First

The Housing First model is a relatively new approach to addressing homelessness that prioritizes providing stable housing to individuals before addressing other needs, such as employment or sobriety. The model differs from traditional approaches that require individuals to meet certain criteria, such as sobriety, before being eligible for housing assistance.

Under the Housing First model, individuals are provided with immediate access to stable housing, with the goal of stabilizing their living situation and allowing them to focus on addressing other needs. This approach recognizes that housing is a fundamental human need, and that addressing homelessness requires first and foremost ensuring that individuals have a safe and stable place to live.

Research has shown that the Housing First model is effective in reducing homelessness and improving housing stability. A 2015 study published in the Journal of the American Medical Association found that Housing First programs led to significant reductions in homelessness and increased housing stability among participants.

Other studies have found that the Housing First model is also cost-effective, as it reduces the use of expensive emergency services, such as hospitals and jails.

The Housing First model has also been shown to be effective in addressing the root causes of homelessness, such as mental illness and substance abuse. By providing stable housing, individuals are better able to access needed services and support, including mental health and addiction treatment. The Housing First model recognizes that addressing these underlying issues is critical to achieving long-term housing stability.

The Housing First model has been successfully implemented in a number of cities across the United States, including Seattle, Los Angeles, and New York City. In Seattle, the Housing First approach has been credited with reducing homelessness by 8% between 2018 and 2019. In New York City, a Housing First program known as "Homebase" has helped more than 30,000 families avoid eviction and homelessness since 2004.

Despite its successes, the Housing First model is not without challenges. One key challenge is the availability of affordable housing, particularly in high-cost cities. The model also requires significant investment in supportive services, such as mental health and addiction treatment, which can be costly.

Overall, the Housing First model offers a promising approach to addressing homelessness that prioritizes stable housing and recognizes the importance of addressing underlying issues, such as mental illness and substance abuse. With continued investment and support, the Housing First model has the potential to significantly reduce homelessness and improve the lives of those impacted by the drug and homelessness crisis.

Harm Reduction

Harm reduction is an approach to addressing drug addiction that seeks to minimize the negative consequences of drug use and promote safety, health, and well-being for individuals who use drugs. The harm reduction approach recognizes that not all individuals are ready or able to stop using drugs, and therefore aims to reduce the risks associated with drug use rather than insisting on abstinence as the only solution.

One key component of harm reduction is the provision of clean needles and syringes to individuals who inject drugs. This reduces the risk of blood-borne infections such as HIV and hepatitis C, which can be transmitted through the sharing of needles. In addition to providing clean needles, harm reduction programs may also provide other supplies such as alcohol swabs, cotton balls, and sterile water to promote safe injection practices.

Another harm reduction approach is the provision of safe injection sites, also known as supervised consumption sites. These are facilities where individuals can safely use drugs under the supervision of trained staff, who can provide overdose prevention measures, medical assistance, and referral to additional services such as counseling and addiction treatment. Safe injection sites have been shown to reduce overdose deaths, reduce the transmission of blood-borne infections, and improve access to addiction treatment.

Medication-assisted treatment is another harm reduction approach that uses medications such as methadone and buprenorphine to manage withdrawal symptoms and cravings for opioids. These medications are considered highly effective in promoting recovery and reducing the risk of overdose, but are often stigmatized due to misconceptions about their effectiveness and concerns about dependence.

The effectiveness of harm reduction approaches has been demonstrated through research and real-world implementation. Studies have shown that the provision of clean needles can reduce the spread of blood-borne infections, while safe injection sites have been shown to reduce overdose deaths and improve access to addiction treatment. Medication-assisted treatment has been found to reduce opioid use, overdose deaths, and criminal activity, and is considered a gold standard for opioid addiction treatment.

However, harm reduction approaches continue to face challenges and barriers to implementation, including resistance from policymakers and community members, funding constraints, and stigma associated with drug use. There is a need for continued advocacy and education to promote harm reduction approaches as a viable and effective strategy for addressing drug addiction and its associated harms.

In summary, harm reduction is an innovative approach to addressing drug addiction that prioritizes safety, health, and well-being for individuals who use drugs. The provision of clean needles, safe injection sites, and medication-assisted treatment are key components of harm reduction, and have been shown to be effective in reducing harm and promoting recovery. However, continued advocacy and education are needed to overcome challenges and promote the widespread implementation of harm reduction approaches.

Community-Based Solutions

Community-based solutions to the drug and homelessness crisis have gained traction in recent years, as grassroots organizations and neighborhood initiatives have emerged to provide support and resources to those impacted. These solutions prioritize community engagement and empowerment, recognizing that local residents are often the most knowledgeable about the needs and challenges facing their communities.

One example of a community-based solution is the Homeless Outreach Program and Empowerment (HOPE) program in Hawaii. HOPE is a partnership between law enforcement, social services, and community leaders, aimed at connecting homeless individuals with services and support to help them get off the streets. Rather than relying on traditional enforcement approaches, HOPE emphasizes compassion and collaboration, building trust with homeless individuals and providing them with the resources they need to rebuild their lives.

Another example is the Chicago Recovery Alliance (CRA), which provides harm reduction services to drug users in Chicago. CRA operates a needle exchange program, distributes naloxone (a medication used to reverse opioid overdoses), and provides education and support to individuals struggling with addiction. CRA is run by people with lived experience of drug use and prioritizes a non-judgmental, client-centered approach.

These community-based solutions have shown promise in addressing the root causes of the drug and homelessness crisis. By prioritizing community engagement and empowerment, these approaches build trust and foster cooperation between local residents, service providers, and those impacted by the crisis. Additionally, community-based solutions often incorporate cultural and contextual knowledge that is specific to the community being served, making them more effective in meeting the unique needs and challenges of that community.

However, community-based solutions also face challenges, including limited funding and resources, as well as the potential for burnout among volunteers and service providers. Additionally, community-based solutions may struggle to scale up to meet the needs of larger populations, requiring collaboration with other organizations and government agencies.

Despite these challenges, community-based solutions offer a promising way forward in addressing the drug and homelessness crisis. By building trust and collaboration within communities, these solutions offer a more sustainable and equitable approach to addressing the root causes of the crisis.

Employment and Job Training Programs

The drug and homelessness crisis is not only a public health and social issue but also an economic issue. The lack of access to employment and stable income is one of the root causes of homelessness and drug addiction. Therefore, employment and job training programs have been developed as innovative approaches to addressing the drug and homelessness crisis.

These programs aim to provide individuals experiencing homelessness or addiction with job training, education, and employment opportunities that can help them transition out of homelessness or addiction and build a stable life. Employment and job training programs vary in their design and approach, but they all share a common goal of creating a pathway to self-sufficiency and long-term stability.

One example of an employment and job training program is the Center for Employment Opportunities (CEO). CEO provides comprehensive employment services to individuals with criminal records, including those who have experienced homelessness and addiction. CEO's program includes job readiness training, paid transitional work, job placement, and retention services. The program has been successful in helping participants secure employment and reduce recidivism rates.

Another example is the Second Chance Employment and Training Program in Portland, Oregon. This program provides job training and employment opportunities to individuals experiencing homelessness, addiction, or other barriers to employment. Participants receive job training and support, as well as access to transitional employment opportunities in industries such as construction, culinary arts, and hospitality. The program has helped participants gain new skills and find stable employment.

The importance of employment and job training programs in addressing the drug and homelessness crisis cannot be overstated. By providing individuals with the skills, resources, and support they need to obtain stable employment, these programs can help break the cycle of poverty, addiction, and homelessness. They also promote self-sufficiency and reduce reliance on social services and public assistance programs.

However, employment and job training programs alone are not enough to address the root causes of the drug and homelessness crisis. These programs must be integrated into a comprehensive and holistic approach that includes access to housing, healthcare, and other essential services. They must also be designed with the input and needs of those impacted by the crisis, ensuring that they are culturally competent and responsive to the unique challenges faced by individuals experiencing homelessness or addiction.

In summary, employment and job training programs have shown promise in addressing the drug and homelessness crisis by providing individuals with the skills and resources they need to obtain stable employment and build a better life. However, these programs must be integrated into a comprehensive and holistic approach that addresses the root causes of the crisis and promotes long-term stability and self-sufficiency.

Peer Support and Recovery Coaching

Peer support and recovery coaching models have gained recognition in recent years as an innovative approach to addressing the drug and homelessness crisis. These models involve individuals with lived experience of addiction and homelessness who work as peers and coaches to support others in their recovery journey. This approach is based on the belief that individuals who have gone through similar experiences are best positioned to provide support and guidance to others who are struggling.

One example of a successful peer support and recovery coaching model is the Recovery Coach Program. This program was developed by the Connecticut Community for Addiction Recovery (CCAR) in 1998 and has since been implemented in various states across the United States. The program trains individuals with lived experience of addiction to become certified recovery coaches, who provide support and guidance to those in recovery. The program has been shown to be effective in improving retention rates in treatment programs and reducing relapse rates.

Another example of a successful peer support and recovery coaching model is the Certified Peer Recovery Specialist (CPRS) program, which was developed by the Georgia Council on Substance Abuse (GCSA). This program trains individuals with lived experience of addiction to become certified peer recovery specialists, who provide support and guidance to others in recovery. The program has been shown to be effective in reducing recidivism rates among individuals involved in the criminal justice system and improving treatment outcomes.

Peer support and recovery coaching models have been found to be effective in addressing the root causes of the drug and homelessness crisis. These models provide individuals with lived experience the opportunity to share their knowledge and experience with others, which can lead to increased empathy and understanding. Additionally, these models provide a sense of community and belonging, which can be essential to supporting individuals in their recovery journey.

Moreover, peer support and recovery coaching models can be more cost-effective than traditional treatment approaches. By utilizing individuals with lived experience, these models can reduce the need for expensive medical interventions and promote a more holistic approach to recovery.

However, it is important to note that peer support and recovery coaching models should not be viewed as a replacement for traditional treatment approaches. Rather, they should be seen as a complementary approach that can be used in conjunction with other treatment modalities to support individuals in their recovery journey.

In conclusion, peer support and recovery coaching models have shown promise in addressing the drug and homelessness crisis. These models provide a unique approach to supporting individuals in their recovery journey and promoting community-based solutions to the crisis. Further research and investment in these models could lead to a more comprehensive and effective approach to addressing the root causes of the crisis.

Healthcare Innovation

Innovative approaches to healthcare can play a vital role in addressing the drug and homelessness crisis. One approach that has shown promise is the integration of healthcare services to address the complex physical and mental health needs of individuals experiencing homelessness and addiction.

Integrated care models provide coordinated healthcare services that address both physical and mental health conditions. These models recognize that individuals experiencing homelessness and addiction often face a range of complex health issues, including chronic physical health conditions, mental health disorders, and substance use disorders. By integrating primary care, behavioral health, and substance use disorder treatment services, these models aim to improve health outcomes and reduce healthcare costs.

One example of an integrated care model is the Healthcare for the Homeless (HCH) program, which provides comprehensive healthcare services to individuals experiencing homelessness. HCH programs offer a range of services, including medical care, dental care, behavioral health services, substance use disorder treatment, and case management. By addressing the multiple and complex health needs of individuals experiencing homelessness, these programs aim to improve health outcomes, reduce healthcare costs, and prevent unnecessary hospitalizations.

Another approach to healthcare innovation is the use of telemedicine to provide healthcare services to individuals experiencing homelessness and addiction. Telemedicine allows healthcare providers to connect with patients remotely, using video conferencing and other communication technologies. This can be particularly helpful in providing healthcare services to individuals who are geographically isolated or who face transportation barriers.

Telemedicine has been used to provide a range of healthcare services to individuals experiencing homelessness and addiction, including substance use disorder treatment, mental health counseling, and primary care. Telemedicine can increase access to healthcare services, reduce costs, and improve health outcomes.

In addition to these innovative approaches to healthcare, there are also efforts underway to address the social determinants of health that contribute to the drug and homelessness crisis. For example, some healthcare providers are working to address food insecurity, housing insecurity, and transportation barriers as part of their healthcare services. These efforts recognize that addressing the social determinants of health is critical to improving health outcomes and reducing healthcare costs.

In conclusion, innovative approaches to healthcare can play a vital role in addressing the drug and homelessness crisis. Integrated care models, telemedicine, and efforts to address social determinants of health can all help to improve health outcomes, reduce healthcare costs, and prevent unnecessary hospitalizations. These approaches should be supported and expanded to ensure that individuals experiencing homelessness and addiction receive the healthcare services they need to achieve recovery and stability.

Public-Private Partnerships

Public-private partnerships can be an effective way to address the drug and homelessness crisis by leveraging the resources and expertise of both the public and private sectors. These partnerships bring together stakeholders from a variety of sectors, including government agencies, nonprofits, and private businesses, to work collaboratively on addressing the root causes of the crisis and supporting those impacted.

One example of a successful public-private partnership is the Homeless Veterans Initiative, launched by the United States Department of Veterans Affairs (VA) in partnership with the Department of Housing and Urban Development (HUD) and community organizations. This initiative provides housing vouchers and supportive services to veterans experiencing homelessness, with the goal of ending veteran homelessness by 2025. The partnership between these agencies and community organizations has resulted in a significant reduction in veteran homelessness across the country.

Another example is the Housing Opportunities and Maintenance for the Elderly (HOME) Investment Partnership Program, which brings together federal funding from HUD with private investment to create affordable housing for elderly individuals. This program has resulted in the creation of thousands of affordable housing units across the United States, improving housing security and reducing homelessness among the elderly population.

Despite these successes, public-private partnerships also face challenges. One challenge is ensuring that the goals and priorities of all stakeholders are aligned, as competing interests can lead to conflict and ineffective collaboration. Another challenge is ensuring that the partnership is equitable and that the benefits of the partnership are distributed fairly among all stakeholders.

To address these challenges, effective communication and collaboration are key. It is important to establish clear goals and priorities from the outset, and to establish open lines of communication between all stakeholders. Regular evaluation and assessment of the partnership's progress can also help to ensure that goals are being met and that the partnership remains effective.

In addition, public-private partnerships can benefit from the involvement of community members and those with lived experience of homelessness and addiction. Including these voices in the partnership can help to ensure that the needs and perspectives of those impacted are represented and that the partnership is centered on their needs.

Overall, public-private partnerships have the potential to be a powerful tool in addressing the drug and homelessness crisis. By bringing together stakeholders from diverse sectors, these partnerships can leverage resources and expertise to support those impacted and address the root causes of the crisis. However, effective communication, collaboration, and equitable distribution of benefits are key to ensuring the success of these partnerships.

Technology and Innovation

Innovative approaches to addressing the drug and homelessness crisis are crucial in tackling this complex and multifaceted issue. While traditional approaches have focused on emergency services, shelters, and treatment programs, innovative models have emerged that prioritize long-term solutions and address the root causes of the crisis.

One promising approach is the Housing First model, which prioritizes providing stable housing to those experiencing homelessness before addressing other needs. By providing individuals with a stable home, they can focus on their physical and mental health needs and have a foundation for rebuilding their lives. Studies have shown that this model can reduce homelessness and improve outcomes for those impacted.

Harm reduction approaches are also gaining traction in addressing drug addiction. These approaches prioritize reducing harm and promoting recovery, rather than focusing solely on abstinence. Examples of harm reduction programs include the provision of clean needles, safe injection sites, and medication-assisted treatment. These programs have been shown to reduce the spread of infectious diseases, prevent overdoses, and promote recovery.

Community-based solutions are also a promising approach, as they are often more responsive to local needs and can be tailored to meet the unique challenges of a particular community. Examples of community-based solutions include grassroots organizations and neighborhood initiatives aimed at providing support and resources to those impacted.

Employment and job training programs are another approach to addressing the drug and homelessness crisis. By providing individuals with the skills and resources necessary to secure stable employment, they can achieve financial stability and reduce their risk of experiencing homelessness or addiction. Examples of successful programs include job training programs for formerly incarcerated individuals and initiatives aimed at connecting individuals with employment opportunities in emerging industries.

Peer support and recovery coaching models have also emerged as a promising approach. These models provide individuals with lived experience with addiction and homelessness the opportunity to support others on their recovery journey. By providing a sense of community and connection, these programs can promote recovery and reduce the risk of relapse.

Innovative healthcare approaches, such as integrated care models, can also address the root causes of the drug and homelessness crisis.

These models prioritize the integration of physical and mental healthcare services, providing individuals with comprehensive care and addressing both their physical and mental health needs.

Public-private partnerships are another approach to addressing the drug and homelessness crisis. These partnerships can leverage the expertise and resources of both the public and private sectors to support those impacted and promote long-term solutions. Examples of successful partnerships include collaborations between healthcare providers and community-based organizations.

Finally, technology and innovation can also play a role in addressing the drug and homelessness crisis. Data analytics, telemedicine, and other technological tools can be used to improve service delivery and support those impacted by the crisis.

In conclusion, innovative approaches to addressing the drug and homelessness crisis are crucial in promoting long-term solutions and addressing the root causes of this complex issue. By prioritizing stable housing, harm reduction, community-based solutions, employment and job training, peer support and recovery coaching, innovative healthcare, public-private partnerships, and technology and innovation, we can make progress towards ending the drug and homelessness crisis.

Conclusion

In conclusion, the drug and homelessness crisis is a complex issue that requires innovative approaches to address the root causes and support those impacted. The approaches discussed in this article, such as Housing First, harm reduction, community-based solutions, employment and job training programs, peer support and recovery coaching, healthcare innovation, public-private partnerships, and technology and innovation, all show promise in improving outcomes for individuals experiencing homelessness and addiction. These approaches demonstrate the importance of collaboration across sectors and the need for evidence-based practices to promote lasting change.

It is crucial that investment in these innovative approaches continues, and that policymakers, service providers, and advocates work together to develop and implement solutions that meet the needs of those impacted by the crisis. By focusing on evidence-based practices and addressing the root causes of homelessness and addiction, we can promote lasting change and improve outcomes for individuals and communities across the country.

Hope and Resilience in the Face of Crisis

The drug and homelessness crisis is a complex issue that has affected individuals, families, and communities across the globe. It is a multifaceted problem that involves economic, social, and health factors, and can have lasting consequences on individuals' well-being and quality of life. Despite the challenges presented by this crisis, there are stories of hope and resilience emerging from communities and individuals who have found ways to overcome adversity and create positive change. In this discussion, we will explore these stories of hope and resilience and examine how they can inspire us to find innovative solutions and a path forward in addressing the drug and homelessness crisis.

Community Resilience

Community resilience plays an important role in addressing the drug and homelessness crisis. Communities affected by the crisis often face significant challenges, including limited resources, stigma, and a lack of support from government agencies. However, many communities have demonstrated remarkable resilience and creativity in addressing these challenges and providing support to those impacted by the crisis.

Grassroots organizations and community-led initiatives have emerged as important drivers of change in many communities. These organizations often work to fill gaps in services and support that are not being adequately addressed by government agencies. For example, some communities have established community-based harm reduction programs, providing clean needles and overdose prevention services to those who use drugs. These programs have been shown to reduce overdose deaths and improve health outcomes for those impacted by drug addiction.

Other communities have established mutual aid networks, providing support and resources to those experiencing homelessness. These networks often operate outside of traditional systems of support, providing direct assistance to those in need. For example, some networks provide tents and other essential supplies to those living in encampments, while others offer transportation to medical appointments or other essential services.

Community resilience can also take the form of advocacy efforts aimed at promoting policy change. Many communities have successfully advocated for increased funding for affordable housing, harm reduction services, and other critical resources. These advocacy efforts have been instrumental in shaping policy and driving change at the local, state, and federal levels.

Overall, community resilience plays a critical role in addressing the drug and homelessness crisis. By working together and finding creative solutions to complex problems, communities can create positive change and support those impacted by the crisis.

Overcoming Stigma

Stigma is one of the significant challenges that individuals and communities impacted by drug addiction and homelessness face. It can prevent those in need from seeking help and accessing essential resources, perpetuating the cycle of addiction and homelessness. However, stories of hope and resilience can play a significant role in overcoming stigma by challenging stereotypes and promoting greater understanding.

Many individuals and communities impacted by the crisis have found ways to challenge stigma and promote positive change. For example, recovery communities and support groups, such as Alcoholics Anonymous and Narcotics Anonymous, provide a safe space for individuals to share their experiences and support one another on their recovery journey. These groups often emphasize the importance of anonymity, allowing individuals to seek help without fear of judgment or stigma.

Community-led initiatives and organizations have also played a significant role in challenging stigma and promoting greater understanding of the root causes of addiction and homelessness. For example, the Voices of Community Advocates and Leaders (VOCAL-NY) is a grassroots organization that advocates for policies and resources to support those impacted by the crisis. The organization includes individuals with lived experience of homelessness and addiction, promoting a more comprehensive and compassionate approach to addressing the crisis.

Moreover, the Faces and Voices of Recovery is a national advocacy organization that seeks to eliminate the stigma of addiction and promote recovery through education, advocacy, and organizing. The organization provides training and resources to individuals and organizations seeking to promote greater understanding and challenge stigma at the community level.

In conclusion, stories of hope and resilience can play a critical role in overcoming the stigma associated with drug addiction and homelessness. Community-led initiatives and organizations, support groups, and advocacy organizations all contribute to promoting greater understanding and challenging stereotypes. By highlighting these stories and promoting more comprehensive and compassionate approaches to addressing the crisis, we can create a society that is more supportive and inclusive of those impacted.

Art and Expression

The drug and homelessness crisis can take a heavy toll on individuals, families, and communities. Yet, despite the many challenges and setbacks, there are also stories of hope and resilience that inspire us and remind us of the human capacity to overcome adversity.

One way that hope and resilience can be expressed is through art and self-expression. Creative outlets such as music, painting, and writing can provide individuals with a means to cope with their struggles, express their feelings, and connect with others who share their experiences.

For example, in some cities, organizations have formed to provide homeless individuals with access to art supplies and spaces to create their own artwork. These programs not only provide a therapeutic outlet for individuals struggling with homelessness, but they also showcase the talent and creativity of individuals who are often overlooked and stigmatized.

Another way that hope and resilience can be seen is through community-led initiatives aimed at providing support and resources to those in need. In some areas, grassroots organizations have formed to provide housing, healthcare, and job training to homeless individuals and those struggling with addiction.

These organizations are often founded and led by individuals who have personally experienced the crisis and have a deep understanding of the challenges faced by those impacted. By working together and drawing on their collective strengths and resources, these communities can create positive change and promote greater understanding and empathy.

Finally, hope and resilience can be seen in the stories of individuals who have overcome addiction and homelessness and gone on to lead successful and fulfilling lives. These individuals often credit their success to a combination of personal determination, community support, and access to effective treatment and resources.

Their stories remind us that recovery is possible and that with the right support and resources, individuals can overcome even the most difficult challenges.

In conclusion, the drug and homelessness crisis is a complex and multifaceted issue that requires a range of approaches and solutions. However, by highlighting the stories of hope and resilience that exist within the crisis, we can promote greater understanding, empathy, and support for those impacted, and work towards a more just and equitable society for all.

Peer Support and Mentorship

Peer support and mentorship have been shown to be powerful tools in promoting resilience and recovery among individuals impacted by the drug and homelessness crisis. Peer support involves individuals with lived experience of addiction and homelessness providing guidance, encouragement, and assistance to others who are going through similar experiences. Mentorship programs, on the other hand, involve pairing individuals with more experienced mentors who can provide guidance and support on their recovery journey.

Research has shown that peer support and mentorship programs can lead to increased engagement in treatment, improved mental health outcomes, and reduced substance use. These programs provide individuals with a sense of community and support, which can be particularly important for those who may feel isolated or stigmatized due to their experiences with addiction or homelessness.

One example of a successful peer support program is the Certified Peer Specialist (CPS) program, which trains individuals with lived experience to provide peer support services to others. CPS programs have been shown to increase engagement in treatment and improve mental health outcomes among participants.

Another example is the Recovery Coach program, which provides individuals with peer support and mentorship from those who have experienced addiction and are now in recovery. These programs have been shown to improve outcomes related to addiction recovery, including reduced rates of relapse and increased employment.

Overall, peer support and mentorship programs can play a critical role in promoting resilience and recovery among individuals impacted by the drug and homelessness crisis. By providing support and guidance from individuals with shared experiences, these programs can help individuals navigate the challenges of addiction and homelessness and build a sense of community and hope.

Innovative Approaches

Innovative approaches have played a key role in addressing the drug and homelessness crisis, with many individuals and organizations finding new and creative ways to support those impacted and promote positive change.

For example, some organizations have started to offer mobile outreach services to individuals experiencing homelessness or drug addiction. These services can include medical care, mental health services, and harm reduction resources, all provided on the street or at encampments. By meeting individuals where they are, these programs are able to provide critical services to those who may not otherwise seek them out.

Another example of innovation in this space is the use of peer support and mentorship programs to promote resilience and recovery. These programs connect individuals who have experienced addiction or homelessness with trained peers who can offer support, guidance, and resources. By leveraging the power of lived experience, these programs have been able to build trust and establish meaningful connections with those in need.

Technology has also played a role in promoting innovation in the fight against the crisis. For example, telemedicine has allowed healthcare providers to offer remote care to individuals experiencing homelessness or living in rural areas. This technology has the potential to increase access to critical healthcare services and reduce barriers to care.

Finally, community-based solutions have also been a key driver of innovation in this space. Grassroots organizations and neighborhood initiatives have been successful in providing support and resources to those impacted by the crisis, often through creative and localized approaches. For example, some communities have established tiny home villages or community gardens to provide stable housing and food resources to those in need.

Overall, these examples of innovative approaches highlight the power of creativity and outside-the-box thinking in addressing complex societal challenges. By continuing to invest in innovation and explore new approaches to the drug and homelessness crisis, we can promote hope and resilience among those impacted and work towards lasting change.

Building Community

Building community is an important aspect of promoting hope and resilience in the face of the drug and homelessness crisis. Communities that come together to support one another can provide a sense of belonging and connection, which can be crucial for individuals who may feel isolated or disconnected.

One example of community building is the creation of neighborhood watch programs. These programs bring together community members to look out for each other and help prevent crime and drug use in their neighborhoods. By working together, community members can feel empowered to take action and make positive change in their communities.

Another example is the formation of support groups for families and friends of individuals struggling with addiction or homelessness. These groups can provide a safe and supportive space for loved ones to share their experiences, find emotional support, and gain practical advice on how to best support their loved ones. By building a sense of community among those impacted by the crisis, these groups can help reduce feelings of isolation and promote resilience.

Community building can also take the form of community-led initiatives aimed at providing resources and support to those in need. For example, some communities have established mutual aid networks to provide food, clothing, and other essentials to individuals experiencing homelessness. These networks are typically run by volunteers and rely on community donations, demonstrating the power of collective action to make a difference.

Ultimately, building community is about creating a sense of connection and support among those impacted by the crisis. By coming together to support one another, individuals and communities can find hope and resilience in the face of adversity.

Celebrating Success

Amidst the drug and homelessness crisis, there are individuals and communities who have overcome adversity and achieved positive outcomes. These success stories serve as a source of inspiration and hope, highlighting the importance of resilience and perseverance. Celebrating these successes can also help to break down stereotypes and challenge the stigma associated with addiction and homelessness.

One example of a success story is that of a man named Jeffery, who experienced addiction and homelessness for many years. With the help of a local non-profit organization, he was able to access treatment and support, eventually securing stable housing and employment. Today, Jeffery is a peer mentor, providing support and guidance to others on their recovery journey.

Another example is the success of the Medicine Wheel Village, a community-led initiative in Minneapolis aimed at providing stable housing and support to Native Americans experiencing homelessness. The program combines traditional healing practices with modern medicine and has achieved a 97% success rate in helping individuals maintain stable housing.

Celebrating these success stories can help to shift the narrative around addiction and homelessness, promoting greater understanding and empathy. It also highlights the importance of investing in evidence-based practices and providing individuals with the support and resources they need to achieve positive outcomes.

In conclusion, highlighting success stories of individuals and communities that have overcome the challenges associated with the drug and homelessness crisis is an important part of promoting hope and resilience. By celebrating these successes, we can inspire others and break down stereotypes, while also emphasizing the need for continued investment in evidence-based approaches to addressing the crisis.

Conclusion

In conclusion, the drug and homelessness crisis is a complex and pressing issue that requires innovative and comprehensive solutions. However, amidst the challenges, there are stories of hope and resilience that can inspire and guide us in addressing the crisis. Communities have come together to support one another, individuals have found creative ways to cope and heal, and innovative approaches have been developed to promote positive change. Peer support, mentorship, art and expression, and community building are just a few examples of the approaches that have been successful in promoting hope and resilience. It is important to celebrate the successes of those impacted by the crisis and continue to support and invest in programs and initiatives that prioritize these values. By working together and embracing hope and resilience, we can make a positive difference in the lives of those impacted by the drug and homelessness   crisis.

The Future of the Crisis

The drug and homelessness crisis on the West Coast of the United States has been an ongoing challenge for decades. In recent years, it has become increasingly visible and urgent, with skyrocketing rates of homelessness, addiction, and related health issues. As we look to the future, it is important to understand how demographic and economic changes will impact the crisis and shape our response. This essay will explore the potential trajectory of the crisis in the coming years, and consider the opportunities and challenges that lie ahead.

Population Trends

Population trends and projections are essential for predicting the future of the drug and homelessness crisis on the West Coast. According to the United States Census Bureau, the population of the West Coast states - California, Oregon, and Washington - is expected to continue growing over the next few decades. Additionally, the West Coast has a high number of immigrants, which has historically been linked to higher levels of homelessness due to barriers to accessing services and discrimination.

The aging population is also a factor that may impact the future of the crisis, as older adults have unique needs and may be at higher risk of homelessness due to factors such as retirement, disability, and loss of social support networks. As such, it is crucial to consider population trends and projections when developing long-term strategies for addressing the crisis.

Economic Factors

As the West Coast continues to experience economic growth and urbanization, rising housing costs and changes in the job market are likely to contribute to the drug and homelessness crisis. With the cost of living in many urban areas on the rise, many individuals and families may struggle to find affordable housing, leading to an increased risk of homelessness. In addition, changes in the job market, such as the growth of the gig economy and a shift away from traditional industries, may leave some workers without stable employment and at risk of poverty and homelessness.

Furthermore, economic inequality and income disparities may exacerbate the drug and homelessness crisis, as those who are already struggling to make ends meet may be more vulnerable to addiction and homelessness due to stress, trauma, and lack of resources. Therefore, addressing economic factors and promoting economic stability and equality may be a key component of addressing the crisis in the future.

Policy Responses

The drug and homelessness crisis on the West Coast has prompted a range of policy responses, from emergency measures such as increased funding for shelters and expanded access to addiction treatment, to longer-term strategies aimed at addressing root causes such as affordable housing and income inequality. Looking to the future, it will be important to consider how these policy responses may evolve in response to changing demographics and economic conditions. For example, as the region's population continues to grow and diversify, policymakers may need to place greater emphasis on culturally responsive services that take into account the unique needs and experiences of different communities.

Additionally, there may be a need to reconsider funding priorities in light of changing economic conditions. With rising housing costs and an increasingly competitive job market, there may be a need for increased investment in affordable housing and job training programs that equip individuals with the skills needed to secure stable employment. At the same time, policymakers may need to reassess the role of criminal justice in responding to the crisis, particularly in light of growing calls for decriminalization and harm reduction.

Overall, the future of policy responses to the drug and homelessness crisis on the West Coast will likely be shaped by a range of factors, from shifting political dynamics to changing social and economic conditions. It will be important for policymakers to remain responsive to these changes and to engage in ongoing dialogue with affected communities to ensure that policy solutions are effective, equitable, and sustainable over the long term.

Technological Innovations

Technological innovations can play a significant role in addressing the drug and homelessness crisis on the West Coast. One area where technology can have an impact is in the use of data analytics. By analyzing data related to drug use, homelessness, and healthcare utilization, policymakers and service providers can gain insights into patterns and trends, which can inform the development of targeted interventions and more effective service delivery. For example, data analytics can help identify neighborhoods or regions with high rates of drug-related hospitalizations or emergency department visits, allowing for the allocation of resources to address those specific areas.

Another area where technology can be effective is in the use of telemedicine. This can involve virtual consultations with healthcare providers, as well as remote monitoring of patients' vital signs and medication adherence. Telemedicine can be particularly valuable in areas with limited access to healthcare, such as rural or low-income communities. It can also be an effective way to provide support and treatment to individuals who may be hesitant to seek care in person due to concerns about stigma or privacy.

In addition to these specific examples, there are many other technological tools and innovations that can help address the drug and homelessness crisis. For example, mobile apps and social media platforms can be used to connect individuals with resources and support networks, while virtual reality and gamification techniques can be employed to enhance engagement and motivation in treatment programs. Overall, the use of technology and innovation can play an important role in improving service delivery and treatment outcomes in the face of the crisis.

Collaborative Efforts

Collaborative efforts between various sectors have been instrumental in addressing the drug and homelessness crisis on the West Coast. In the future, there will be a need for continued collaboration and new partnerships to address the evolving challenges of the crisis.

Examples of successful collaborative efforts include joint initiatives between government agencies and non-profit organizations to provide comprehensive services to those in need. For instance, the City of Seattle's Navigation Team, which includes outreach workers, police officers, and sanitation workers, collaborates with non-profit organizations to provide outreach and connect people experiencing homelessness with services and shelter.

There have also been successful partnerships between the private sector and non-profit organizations. For example, in Los Angeles, the Skid Row Housing Trust, a non-profit organization that provides permanent supportive housing, has partnered with private developers to build affordable housing for people experiencing homelessness.

As the crisis continues to evolve, there will be a need for new and innovative partnerships to address emerging challenges. One potential area for collaboration is the use of technology to improve service delivery and support. For example, partnerships between technology companies and non-profit organizations could result in the development of new tools and resources to support people experiencing homelessness, such as mobile apps that connect people to services and resources.

Collaborative efforts will continue to play a crucial role in addressing the drug and homelessness crisis on the West Coast, and there will be a need for ongoing partnerships and new collaborations to address emerging challenges.

Mental Health

The role of mental health is a critical factor in understanding and addressing the drug and homelessness crisis on the West Coast. Research has consistently shown that individuals experiencing homelessness and substance use disorders are more likely to have mental health challenges, with estimates indicating that up to 70% of individuals experiencing homelessness have a mental health condition.

Despite the high prevalence of mental health challenges, access to mental health care for those experiencing homelessness and substance use disorders is often limited, resulting in a lack of proper diagnosis and treatment. This can exacerbate the symptoms of mental health conditions, leading to an increased risk of substance use and homelessness.

To address this issue, future efforts must prioritize improving access to mental health care for individuals experiencing homelessness and substance use disorders. This could include expanding mental health services and resources within existing programs, such as homeless shelters and substance use treatment centers.

Reducing the stigma associated with mental health conditions is also crucial in improving outcomes for individuals experiencing homelessness and substance use disorders. This could involve increasing public education and awareness about mental health, as well as developing targeted outreach programs to provide support and resources to individuals who may be hesitant to seek care.

Additionally, future efforts must prioritize the integration of mental health care and substance use treatment, recognizing that these issues are often intertwined and require a comprehensive approach. By addressing mental health challenges and substance use disorders simultaneously, individuals experiencing homelessness can be better equipped to achieve long-term recovery and stability.

Public Perception

Public perception and media coverage can have a significant impact on the drug and homelessness crisis by shaping public attitudes, policy decisions, and resource allocation. Negative stereotypes and stigmatizing language can contribute to further marginalization and discrimination against those impacted by the crisis, making it more difficult for individuals to access resources and support.

One strategy for changing negative stereotypes and promoting empathy is through education and awareness campaigns that highlight the complex and multi-faceted nature of the crisis. This includes emphasizing the root causes of the crisis, such as economic inequality and lack of affordable housing, as well as the diverse backgrounds and experiences of those impacted.

Another approach is to involve individuals with lived experience in advocacy and public awareness efforts, giving them a platform to share their stories and challenge stereotypes. Media outlets can also play a critical role by changing the way they report on the crisis, avoiding stigmatizing language and highlighting positive examples of community resilience and solutions.

Ultimately, changing public perception and promoting empathy will require a sustained and collaborative effort across sectors, including government, non-profit organizations, media outlets, and community members. By working together to challenge negative stereotypes and promote understanding, we can create a more compassionate and effective response to the drug and homelessness crisis.

Conclusion

In conclusion, the drug and homelessness crisis on the West Coast is a complex and multifaceted issue that will require ongoing attention and investment. Changes in demographics, economic factors, and policy responses will likely impact the trajectory of the crisis in the years to come. Addressing the crisis will require a collaborative effort between government, non-profit organizations, and the private sector, as well as innovative approaches that leverage technology and evidence-based practices. Changing negative stereotypes and promoting empathy will also be important in combatting the public perception and media coverage of the crisis. Despite these challenges, there is hope for positive change, and continued investment in addressing the crisis can help create a better future for all those impacted.

Closing Statements

As I reflect on the content of this book, I am struck by the incredible resilience and hope demonstrated by individuals and communities impacted by the drug and homelessness crisis on the West Coast. It is clear that this crisis is one of the most pressing social issues facing our country today, and it is essential that we continue to examine it from all angles in order to make progress toward lasting solutions.

I must acknowledge the role that the Soft White Underbelly YouTube channel played in inspiring me to explore this topic further. Without the powerful and authentic stories shared on that platform, I may not have fully grasped the depth and complexity of this crisis. I am grateful for the opportunity to learn from those who have experienced drug addiction and homelessness firsthand, and to have been able to share their stories through this book.

It is important to recognize that while the West Coast is where this crisis is most prevalent, it is not unique to this region. Communities across the country are grappling with similar issues, and we must work together to find solutions that can be applied in a variety of contexts.

As we move forward, we must continue to prioritize collaboration, innovation, and evidence-based practices in our efforts to address this crisis. This requires the involvement and investment of a broad range of stakeholders, including government agencies, non-profit organizations, private businesses, and individuals from all walks of life.

But most importantly, we must approach this crisis with empathy and compassion. We must recognize that those who are impacted by drug addiction and homelessness are individuals with unique stories and struggles, and that they deserve our support and understanding. By working together with a shared sense of purpose and a commitment to hope and resilience, we ca

References

Books:
"The Body Keeps the Score: Brain, Mind, and Body in the Healing of Trauma" by Bessel van der Kolk
"Lost Connections: Why You're Depressed and How to Find Hope" by Johann Hari
"Unbroken Brain: A Revolutionary New Way of Understanding Addiction" by Maia Szalavitz
"The Power of Vulnerability: Teachings on Authenticity, Connection and Courage" by Brené Brown
"A First-Rate Madness: Uncovering the Links between Leadership and Mental Illness" by Nassir Ghaemi

Articles:
"Mental Illness and Addiction: What is the Connection?" by National Alliance on Mental Illness (NAMI)
"Why Mental Illness is More Common Than You Think" by Harvard Health Publishing
"The Stigma of Mental Illness" by American Psychological Association (APA)
"The Homeless and the Mentally Ill" by The Atlantic
"Trauma, Homelessness, and the Limits of Self-Regulation" by SAMHSA

Documentaries:
"The Adverse Childhood Experiences Study: The Largest Public Health Study You Never Heard Of" by KPJR Films
"The Mind, Explained" by Vox and Netflix
"Generation Addicted" by PBS NewsHour
"Crazywise" by Phil Borges
"Invisible People" by Mark Horvath

These resources cover a range of topics related to mental health, substance abuse, trauma, homelessness, and stigma. They may provide valuable insights and information for readers interested in learning more about these issues.

www.ingramcontent.com/pod-product-compliance
Lightning Source LLC
Chambersburg PA
CBHW061025250726

48662CB00011B/1034